THE

American Heritage

Series

UNDER THE GENERAL EDITORSHIP OF

LEONARD W. LEVY AND ALFRED YOUNG

The Social Thought of Jane Addams

EDITED BY

CHRISTOPHER LASCH

THE BOBBS-MERRILL COMPANY, INC.
INDIANAPOLIS · NEW YORK

Printed in the United States of America
Library of Congress Catalog Card Number 65-22345
Designed by Stefan Salter Associates
ISBN 0-672-60110-9 (pbk)
Seventh Printing

The Social Thought of Jane Addams

FOREWORD

To comfortable middle-class Americans who owned their own homes on elm-shaded streets, Jane Addams was a prickly maiden aunt. She embarrassed them by her moral earnestness; she disturbed them by her appeals to conscience—but they admired her. She shocked them by her advocacy of strange, even radical causes, but they respected her courage. To the poor and exploited, she was not merely a kindly benefactor, a champion, or a missionary; she was a warm, understanding friend. Even ward bosses, trade unionists, and business leaders grudgingly acknowledged her ability. As one of America's foremost moralists, social reformers, and humanitarians, she helped make "progressivism" and "social justice" respectable causes to be taken seriously.

But Jane Addams was more than a practical activist, more than a great spirit. She was more, indeed, than the sum of her achievements or of her extraordinarily diverse interests, which ranged from child-labor legislation, tenement reform, and public health to pacifism, internationalism, and feminism. She was a first-rate intellect who has not been accorded the place that she deserves as one of our leading social critics.

This collection of her writings has the unusual merit of recognizing her intellectual and literary talents. Professor Lasch, in his graceful introduction, describes Jane Addams as an "intellectual—a thinker of originality and daring," who wrote superbly about most of the many subjects that absorbed her life and are still of continuing concern. Her radiance, goodness, and touching qualities are abundantly evident in the selections

presented by Professor Lasch, but so too are the wisdom, analytical sharpness, and boldness that he detects in her writings
on politics, the city, the revolt of youth, immigrants, social
work, civil rights, pacifism, and family life. From her letters,
lectures, articles, and books, Professor Lasch has given us the
materials that warrant a fresh assessment of Jane Addams as
more than the universal maiden aunt who founded Hull-House,
won a Nobel Peace Prize, and aroused the social conscience
of America.

This book is part of a series whose aim is to provide the
essential primary sources of the American experience, especially of American thought, from the colonial period to the
present. The series when completed will constitute a documentary library of our history. These volumes will fill a need
of libraries, scholars, students, and even general readers for
authoritative collections of original material. These materials
will illuminate the thought of significant individuals, such as
James Madison and Louis Brandeis; groups, such as Puritan
political theorists and American Catholic leaders on social
policy; and movements, such as those of the Anti-Federalists or
the Populists. There are a surprising number of subjects traditionally studied in American history for which there are no
documentary anthologies. This series will be by far the most
comprehensive and authoritative of its kind. It will also have
the distinction of presenting representative pieces of substantial length that have not been butchered into snippets.

Leonard W. Levy
Alfred Young

CONTENTS

PART I

THE SNARE OF PREPARATION

PART III

REFORM, POLITICAL AND SOCIAL

PART IV

DEMOCRACY AND EDUCATION

P A R T   V

PEACE

INTRODUCTION

"I think that her greatness has been veiled by her goodness," said Emily Balch when Jane Addams died. "Men have a curious tendency to turn those of eminent stature into plaster images."[1] Another friend of Jane Addams', the social worker Mary Simkhovitch, made a similar observation. "Jane Addams," she said, "was an intellectual woman, but I don't think we think enough about that, perhaps because she was so natural."[2]

She was "natural" indeed, gentle and compassionate—the very model of Christian charity. And because of this, many people forgot that Jane Addams wrote some of the most discerning studies of industrial society to be found in the literature of social criticism. The shape of her career, moreover, easily lent itself to sentimentality. Like St. Francis of Assisi, to whom she was often compared, Jane Addams left the comfortable surroundings of her youth to live among the poor. It was probably inevitable that people should call her a saint—a woman who sacrificed herself to the welfare of the wretched masses.

Jane Addams herself had no taste for self-sacrifice and no condescension, it might be added, toward the poor. Hull-House, as she conceived it, did not represent a renunciation of the world. It was not even principally a form of good works. It aimed not so much at helping the poor as at understanding them; and by understanding them, at bridging the chasm that

[1] *Unity*, CXV (July 15, 1935), 200.

[2] Speech at the memorial service conducted by the National Conference of Social Work in Montreal, June 10, 1935; clipping in Graham Taylor MSS (Newberry Library, Chicago, Illinois).

industrialism had opened between social classes. Observation and analysis, therefore, were built into the enterprise from the beginning. It was imperative, from Miss Addams' point of view, that the settlement worker articulate his experience; otherwise, the middle class, which had cut itself off from the proletariat, would never begin to understand the degree to which its own culture had been impoverished thereby. It was also imperative that the social worker not only help people but also study the conditions under which they lived. Social work, in her opinion, was a form of sociology.

Why was it so difficult even for some of Jane Addams' admirers to grasp this point? It was only partly because her life so easily lent itself to romance. The speed with which Jane Addams became a national myth suggests that the *need* to romanticize her must have been very great. What Jane Addams discovered about American life by exposing herself to the West Side of Chicago disturbed the national complacency. Her greatness, as Emily Balch called it, lay precisely in her capacity to ask the kind of questions most people prefer to ignore. Praising her goodness, her saintliness, was a way to avoid answering her questions. The myth of Jane Addams served to render her harmless. The process by which Jane Addams, the social critic, became Saint Jane is an excellent example of the way in which American society manages to incorporate its critics into itself, thereby blunting the edge of their criticism.

Jane Addams' works, however, remain; and with them the question they raise, implicitly, on practically every page: is industrialism compatible with humanity? What happens to the human spirit, as she put it in *The Spirit of Youth and the City Streets* (see this volume, Document 7) when young girls are "prized more for their labor power than for their innocence, their tender beauty, their ephemeral gaiety, . . . more for the products they manufacture than for their immemorial ability to reaffirm the charm of existence"? The question is as disturbing today as it was when Miss Addams began to write, and her books, accordingly, remain as fresh and relevant today as when they first appeared. I hope that readers of these selections will be encouraged to read the original books whole and to expose themselves to the full force of her critique of industrial society. Meanwhile, the following selections will indicate the main outlines of that critique and something of the flavor of Miss Addams' superb prose. Beyond that, I trust that they will help dispel the impression that Miss Addams was important solely for her services to the poor. She was an activist, to be sure, an accomplished organizer and promoter, and I have admittedly minimized that aspect of her career, on the grounds that it is already sufficiently familiar. This anthology tries to rescue the less familiar, but to my mind more important, side of Jane Addams' life. It shows her as theorist and intellectual—a thinker of originality and daring.

EARLY LIFE AND SOCIAL WORK

Jane Addams, born on September 6, 1860, was the youngest of the eight children of John and Sarah Addams of Cedarville, Illinois. Sarah Addams died when Jane was less than three years old. John Addams remarried five years later, but his influence dominated the family. Jane in particular showed the stamp of her father's example and training—quick intelligence combined with a serious disposition; a powerful concern with personal morality combined with an impatience with formal theology; above all, a wish to live up to her father's example in all things. John Addams was both a virtuous and distinguished man. Coming to Illinois in the 1840's, he built a mill, acquired a bank, went to the state Senate, and died a leading citizen of the state. It seems to have been taken for granted that his daughter would likewise distinguish herself; that she, too, notwithstanding her sex, would embark upon a

suitable career. Accordingly, she was given the equivalent
of a college education at the nearby Rockford Seminary (later
Rockford College); and resisting the efforts of her teachers to
enlist her in missionary work, she set out in 1881 to study
medicine at the Woman's Medical College in Philadelphia.

If John Addams inspired his daughter to push beyond the
conventional circle of women's rights and duties, he also set
a demanding standard of moral rectitude. A Quaker—though
not a pacifist—he cared little for doctrine. What mattered, he
told his daughter, was that you "be honest with yourself inside,
whatever happened." His insistence on "mental integrity above
everything else," when ripped out of the context of formal
religion, was a heavy load for a young woman to bear.[3] As long
as her father was alive, it was enough for Jane Addams to
work for his approval. But when he died, a few weeks after
her graduation from Rockford Seminary, she found herself
abruptly cast adrift with no support except her own somewhat
overdeveloped conscience, the demands of which, she now discovered, she could not possibly meet. Her sister tried to comfort her: "You need not think that because he is gone, your
incentive has perished."[4] That, however, was precisely what
Jane could not help thinking. Her father's death precipitated
a nervous crisis that came to an end only in 1888, with the
decision to found Hull-House.

Ill health—a chronic spinal condition—forced her to withdraw from her medical studies in the winter of 1881–1882,
thereby compounding her difficulties. An operation in 1882
partially corrected the condition, but she had never been robust
and continued, for the rest of her life, to suffer periodic bouts
with illness. Characteristically, she blamed not her health but

---

[3] Jane Addams, *Twenty Years at Hull-House* (New York: The Macmillan Company, 1910), p. 15.

[4] Mary Addams Linn to Jane Addams, August 26 [?], 1881; Jane
Addams MSS (Swarthmore College Peace Collection, Swarthmore, Pennsylvania).

herself: "Failure through ill-health is just as culpable and miserable as failure through any other cause."[5] For seven years she drifted, unable to settle on a career. She went with her stepmother to Europe in dutiful pursuit of "culture" and returned convinced that culture for its own sake was a sterile pursuit—without, however, finding a better object of her own. Meanwhile, her idleness deepened day by day.

Her father had encouraged her to follow a career; her stepmother, a handsome, forceful, gregarious woman, actively discouraged her. She wished Jane to cultivate the traditional refinements and graces of womanhood. She also wished Jane to marry. A silent, prolonged conflict ensued—the source of Jane Addams' intuitions, later integrated into her social philosophy, about the tragic failure of the generations to understand each other. In 1887 Jane sailed once again for Europe, this time without her stepmother; and it was during this trip that her mounting disgust with a life of cultured ease crystallized into a plan of action. When she returned, she bought an old mansion, once a solitary estate, now an island of earlier affluence in a sea of slums, and plunged into the seething life of industrial Chicago.

The manner in which Jane Addams reached her decision to found a settlement on the West Side helps explain why she did not conceive of social work as a form of charity. Hull-House gave her a chance to do good, but it also provided the focus for her ambition to distinguish herself in some form of intellectual effort. Her first attempt to formulate the meaning of her decision was an essay entitled "The Subjective Necessity for Social Settlements,"[6] in which she argued that it was precisely the futility of the pursuit of culture for its own sake that had driven young women like herself into the settlement move-

---

[5] Jane Addams to Ellen Starr, June 8, 1884; Ellen Gates Starr MSS (Smith College Library, Northampton, Massachusetts).

[6] See this volume, Document 4.

ment. She never ceased to insist on the subjective necessity of social reform, and it was her awareness of the complexity of her own motives that saved her from the reformer's habitual self-righteousness. It also made her aware of the complexity of the motives of others, particularly those motives that divided parents and children. Her own rebellion, she found, had echoes in the rebellion of the children of immigrants and in the revolt of youth in general. Because her own experience approximated theirs, she was able to write about the aspirations of young people—even "juvenile" delinquents—and about the agonies of their parents, with an understanding that none of her predecessors in social work had been able to achieve.

With the founding of Hull-House, Jane Addams' remarkable energies, so long unused, exploded in simultaneous and seemingly incompatible lines of activity. She tried to do what she could to help her "neighbors" in immediate and tangible ways. Hundreds of people came to the house every day for help, advice, and comfort. Jane Addams and the other residents talked to them all. They taught classes—small children in the morning, older ones in the afternoon, adults in the evening. They tried to find jobs for men who needed work. A burglar broke into the house one night; Jane Addams told him to come back at nine the next morning, and she found him a job. Once, she even delivered a baby. The baby was illegitimate, and the neighbors, whose kindness to one another Jane Addams so often admired, "would not touch the likes of her." The house in which the pregnant girl was staying, moreover, was in a "bad" part of town. Nevertheless, she went when summoned, "just as if she was a doctor."[7]

Meanwhile, she talked wherever she could. She wanted to explain to the middle class "how the other half lived," but she also needed to raise money. As her nephew has explained,

---

[7] Jane Addams, *Twenty Years*, p. 110; James Weber Linn, *Jane Addams* (New York: D. Appleton-Century Company, 1935), p. 113.

Hull-House, being "personal" and "experimental," could not afford deficits.[8] At the same time it was costing far more than Jane Addams had expected. The need for money, therefore, was imperative, but that did not prevent her from refusing a gift of $20,000 from a man whose employees, mostly young girls, were notoriously underpaid. Another offer of $50,000 was easier to refuse, because it was made on condition that the residents desist from their agitation for a state factory-law. Characteristically, Jane Addams blamed not the offerer of the bribe but herself. Her father, she recalled, was "the one man in the Senate of Illinois" who had never been offered a bribe. "What had befallen the daughter of my father, that such a thing could happen to her? The salutary reflection that it could not have occurred unless a weakness in myself had permitted it, at least withheld me from any heroic display of indignation."[9]

Somehow money was raised, and Hull-House grew into a great complex of buildings and programs. Two friends, Mary Rozet Smith and Louise Bowen, contributed again and again. The first new building, an art gallery, was a reminder that the social settlement, as Jane Addams understood it, defied any narrow, utilitarian interpretation of its function. Other buildings were more practical—a coffeehouse, a gymnasium, an addition to the original building, a children's building, a house for the Jane Club (a cooperative boarding club for working girls), the Hull-House Apartments, a woman's club, a boys' club, a nursery. The supervision of this array of enterprises called forth in Jane Addams executive abilities that must have astonished even herself. Her correspondence for these years is that of an overworked executive—scribbled notes to her innumerable lieutenants. She no longer had time for letters or even, until Hull-House was ten years old, for more than occasional

---

[8] *Jane Addams*, p. 120.
[9] Jane Addams, *Twenty Years*, p. 33.

articles. Yet, all this bustle, this organizing and fund raising and politicking, never seems to have distracted her from the neighbors themselves, and in the midst of it she could write to a friend:

The playground this year is a fine affair, the willows wave in the breeze likewise clover, the children . . . play in the sand, build block houses and the Mothers sit in the shelter and sew—quite like a story book. My fund is up to $65150. and as soon as we move into the new building we will move the gym and clap onto it the third story. It will really be a great addition.[10]

Apart from the growth of Hull-House itself, she had increasingly to think of politics; for much of what she and her friends were trying to do depended on political and social reforms in the city as a whole, and beyond the city, in the state and in the nation. She campaigned for the abolition of child labor, for factory laws, for the reform of the courts, for temperance, for women's suffrage. These causes swept her into the Progressive Party in 1912. By that time she had acquired a national reputation. She seconded the nomination of Theodore Roosevelt and took a prominent part in the campaign for his election. But she never lost sight of the prosaic details of ward politics. These, more than the national experience, had been her political education.

She found very early, for instance, that even so basic a service as the removal of garbage was apparently beyond the resources of the local politicians. In 1895 she herself put in a bid for the garbage-removal contract of Chicago's 19th ward. The bid was rejected, but the mayor appointed her garbage inspector for the ward at a salary of $1,000 a year. "The position," she wrote, "was no sinecure."[11] She found herself, for a time, involved in the struggle against the Democratic machine headed by John Powers. The campaign failed, but Jane Addams

---

[10] Jane Addams to Mary Rozet Smith, July 31, 1889; Addams MSS.
[11] Jane Addams, *Twenty Years*, p. 203.

had already begun to wonder in any case whether reformers like herself did not make too much of the abstract virtue of political purity. Seeking to oust the machine, she came to understand it. She came to see the ward boss from the point of view of his constituents, not as a spoilsman but as the embodiment of neighborly generosity. She wondered now whether the ethics of the poor, in politics as in so many other things, were not after all more sophisticated than those of her own class.

That she could arrive at so charitable a view of machine politics was the more remarkable in view of the attacks to which she was subjected by Powers' supporters—attacks that were always violent and sometimes obscene. One voter objected not only to her campaign against Powers but to her entire career. "No man," he wrote,

can love a woman who takes her place among men as you do. . . . And now for a little advice to help you defeat the good man you have so often tried to do without success of course I can speak very plain to you, as your highest ambition is to be recognized as capable of doing a man's work. . . . Did it ever occur to you while on a tour of inspection, through alleyways old barns and such places where low depraved men with criminal records may be found (such a place a virtuous woman would be afraid to go.) You might for a small sum induce one of such men to sell you his pecker and balls, It would not be much loss to him, and will be your only chance to prove yourself a man. You could then go before a board of examiners chosen from the 19th ward prove yourself capable of filling a man's place, You could then have the privelage of casting a vote, and should that bold bad Johnny Powers challenge you you could produce your pecker cast your vote, and probably defeat him[.][12]

At the time of this attack Jane Addams was still a young woman—not the portly matron we picture—and it was not difficult to detect the prurience beneath such obscenity. An attack like this was also in some sense a sexual advance—the

---

[12] "A Voter" to Jane Addams, January 17, 1898; Addams MSS.

most outrageous, perhaps, of all the indignities to which a
practicing feminist exposed herself.[13] Such incidents were more
than personal affronts. They showed how easy it was to carica-
ture and vulgarize the feminists' actions—all actions. They
testified to the meanness of the human spirit, its seemingly
irresistible affinity, against which every countervailing influence
was impotent, for whatever was sordid; and it would have been
easy, in the face of such evidence of the intractability of human
nature, to despair of the effort to go against the grain. The
wretchedness of the 19th ward was appalling enough, but to
find its wretchedness directed against oneself must have been,
for someone who loved her neighbors, inexpressibly humiliat-
ing. At the least, Jane Addams might have wished to destroy
the letter. But she merely laid it by, and it survives today
along with the rest of her papers, side by side with the tributes
of statesmen and philosophers.

PROGRESSIVISM AND PACIFISM

The first twenty years at Hull-House—the period described
in Miss Addams' masterpiece, *Twenty Years at Hull-House*—
were a time of discovery. It was during this period that she
produced—except for *Peace and Bread*—her finest writings:

---

13 Emma Goldman once spent the night in a hotel in Cincinnati. A
brewer knocked on the door, expecting to be admitted; presumably,
Emma Goldman, who was not only a feminist but an advocate of free
love, would make love to anyone. Wasn't that what free love meant?
Free love was a pernicious doctrine, of course, and Emma Goldman a
dangerous woman, but as long as she was available, why shouldn't a man
take advantage of her permissiveness and accept what was so freely
offered?

Miss Goldman jumped out of bed and threatened to wake the whole
hotel.

"Please, please!" cried the brewer. "Don't make any scene. I'm a mar-
ried man, with grown children. I thought you believed in free love."
(Richard Drinnon, *Rebel in Paradise: A Biography of Emma Goldman*
[Chicago: University of Chicago Press, 1961], p. 151.)

Democracy and Social Ethics (1902), *The Spirit of Youth and the City Streets* (1909), and *Twenty Years at Hull-House* (1910). The following years, by contrast, were a time of suffering and trial. The outbreak of the First World War put progressivism to the test. Most progressives—John Dewey was a good example—eventually worked out a rationalization for support of the war as an agency of "socialization." As a political pragmatist and a friend and follower of Dewey, Miss Addams found this argument congenial and even tempting; she sometimes fell into it herself. She could not, however, accept the fact of the war itself. She had labored in the peace movement for many years; she continued to work for peace during the war.

Not that she was a doctrinaire nonresistant. Her father's Quakerism had not prevented him from raising a company of volunteers—the Addams Guards—to fight in the Civil War; and she herself was not even a Quaker. Her temperament was far from that of an enthusiast, a single-minded seeker of a single Truth. If she had had any doubts about her essential moderation, they had been dispelled by her exposure to the Chicago radicals of the 1890's, whose dogmatism repelled her, and by a memorable visit to Leo Tolstoy in the summer of 1896. Tolstoy, who had somewhat ostentatiously renounced his wealth for the life of a Russian peasant, questioned Jane Addams' devotion to the people. The sleeves of her dress, he pointed out, were so full that "there was enough stuff on one arm to make a frock for a little girl." She lived, moreover, on the unearned increment from her land in northern Illinois. "So you are an absentee landlord?" Chagrined, Jane Addams returned to Chicago determined to spend two hours a day in the Hull-House bakery, laboring with her own hands. But when she arrived in Chicago,

the whole scheme seemed to me as utterly preposterous as it doubtless was. The half dozen people invariably waiting to see me after breakfast, the piles of letters to be opened and answered, the demand of actual and pressing human wants—were these all to be pushed aside and asked to wait while I saved my soul by two hours' work at baking bread?

It was possible, after all, that Tolstoy was "more logical than life warrants."[14]

Jane Addams' pacifism, then, was pragmatic, resting on a sense that conflict, whatever else it might be, was inexcusably inefficient; but her opposition to the First World War inevitably made people identify her with the most intransigent type of dogmatism. Her position proved to be almost impossible to explain. The experience of being consistently misunderstood, together with that of standing almost alone, tempted her more than once to self-pity; it made her wish, at times, for martyrdom. The way in which she wrestled with these intricate and subtle dangers was in many ways her finest achievement, surpassed only by her brilliant analysis of it in *Peace and Bread in Time of War* (1922).

The war did not lead Jane Addams, as it led Randolph Bourne,[15] to reconsider the assumptions about the orderly progress of humanity that she shared with other progressives of her time. Despair was as foreign to her temperament as unreasoned optimism. In her writings she had always acknowledged the darker side of things, at the same time arguing that an understanding of evil would lead people to undertake the solution of problems that her own experience seemed to show were far from hopeless. She remained cautiously cheerful in her later years. Her energies, however, declined, especially after a heart attack in 1926. She wrote three more books—*The Second Twenty Years at Hull-House* (1930), *The Excellent Becomes*

---

14 Jane Addams, *Twenty Years*, pp. 268–277.

15 Randolph Bourne (1886–1918) was a literary essayist and social critic, whose opposition to the war combined with his premature death made him a hero of the intellectual Left in the 1920's.

the Permanent (1932), and *My Friend, Julia Lathrop* (1935)—
but none of them approached the high standard of her earlier
work. Meanwhile, Hull-House continued to grow and Miss
Addams' fame spread throughout the world. To her great
amusement, she found herself honored by people who had
formerly criticized her lack of patriotism. In 1931 a jury of
men named her first among the "twelve greatest living women
of America." "One of the committee," she said, "formerly regarded me as a traitor, and I am quite sure that two at least
of the others had never heard of me before this 'contest.' "[16]
In the same year she won the Nobel Peace Prize, along with
Nicholas Murray Butler, who had strongly supported the war
and denounced its opponents. Her errors forgiven, she found
herself in strange company. She was worse than famous; she
was respectable. But she refused to play the part. In 1932 she
gave a vigorous address at Swarthmore College, "Our National
Self-Righteousness." "Perhaps never before in our history," she
said, "has there been within the framework of orderly government such impatience with differing opinion."[17] "She had no
idea," her nephew wrote, "of 'departing in peace.' "[18]

On May 18, 1935, she underwent an intestinal operation,
which revealed, to her doctors' surprise and distress, that she
was also suffering from cancer. Three days later she died in
Passavant Hospital in Chicago.

THE DISCOVERY OF POVERTY AND THE SELF

Perhaps it is pointless to try to summarize the distinctive
quality of Jane Addams' intelligence. She loved the concrete,
but she was always earnestly seeking the general. She theor-

---

[16] James Weber Linn, *Jane Addams,* p. 380.
[17] "Our National Self-Righteousness," *University of Chicago Maga-
zine, XXCI* (November 1933), 9.
[18] James Weber Linn, *Jane Addams,* p. 386.

ized about every subject she ever touched, but without arriving at a general theory of modern society—doubtless because she distrusted the dogmatism with which such theories are often associated. Her method was essentially autobiographical, and the virtues and defects of her work were those that come from writing directly out of one's experience. She wrote superbly about the revolt of youth, the plight of women, the uprooting of immigrants, and the disintegration of family life under the conditions of industrialism. On subjects like prostitution, she wrote much less effectively, because there was no parallel in her experience to the bottomless cynicism that was so essential a feature of the "social evil."

The period in which Jane Addams lived was a time of social exploration, during which the "submerged tenth" of society was "discovered" by the comfortable classes. Autobiography was on the whole well-suited to such a time. The shock of discovery and the reversal of conventional perspectives that it implied were the persistent themes of Jane Addams' work, and they were themes that could best be treated by re-creating, again and again, the experience of one who had felt the shock at first hand. The social theories of the progressive period have not held up very well over the years, but the autobiographies—Lincoln Steffens', Jane Addams'—the books which describe how it felt to stumble upon a whole realm of social existence that the conventions of middle-class culture and education had completely concealed—these books are not likely to grow stale. Where the discovery of the poor was bound up with the discovery of the self, the result was a literature notable for its clarity, its immediacy, and its power to evoke in the reader sympathies whose existence he scarcely suspected.

I should like to thank the Smith College Library, the University of Kansas Library, and the Swarthmore College Library for permission to quote from Jane Addams' letters. I should also like to take this opportunity to thank Marjorie Edwards and Ardith L. Emmons, of the Swarthmore College Peace Collection, for their generous help on many occasions. Finally, I am indebted to Jane L. Rogers and Elizabeth Linn Murray for their assistance in my unsuccessful search for the holders of the literary rights to those works of Jane Addams to which the Macmillan Company no longer holds the copyright—*The Spirit of Youth and the City Streets* (1909), and *Peace and Bread in Time of War* (1922).

Christopher Lasch

August 1965

CHRONOLOGY

1860, September 6. Born at Cedarville, Illinois.

1863 Jane Addams' mother, Sarah Addams, dies.

1868 John Addams marries Anne Haldeman, widow of a prominent merchant.

1877–1881 Jane Addams attends Rockford Seminary.

1881, August 17. John Addams dies.

1881–1882 Jane Addams studies at Woman's Medical College, Philadelphia.

1882 Spinal operation, partially successful.

1883–1885 Tour of England and Continent.

1885 Joins Presbyterian Church.

1887–1888 Second trip to Europe.

1889, September 18. Opens Hull-House.

1891 Edward Butler, Chicago merchant, gives $5,000 for an art gallery at Hull-House.

Jane Club founded at Hull-House, a cooperative boarding-club for working girls.

1893 Coffeehouse and gymnasium built at Hull-House.

1894 Pullman strike.

1895 Appointed garbage inspector for 19th ward.

Elected to D.A.R.

Typhoid fever.

1896 Visits England and Russia; meets Tolstoy.

1898 Opposes United States acquisition of Philippine Islands.

1901 Defends the anarchist Abraham Isaak, arrested following assassination of McKinley.

1905 First of many summers in Bar Harbor, Maine.

1905–1909 Member Chicago School Board.

1907 Delegate to first National Peace Congress.

1909 Appendicitis.

1912 Delegate to Progressive National Convention and member of platform committee.

1914 First World War begins.

1915 Attends first congress of Women's International League for Peace and Freedom, The Hague.

Supports Henry Ford's peace ship, but pneumonia prevents her from sailing on the *Oskar II*.

1916 Tuberculosis of kidneys; one kidney removed.

Votes for Wilson ("he kept us out of war").

1917 United States declares war on Germany.

"It has been very painful to many of us who hold Miss Addams in deep affection . . . to find that we cannot think or act in unison with her." (Mary Simkhovitch, president, National Federation of Settlements)

"I have always been a friend of Miss Addams, but—" (Judge Orrin Carter, United States Superior Court).

1919 Presides over second congress of Women's International League for Peace and Freedom, Zurich.

Tours postwar France, Holland, Germany.

Blacklisted by Lusk Committee, New York legislature.

1920 Votes for Debs.

1921 Third congress of Women's International League for Peace and Freedom, Vienna.

1923 Trip around the world.

1924 Fourth congress of Women's International League for Peace and Freedom, Washington, D. C.

Votes for La Follette.

1926 Fifth congress of Women's International League for Peace and Freedom, Dublin.

Heart attack.

1928 Votes for Hoover.

1929 Sixth congress of Women's International League for Peace and Freedom, Prague; resigns as president; elected honorary president for life.

1930 Honorary LL.D., University of Chicago.

1931 Operation for tumor, apparently successful.

Receives Nobel Peace Prize, with Nicholas Murray Butler.

1932 Votes for Hoover again.

1935, May 21. Dies in Chicago of cancer; buried in Cedarville, Illinois.

SELECTED BIBLIOGRAPHY

ORIGINAL SOURCES
Manuscripts

Jane Addams MSS. Swarthmore College Peace Collection. Both incoming and outgoing correspondence, together with scrapbooks, clippings, articles.

Alice Haldeman MSS. University of Kansas Library. Letters from Jane Addams to her family from Europe, 1883–1885 and 1887–1888.

Ellen Gates Starr MSS. Smith College Library. Jane Addams' letters to Ellen Starr.

Graham Taylor MSS. Newberry Library. A few letters from Jane Addams.

Lillian D. Wald MSS. The New York Public Library. Letters from Jane Addams.

Principal Works of Jane Addams

"The Subjective Necessity for Social Settlements" and "The Objective Value of a Social Settlement." *Philanthropy and Social Progress.* New York: Thomas Y. Crowell & Company, 1893. Pp. 1–26, 27–56.

"A Function of the Social Settlement." *Annals of the American Academy of Political and Social Science,* XIII (May 1899), 323–345.

Democracy and Social Ethics. New York: The Macmillan Company, 1902.

Newer Ideals of Peace. New York: The Macmillan Company, 1907.

The Spirit of Youth and the City Streets. New York: The Macmillan Company, 1909.

Twenty Years at Hull-House. New York: The Macmillan Company, 1910.

A New Conscience and an Ancient Evil. New York: The Macmillan Company, 1912.

"A Modern Lear." *Survey,* XXIX (November 2, 1912), 131–137.

"The Revolt Against War," "Factors in Continuing the War," and "Women in Internationalism." *Women at The Hague: The International Congress and Its Results.* New York: The Macmillan Company, 1915. Pp. 55–81, 82–98, 124–141.

The Long Road of Woman's Memory. New York: The Macmillan Company, 1917.

Peace and Bread in Time of War. New York: The Macmillan Company, 1922.

The Second Twenty Years at Hull-House. New York: The Macmillan Company, 1930.

The Excellent Becomes the Permanent. New York: The Macmillan Company, 1932.

My Friend, Julia Lathrop. New York: The Macmillan Company, 1935.

Jane Addams: A Centennial Reader. New York: The Macmillan Company, 1960.

COLLATERAL READING

BOWEN, LOUISE DE KOVEN. *Open Windows: Stories of People and Places.* Chicago: R. F. Seymour and Company, 1946.

COMMAGER, HENRY STEELE. Foreword, *Twenty Years at Hull-House.* New York: New American Library of World Literature (Signet Books), 1961. Pp. vii-xvi.

CONWAY, JILL. "Jane Addams: An American Heroine," *Dædalus,* XCIII (Spring 1964), 761-780.

LINN, JAMES WEBER. *Jane Addams.* New York: D. Appleton-Century Company, 1935.

LOVETT, ROBERT MORSS. "Jane Addams," *World Tomorrow,* VIII (November 1925), 345.

LYND, STAUGHTON. "Jane Addams and the Radical Impulse," *Commentary,* XXXII (July 1961), 54-59.

TAYLOR, GRAHAM. "Jane Addams's Twenty Years of Industrial Democracy," *Survey* XXV (December 3, 1920), 405-409.

Unity, CXV (July 15, 1935), Memorial Issue.

TIMS, MARGARET. *Jane Addams of Hull-House.* London: George Allen & Unwin, 1961.

WILSON, EDMUND. "Hull-House in 1932," *American Earthquake.* Garden City: Doubleday & Company, 1958. Pp. 447-464.

WISE, WINIFRED E. *Jane Addams of Hull-House.* New York: Harcourt, Brace and Company, 1935.

EDITOR'S NOTE

In order to include a wide variety of Jane Addams' writings, I have had to abridge some of the selections; these abridgments are indicated in the text by ellipses. Jane Addams often borrowed from herself. Thus, parts of "The Objective Value of a Social Settlement" reappear verbatim in the chapter "Immigrants and Their Children" in *Twenty Years at Hull-House*. Most of my deletions involve such duplicating passages; and the reader may be assured, therefore, that nothing essential has been lost.

I have added footnotes to the text only to clarify references (a) that are sufficiently unfamiliar to require explanation and (b) that are necessary to an understanding of the passage in question. Nothing is more infuriating, in collections of this sort, it seems to me, than explanations of obvious or inconsequential references. A strong desire to spare the reader such explanations—which usually serve only to parade the editor's own erudition—has led me to keep my notes to an absolute minimum. In cases where an editorial footnote was essential, I have inserted a bracketed "Ed." to distinguish my annotation from that of Jane Addams.

PART I

THE SNARE OF PREPARATION

---

1. "With All My Apparent Leisure I Do Nothing at All"

1879, 1886

The sentimental version of Jane Addams' career has long obscured one of the most important things about it: she did not discover the "other half" until she was in her late twenties, old enough to experience it as a challenge to all her previous assumptions about the world. Without this discovery, without this shock, Jane Addams would not have been Jane Addams. But the creators of the Addams myth, in their effort to show that it was a sense of pity and compassion, and pity and compassion alone, that drove her into social work, insist that she had dedicated herself to the service of humanity practically from birth. The "master-motive" of her life, wrote Graham Taylor, a fellow settlement worker, "began to possess her . . . from her sixth year."[1] Robert Morss Lovett declared: "When a child of seven, she had her first sight of 'the poverty which implies squalor.' "[2] As late as 1955 Violet Oakley wrote a "dramatic outline of the life of

---

From Ellen Gates Starr MSS (Smith College Library, Northampton, Massachusetts). Printed with the permission of the Smith College Library and the directors of Hull-House Association.

[1] Graham Taylor, "Jane Addams's Twenty Years of Industrial Democracy," *Survey*, XXV (December 3, 1910), 405.

[2] Robert Morss Lovett, "Jane Addams," *World Tomorrow*, VIII (November 1925), 345.

Jane Addams," in which she depicted Jane as a girl of seven discussing with her brother her plans to "have a lot of money saved up to build the Great Big House."[3]

All the contemporary evidence that I have been able to find suggests that the problem of poverty was far from Jane Addams' thoughts during her formative years. Her letters to her friends show her to have been a pious young woman conscientiously pursuing a program of self-education in the cultural classics esteemed by the genteel tradition in which she was brought up. Particularly revealing are her letters to Ellen Gates Starr, a fellow student at Rockford Seminary and later cofounder of Hull-House. The two letters that follow, one written before, the other during, Jane Addams' period of nervous depression, give something of the flavor of the correspondence.

Cedarville, Ill

Aug 11, 1879

Beloved Friend:

You confuse me by writing about so many things at once, I don't exactly follow your transition of moods. Yet I truly thank you for all you said to me concerning your "incomprehensible news".[4] I catch your idea, of course I do. Don't you see that

---

[3] Violet Oakley, *Cathedral of Compassion* (Philadelphia: Privately Published, 1955), p. 12.

[4] Ellen had written:

Do you know, Jane, there is something in myself incomprehensible to me, in my views & feelings concerning religious subjects & especially [the] subject of the divinity of Christ. I should be glad to believe it. . . . And yet when I ask myself if I believe it, I know that I don't. The reality is about like that of certain characters in fiction, Dicken's especially.

(Ellen Starr to Jane Addams, July 27, 1879; Jane Addams MSS [Swarthmore College Peace Collection, Swarthmore, Pennsylvania] [Ed.].)

you are all right. What do you understand by being saved? I
don't know, of course, whether I have the correct idea or not,
but what I call it is this—that a people or a nation are saved
just as soon as they comprehend their god; almost every nation
has a beautiful divinity to start with, if they would only keep
right to that they would be all right, but they don't. They keep
getting farther away & lowering their ideal until at last they
are lost. Comprehending your deity & being in harmony with
his plans is to be saved. If you realize God through Christ, it
don't make any difference whether you realize Christ or not,
that is not the point. If God has become nearer to you, more
of a reality through him, then you are a Christian, Christ's
mission to you has been fulfilled. Don't you see what I mean.
If you have a God you are a Deist, if you more clearly comprehend that God through Christ then you are a Christan. I
am afraid I haven't expressed my idea very clearly, if you read
Tennyson's "In Memoriam" & look out for it, maybe you can
see something that will be exactly what you need. I did once
but I am far enough away now, & I beg you not to think that
I am trying to "preach," it don't sound like what I meant it
should if you think that I wish I was where you are. Christ
don't help me in the least, I know it is because I don't appreciate him, sometimes I can work myself into great admiration
for his life & occasionally I can catch something of his philosophy, but he don't bring me any nearer the Deity. I think of him
simply as a Jew living hundreds of years ago, surrounding
whom there is a mystery & a beauty incomprehensible to me.
I feel a little as I do when I hear very fine music—that I am
incapable of understanding. This is the nearest that I get to
it & it is very rare. As a general thing I regard it with indifference, think of the Jewish faith just as I do of Mohammadism
or any other system of religion. Lately it seems to me that I
am getting back of all of it—superior to it, I almost feel. Back
to a great *Primal Cause;* not Nature exactly, but a fostering
mother, a necessity, brooding and watching over all things,

above every human passion & yet not passive, the mystery of creation. I make a botch trying to describe it & yet the idea has been lots of comfort to me lately. The idea embodied in the sphinx—peace. Every time I talk about religion I vow a great vow never to do it again; I find myself growing indignant & sensitive when people speak of it lightly, as if they had no right to, you see I am not so *un*settled, as I *re*settle so often, but my creed is ever *be sincere* & don't fuss. I began with an honest desire to say something that might help you & end by trying to describe something in myself which is intangible— "impale a man on the personal pronoun."—I give you my blessing, my dear, & I'm quite sure you are all right. . . .

144 Washington Place

Baltimore, Feb. 7th 1886

My dear Ellen

I have been reading "Modern Painters" most of the afternoon. I have remembered your injunction you see "Read it, and don't let the grass grow under your feet." One is always impressed by Ruskin, in addition to the fine things he says, the air of authority with which he asserts them would make his readers believe any-thing much less fine. The assumption of superiority is always impressive, much more so where the superiority is real.

Your letter, my dear, did me much good. I was not waiting to be put in the position of a debtor but the desire to speak to you comes with increasing force after reading your words. You will never forget that wretched scolding I gave you at Cedarville last summer. You refer to it again in your "handicapping."[5] Don't you know, my dear, that you do as much work as I do, and more, in addition to all the time and vitality you give to your girls and that I am filled with shame that with all my apparent leisure I do nothing at all. I have had the strangest experience since I have been in Baltimore, I have found my faculties, memory receptive faculties and all, perfectly inaccessible locked up away from me. It may have been the culmination of the dreadful [*illegible*], or it may have been that I was bilious (the dreadful liver at the base of all our woes) at any rate I am only beginning to recover. I have been taking two French lessons a week with Mademoiselle Rabillon. The air of pity and consideration with which she has treated my feeble faculties is only equalled by her air of surprise since I have begun to wake up. Her father is the lecturer in French literature in the University. I attend a lecture every Saturday evening at five which I manage to translate and find very interesting. His view of Rabelais has been a perfect revelation to me. Beyond reading a little French I have done almost nothing, if you find Voltaire's Life of Charles XII, whether in English or French *be sure to read it*. It is one of the most fascinating little books I have ever read. The combination of gossip and philosophy, the subtle distinction between men who

---

[5] Ellen's previous letter alludes to some former reproach:

Be a little good to me, Jane dear. I am a good deal 'handicapped' by a [mere?] mass of drudgery in the way of huge piles of worthless compositions to correct weekly, consuming evening after evening [she was then teaching school in Chicago]; and my best material is a good deal drawn upon by the individual minds, ethical and other, of girls who seem to be my mission, and whom I wouldn't dare to neglect for anything. I would be glad to give you my best, and would still feel in your debt—but sometimes it isn't mine to give.

(Ellen Starr to Jane Addams, January 31, 1886; Addams MSS. [Ed.]

had brains & men who thought they had, is delicious. I have never seen Lewes History of Philosophy. I imagine that it would be entertaining and not much of an undertaking. If we are to meet next summer, we might try reading something before then and have opinions and sentiments ready to "exchange." I am impressed with the necessity of forming opinions, and amused by the southern people always assuming that Americans are so opinionated. I had a pleasant experience yesterday, took lunch with Mrs Dr Brooks, the little hostess, quite as cultivated as ladies I am accustomed to meet, said with great surprise "I thought northern people always talked about books, and I have been waiting to have you ask me about Henry James' last novel." This was said in all seriousness & is only a phase of the misconception they have of the severe and terrible northern young lady.

I am becoming much attached to Browning, not quite as to a poet but as an essayist. I read Carson's pamphlet devoted an entire day to it on "The Idea of Personality as embodied in Browning's poetry," it was a trifle obscure and mystical, it might have been written by a pantheist, but it showed B.'s continuous effort to reveal again "the fair fine trace of what was written once," his veneration and hope in the power of personality which each man owes to the world. Do you know anything of Russell Sturgis of New York? He gave a series of four lectures on Decorative Art at the Peabody, which were very fine. He was full of matter and overflowing with his subjects. I have never read Farrar's Life of Christ but have always felt drawn toward it. The finest minister in the city whom I have heard is a Unitarian, the church is near us, and I am rather afraid that I shall settle down to it. The sermon is more to me than the service. Grace Church is near us to which I have gone oftener than any other but it is not quite what I want. My mother sends you her love. Write to me when you can, my dear, and please don't imply that your letters are stupid. I object to the term in connection with anything of yours. I am always dear Ellen your unchanging friend

Jane Addams

2. "I Would Rather Not Have the Children Know"

1883, 1888

Those who hold that compassion was the "master-motive" of Jane Addams' life attach great importance to her two trips to Europe in the 1880's (1883–1885 and 1887–1888), because it was during these expeditions that she is said to have come face to face with industrial poverty. Jane Addams herself, in her autobiography, claimed that her first glimpse of poverty in the East End of London had decisively influenced her subsequent career.[1] The first of the following letters, however—the only surviving contemporary record of this event—suggests that she may have exaggerated its importance in retrospect. She makes only a passing reference to the scene she later described so vividly, and even this reference has a curiously literary and derivative flavor. Whatever her reactions to this first confrontation with large-scale human suffering, they had hardly reached the level of articulation, much less of action. She remained, throughout the first of these European trips and even through much of the second, an American girl in conscientious pur-

From Alice Haldeman MSS (University of Kansas Library, Lawrence, Kansas). Printed with the permission of the University of Kansas Library and the directors of Hull-House Association.

[1] See this volume, Document 3 [Ed.].

suit of the "advantages" associated with travel, leisure, and refinement.

The second of these letters, written toward the end of the second journey, describes a curious incident in Jane Addams' personal history. The more ample account in *Twenty Years at Hull-House*[2] shows that it had important consequences. What is interesting, however, is that the two accounts do not altogether agree. In her autobiography Miss Addams takes all the guilt associated with the incident upon herself; whereas the contemporary letter makes it clear that if it was wrong to enjoy a bullfight, she shared the fault with the rest of her companions. The discrepancy suggests that Miss Addams, like other autobiographers, was not above improving on the bare facts of her life when it suited her purpose to do so—even if it meant depicting herself as guiltier than she had actually felt at the time.

32, Dorset Square, London

Oct 29, 1883.

My dear Web,[3]

We have been devoting our energies so thoroughly to London for the last two weeks, that journalistic letter writing has rather dropped into the background. We leave the big town with the comfort of saying that we will certainly come back on our way home, for it seems otherwise impossible to go away. We bought our tickets this morning for Dresden. We will go by the way of Rotterdam & take about a week of sightseeing in Holland. We had quite an adventure last Saturday morning. Miss Warner the lady of the house took nine of the guests down into the "East end" to see the Saturday night marketing. The poorest people wait until very late Saturday night as

---

[2] *Ibid.*

[3] Weber Addams, Jane Addams' brother [Ed.].

meats and vegetables which cannot be kept on Sunday are sold cheaper. We reached the neighborhood by the underground railway & rode on top of a street car for five miles through [rows?] of booths and stalls, and swarming thousands of people. At one time we found ourselves in a Dickens neighborhood past Mrs Bardell's house, the old debtor prison, & Louis all alone. We took a look down into dingy old Grub St. It was simply an outside superficial survey of the misery & wretchedness, but it was enough to make one thoroughly sad & perplexed. Yesterday morning we heard Joseph Parker certainly the most powerful man we have heard since we came to London. He is large and his head looks not unlike a lion. The large handsome church or rather temple with the immense congregation was quite a contrast to the Sunday before which we spent at the old foundling Hospital. . . .

Madrid, Spain, April 25, 1888.

My dear Laura,[4]

I sent some photographs of the gallery to your address today. The small Murrillo I took from your ten dollars, saving the most of it for Cathedral views and I am very much tempted to save half of it for some Carbon points[5] in Paris. I couldn't find anything of the exterior of the Barcelona cathedral, and doubt if any are taken, as it is not interesting at least the view we had of it.

. . . There is nothing characteristic about Madrid as a whole although it is attractive and handsome in its way. The large old palace and stables are more interesting than the trappings of royalty usually are because more pretentious & showy. The

---

[4] I have not been able to identify "Laura" [Ed].
[5] Etchings.

carriages were marvels of gold and lace and the horses are valued at a million dollars, although the man insisted upon showing us the English breeds instead of the Arab.

We went to the Escorial one rainy day gloomy enough to suit the character of the place. The great stone building, neither monastery, church or palace, or rather the three combined in enormous proportions was very interesting because it was a complete expression of Philip II['s] mind and so carefully preserved as he left it. The tapestries are handsome and the library exceedingly interesting, but the effect of the building as a whole was so unimpressive that it was quite impossible to remember details. We went to the gallery every day, and could have gone many more times with profit. The portraits by Valezquez are magnificent & he liberally exposed any thought in Philip IV['s] mind. The great event of our stay in Madrid after all was the thing we are all rather ashamed of—and that was a bull fight or Festa del Toros as we rather prefer to call it. The ring or amphitheater itself was an immense affair with stone seats for eight or ten tiers, and the upper rows of wooden seats with a covering where we sat. Mrs. Rowell decided not to go finally, and we took as protector and guide, one of the men from the hotel, who wore a gorgeous Spanish cloak and regarded it all in a true Spanish light. We got there just as the first grand procession was in the ring, and just as they went out the bull came rushing in. He was a beautiful creature, as lithe and active as a cat, and as fleet and graceful as a deer with nothing of the awkwardness one associates with a bull. The *picadors* are the two men mounted on horses who irritate the bull with long wooden lances until he rushes into them and kills the horses. The first bull killed four horses, two under each picador, he made a wild rush followed by a grand melée of horse and rider, the rider invariably being pulled out unhurt and the horse lying dead. That was the worst part of it. The second act of six men tiring and bewildering the bull with their bright red cloaks was graceful and brilliant with no suggestion of danger. The *bandilleros* who struck the victim with the gaily decorated little swords were in apparently greater danger than the *matador* himself, who did not come in until the bull was so tired out that it was a comparatively easy matter to kill, by one clever stroke into his spinal cord. There were six bulls killed that afternoon, but we did not stay until the bitter end although we were rather ashamed and surprised to find that we were brutal enough to take a great interest in it. The immense audience was either wild with delight or uproarious with hisses every minute, even throwing hats and oranges at the head of our awkward matador. . . .

I will ask you to send this to Alice,[6] it is fearfully stupid but it is about all I am able to write. I think I would rather not have the children of the family know of the bullfight.

3. *Twenty Years at Hull-House*

1910

The contrast between her youthful letters and essays and her autobiography, written when she was in her late forties, is the best indication that Jane Addams, in discovering industrial poverty, also discovered in herself powers of self-expression of which her early writings gave only the barest hint. She had perfected a distinctive literary style, at once simple and marvelously subtle, and she was in absolute control of her material. Hardly a line of her autobiog-

---

Reprinted with the permission of The Macmillan Co. from *Twenty Years at Hull-House* by Jane Addams, pages 65–88. Copyright 1910 by The Phillips Publishing Co., copyright 1910 by The Macmillan Co., renewed 1938 by James W. Linn.

[6] Alice was Jane's elder sister, Alice Addams Haldeman [Ed.].

raphy does not testify to the quiet self-assurance that followed Jane Addams' years of doubt and uncertainty—themselves the subject of the remarkable chapter that follows.

THE SNARE OF PREPARATION

The winter after I left school was spent in the Woman's Medical College of Philadelphia, but the development of the spinal difficulty which had shadowed me from childhood forced me into Dr. Weir Mitchell's hospital for the late spring, and the next winter I was literally bound to a bed in my sister's house for six months. In spite of its tedium, the long winter had its mitigations, for after the first few weeks I was able to read with a luxurious consciousness of leisure, and I remember opening the first volume of Carlyle's "Frederick the Great" with a lively sense of gratitude that it was not Gray's "Anatomy," having found, like many another, that general culture is a much easier undertaking than professional study. The long illness inevitably put aside the immediate prosecution of a medical course, and although I had passed my examinations creditably enough in the required subjects for the first year, I was very glad to have a physician's sanction for giving up clinics and dissecting rooms and to follow his prescription of spending the next two years in Europe.

Before I returned to America I had discovered that there were other genuine reasons for living among the poor than that of practicing medicine upon them, and my brief foray into the profession was never resumed.

The long illness left me in a state of nervous exhaustion with which I struggled for years, traces of it remaining long after Hull-House was opened in 1889. At the best it allowed me but a limited amount of energy, so that doubtless there was much nervous depression at the foundation of the spiritual struggles which this chapter is forced to record. However, it could not have been all due to my health, for as my wise little notebook sententiously remarked, "In his own way each man must struggle, lest the moral law become a far-off abstraction utterly separated from his active life."

It would, of course, be impossible to remember that some of these struggles ever took place at all, were it not for these selfsame notebooks, in which, however, I no longer wrote in moments of high resolve, but judging from the internal evidence afforded by the books themselves, only in moments of deep depression when overwhelmed by a sense of failure.

One of the most poignant of these experiences, which occurred during the first few months after our landing upon the other side of the Atlantic, was on a Saturday night, when I received an ineradicable impression of the wretchedness of East London, and also saw for the first time the overcrowded quarters of a great city at midnight. A small party of tourists were taken to the East End by a city missionary to witness the Saturday night sale of decaying vegetables and fruit, which, owing to the Sunday laws in London, could not be sold until Monday, and, as they were beyond safe keeping, were disposed of at auction as late as possible on Saturday night. On Mile End Road, from the top of an omnibus which paused at the end of a dingy street lighted by only occasional flares of gas, we saw two huge masses of ill-clad people clamoring around two hucksters' carts. They were bidding their farthings and ha'pennies for a vegetable held up by the auctioneer, which he at last scornfully flung, with a gibe for its cheapness, to the successful bidder. In the momentary pause only one man detached himself from the groups. He had bidden in a cabbage, and when it struck his hand, he instantly sat down on the curb, tore it with his teeth, and hastily devoured it, unwashed and uncooked as it was. He and his fellows were types of the "submerged tenth," as our missionary guide told us, with some little satisfaction in the then new phrase, and he further added that so many of them could scarcely be seen in one spot save at this Saturday night auction, the desire for cheap food being apparently the one thing which could move them simultaneously. They were huddled into ill-fitting, cast-off clothing, the ragged finery which one sees only in East London. Their pale faces were dominated by that most unlovely of human expressions, the cunning and shrewdness of the bargain-hunter who starves if he cannot make a successful trade, and yet the final impression was not of ragged, tawdry clothing nor of pinched and sallow faces, but of myriads of hands, empty, pathetic, nerveless and workworn, showing white in the uncertain light of the street, and clutching forward for food which was already unfit to eat.

Perhaps nothing is so fraught with significance as the human hand, this oldest tool with which man has dug his way from savagery, and with which he is constantly groping forward. I have never since been able to see a number of hands held upward, even when they are moving rhythmically in a calisthenic exercise, or when they belong to a class of chubby children who wave them in eager response to a teacher's query, without a certain revival of this memory, a clutching at the heart reminiscent of the despair and resentment which seized me then.

For the following weeks I went about London almost furtively, afraid to look down narrow streets and alleys lest they disclose again this hideous human need and suffering. I carried with me for days at a time that curious surprise we experience when we first come back into the streets after days given over to sorrow and death; we are bewildered that the world should be going on as usual and unable to determine which is real, the inner pang or the outward seeming. In time all huge London came to seem unreal save the poverty in its East End. During the following two years on the continent, while I was irresistibly drawn to the poorer quarters of each city, nothing among the beggars of South Italy nor among the saltminers of Austria carried with it the same conviction of human wretchedness which was conveyed by this momentary glimpse of an East London street. It was, of course, a most fragmentary and lurid view of the poverty of East London, and quite unfair. I should have been shown either less or more, for I went away with no notion of the hundreds of men and women who had gallantly identified their fortunes with these empty-handed people, and who, in church and chapel, "relief works," and charities, were at least making an effort towards its mitigation.

Our visit was made in November, 1883, the very year when the *Pall Mall Gazette* exposure started "The Bitter Cry of Outcast London," and the conscience of England was stirred as never before over this joyless city in the East End of its capital. Even then, vigorous and drastic plans were being discussed, and a splendid program of municipal reforms was already dimly outlined. Of all these, however, I had heard nothing but the vaguest rumor.

No comfort came to me then from any source, and the painful impression was increased because at the very moment of looking down the East London street from the top of the omnibus, I had been sharply and painfully reminded of "The Vision of Sudden Death" which had confronted De Quincey one summer's night as he was being driven through rural England on a high mail coach. Two absorbed lovers suddenly appear between the narrow, blossoming hedgerows in the direct path of the huge vehicle which is sure to crush them to their death. De Quincey tries to send them a warning shout, but finds himself unable to make a sound because his mind is hopelessly entangled in an endeavor to recall the exact lines from the "Iliad" which describe the great cry with which Achilles alarmed all Asia militant. Only after his memory responds is his will released from its momentary paralysis, and he rides on through the fragrant night with the horror of the escaped calamity thick upon him, but he also bears with him the consciousness that he had given himself over so many years to classic learning—that when suddenly called upon for a quick decision in the world of life and death, he had been able to act only through a literary suggestion.[1]

This is what we were all doing, lumbering our minds with literature that only served to cloud the really vital situation spread before our eyes. It seemed to me too preposterous that in my first view of the horror of East London I should have recalled De Quincey's literary description of the literary suggestion which had once paralyzed him. In my disgust it all appeared a hateful, vicious circle which even the apostles of culture themselves admitted, for had not one of the greatest among the moderns plainly said that "conduct, and not culture is three fourths of human life."

For two years in the midst of my distress over the poverty which, thus suddenly driven into my consciousness, had become to me the "Weltschmerz," there was mingled a sense of futility, of misdirected energy, the belief that the pursuit of cultivation would not in the end bring either solace or relief. I gradually reached a conviction that the first generation of college women had taken their learning too quickly, had departed too suddenly from the active, emotional life led by their grandmothers and great-grandmothers; that the contemporary education of young women had developed too exclusively the power of acquiring knowledge and of merely receiving impressions; that somewhere in the process of "being educated" they had lost that simple and almost automatic response to the

----

[1] See Thomas De Quincey, "The Vision of Sudden Death," in *The English Mail Coach and Other Writings* (Edinburgh: Adam and Charles Black, 1863), pp. 336–337. But Jane Addams remembered the passage incorrectly, attributing her own condemnation of culture to De Quincey. His meaning was precisely the reverse: the passage from Homer, far from "paralyzing" him, prompted him to shout, "Oh heavens! What is it that I shall do? Speaking or acting, what help can I offer? Strange it is, and to a mere auditor of the tale might seem laughable, that I should need a suggestion from the 'Iliad' to prompt the sole resource that remained. Yet so it was. Suddenly I remembered the shout of Achilles . . . I shouted . . ." [Ed.].

human appeal, that old healthful reaction resulting in activity from the mere presence of suffering or of helplessness; that they are so sheltered and pampered they have no chance even to make "the great refusal."

In the German and French *pensions*, which twenty-five years ago were crowded with American mothers and their daughters who had crossed the seas in search of culture, one often found the mother making real connection with the life about her, using her inadequate German with great fluency, gayly measuring the enormous sheets or exchanging recipes with the German Hausfrau, visiting impartially the nearest kindergarten and market, making an atmosphere of her own, hearty and genuine as far as it went, in the house and on the street. On the other hand, her daughter was critical and uncertain of her linguistic acquirements, and only at ease when in the familiar receptive attitude afforded by the art gallery and the opera house. In the latter she was swayed and moved, appreciative of the power and charm of the music, intelligent as to the legend and poetry of the plot, finding use for her trained and developed powers as she sat "being cultivated" in the familiar atmosphere of the classroom which had, as it were, become sublimated and romanticized.

I remember a happy busy mother who, complacent with the knowledge that her daughter daily devoted four hours to her music, looked up from her knitting to say, "If I had had your opportunities when I was young, my dear, I should have been a very happy girl. I always had musical talent, but such training as I had, foolish little songs and waltzes and not time for half an hour's practice a day."

The mother did not dream of the sting her words left and that the sensitive girl appreciated only too well that her opportunities were fine and unusual, but she also knew that in spite of some facility and much good teaching she had no genuine talent and never would fulfill the expectations of her friends. She looked back upon her mother's girlhood with positive envy because it was so full of happy industry and extenuating obstacles, with undisturbed opportunity to believe that her talents were unusual. The girl looked wistfully at her mother, but had not the courage to cry out what was in her heart: "I might believe I had unusual talent if I did not know what good music was; I might enjoy half an hour's practice a day if I were busy and happy the rest of the time. You do not know what life means when all the difficulties are removed! I am simply smothered and sickened with advantages. It is like eating a sweet dessert the first thing in the morning."

This, then, was the difficulty, this sweet dessert in the morning and the assumption that the sheltered, educated girl has nothing to do with the bitter poverty and the social maladjustment which is all about her, and which, after all, cannot be concealed, for it breaks through poetry and literature in a burning tide which overwhelms her; it peers at her in the form of heavy-laden market women and underpaid street laborers, gibing her with a sense of her uselessness.

I recall one snowy morning in Saxe-Coburg, looking from the window of our little hotel upon the town square, that we saw crossing and recrossing it a single file of women with semi-circular heavy wooden tanks fastened upon their backs. They were carrying in this primitive fashion to a remote cooling room these tanks filled with a hot brew incident to one stage of beer making. The women were bent forward, not only under the weight which they were bearing, but because the tanks were so high that it would have been impossible for them to have lifted their heads. Their faces and hands, reddened in the cold morning air, showed clearly the white scars where they had previously been scalded by the hot stuff which splashed if they stumbled ever so little on their way. Stung into action by one of those sudden indignations against cruel conditions which at times fill the young with unexpected energy, I found myself across the square, in company with mine host, interviewing the phlegmatic owner of the brewery who received us with exasperating indifference, or rather received me, for the innkeeper mysteriously slunk away as soon as the great magnate of the town began to speak. I went back to a breakfast for which I had lost my appetite, as I had for Gray's "Life of Prince Albert" and his wonderful tutor, Baron Stockmar, which I had been reading late the night before. The book had lost its fascination; how could a good man, feeling so keenly his obligation "to make princely the mind of his prince," ignore such conditions of life for the multitude of humble, hardworking folk. We were spending two months in Dresden that winter, given over to much reading of "The History of Art" and to much visiting of its art gallery and opera house, and after such an experience I would invariably suffer a moral revulsion against this feverish search after culture. It was doubtless in such moods that I founded my admiration for Albrecht Dürer, taking his wonderful pictures, however, in the most unorthodox manner, merely as human documents. I was chiefly appealed to by his unwillingness to lend himself to a smooth and cultivated view of life, by his determination to record its frustrations and even the hideous forms which darken the day for our human imagination and to ignore no human complications. I believed that his canvases intimated the coming religious and social changes of the Reformation and the peasants' wars, that they were surcharged with pity for the downtrodden, that his sad knights, gravely standing guard, were longing to avert that shedding of blood which is sure to occur when men forget how complicated life is and insist upon reducing it to logical dogmas.

The largest sum of money that I ever ventured to spend in Europe was for an engraving of his "St. Hubert," the background of which was said to be from an original Dürer plate. There is little doubt, I am afraid, that the background as well as the figures "were put in at a later date," but the purchase at least registered the high-water mark of my enthusiasm.

The wonder and beauty of Italy later brought healing and

some relief to the paralyzing sense of the futility of all artistic and intellectual effort when disconnected from the ultimate test of the conduct it inspired. The serene and soothing touch of history also aroused old enthusiasms, although some of their manifestations were such as one smiles over more easily in retrospection than at the moment. I fancy that it was no smiling matter to several people in our party, whom I induced to walk for three miles in the hot sunshine beating down upon the Roman Campagna, that we might enter the Eternal City on foot through the Porta del Popolo, as pilgrims had done for centuries. To be sure, we had really entered Rome the night before, but the railroad station and the hotel might have been anywhere else, and we had been driven beyond the walls after breakfast and stranded at the very spot where the pilgrims always said "Ecco Roma," as they caught the first glimpse of St. Peter's dome. This melodramatic entrance into Rome, or rather pretended entrance, was the prelude to days of enchantment, and I returned to Europe two years later in order to spend a winter there and to carry out a great desire to systematically study the Catacombs. In spite of my distrust of "advantages" I was apparently not yet so cured but that I wanted more of them.

The two years which elapsed before I again found myself in Europe brought their inevitable changes. Family arrangements had so come about that I had spent three or four months of each of the intervening winters in Baltimore, where I seemed to have reached the nadir of my nervous depression and sense of maladjustment, in spite of my interest in the fascinating lectures given there by Lanciani of Rome, and a definite course of reading under the guidance of a Johns Hopkins lecturer upon the United Italy movement. In the latter I naturally encountered the influence of Mazzini, which was a source of great comfort to me, although perhaps I went too suddenly from a contemplation of his wonderful ethical and philosophical appeal to the workingmen of Italy, directly to the lecture rooms at Johns Hopkins University, for I was certainly much disillusioned at this time as to the effect of intellectual pursuits upon moral development.

The summers were spent in the old home in northern Illinois, and one Sunday morning I received the rite of baptism and became a member of the Presbyterian church in the village. At this time there was certainly no outside pressure pushing me towards such a decision, and at twenty-five one does not ordinarily take such a step from a mere desire to conform. While I was not conscious of any emotional "conversion," I took upon myself the outward expressions of the religious life with all humility and sincerity. It was doubtless true that I was

> "Weary of myself and sick of asking,
> What I am and what I ought to be,"

and that various cherished safeguards and claims to self-dependence had been broken into by many piteous failures. But certainly I had been brought to the conclusion that "sincerely to give up one's conceit or hope of being good in one's own right is the only door to the Universe's deeper reaches." Perhaps the young clergyman recognized this as the test of the Christian temper, at any rate he required little assent to dogma or miracle, and assured me that while both the ministry and the officers of his church were obliged to subscribe to doctrines of well-known severity, the faith required of the laity was almost early Christian in its simplicity. I was conscious of no change from my childish acceptance of the teachings of the Gospels, but at this moment something persuasive within made me long for an outward symbol of fellowship, some bond of peace, some blessed spot where unity of spirit might claim right of way over all differences. There was also growing within me an almost passionate devotion to the ideals of democracy, and when in all history had these ideals been so thrillingly expressed as when the faith of the fisherman and the slave had been boldly opposed to the accepted moral belief that the well-being of a privileged few might justly be built upon the ignorance and sacrifice of the many? Who was I, with my dreams of universal fellowship, that I did not identify myself with the institutional statement of this belief, as it stood in the little village in which I was born, and without which testimony in each remote hamlet of Christendom it would be so easy for the world to slip back into the doctrines of selection and aristocracy?

In one of the intervening summers between these European journeys I visited a western state[2] where I had formerly invested a sum of money in mortgages. I was much horrified by the wretched conditions among the farmers, which had resulted from a long period of drought, and one forlorn picture was fairly burned into my mind. A number of starved hogs— collateral for a promissory note—were huddled into an open pen. Their backs were humped in a curious, camel-like fashion, and they were devouring one of their own number, the latest victim of absolute starvation or possibly merely the one least able to defend himself against their voracious hunger. The farmer's wife looked on indifferently, a picture of despair as she stood in the door of the bare, crude house, and the two children behind her, whom she vainly tried to keep out of sight, continually thrust forward their faces almost covered by masses of coarse, sunburned hair, and their little bare feet so black, so hard, the great cracks so filled with dust that they looked like flattened hoofs. The children could not be compared to anything so joyous as satyrs, although they appeared but half-human. It seemed to me quite impossible to receive interest from mortgages placed upon farms which might at any season be reduced to such conditions, and with great inconvenience to my agent and doubtless with hardship to the farmers, as speedily as possible I withdrew all my investment.

---

[2] Illinois [Ed.].

But something had to be done with the money, and in my reaction against unseen horrors I bought a farm near my native village and also a flock of innocent-looking sheep. My partner in the enterprise had not chosen the shepherd's lot as a permanent occupation, but hoped to speedily finish his college course upon half the proceeds of our venture. This pastoral enterprise still seems to me to have been essentially sound, both economically and morally, but perhaps one partner depended too much upon the impeccability of her motives and the other found himself too preoccupied with study to know that it is not a real kindness to bed a sheepfold with straw, for certainly the venture ended in a spectacle scarcely less harrowing than the memory it was designed to obliterate. At least the sight of two hundred sheep with four rotting hoofs each, was not reassuring to one whose conscience craved economic peace. A fortunate series of sales of mutton, wool, and farm enabled the partners to end the enterprise without loss, and they passed on, one to college and the other to Europe, if not wiser, certainly sadder for the experience.

It was during this second journey to Europe that I attended a meeting of the London match girls who were on strike and who met daily under the leadership of well-known labor men of London. The low wages that were reported at the meetings, the phossy jaw which was described and occasionally exhibited, the appearance of the girls themselves I did not, curiously enough, in any wise connect with what was called the labor movement, nor did I understand the efforts of the London trades-unionists, concerning whom I held the vaguest notions. But of course this impression of human misery was added to the others which were already making me so wretched. I think that up to this time I was still filled with the sense which Wells describes in one of his young characters, that somewhere in Church or State are a body of authoritative people who will put things to rights as soon as they really know what is wrong. Such a young person persistently believes that behind all suffering, behind sin and want, must lie redeeming magnanimity. He may imagine the world to be tragic and terrible, but it never for an instant occurs to him that it may be contemptible or squalid or self-seeking. Apparently I looked upon the efforts of the trades-unionists as I did upon those of Frederic Harrison and the Positivists whom I heard the next Sunday in Newton Hall, as a manifestation of "loyalty to humanity" and an attempt to aid in its progress. I was enormously interested in the Positivists during these European years; I imagined that their philosophical conception of man's religious development might include all expressions of that for which so many ages of men have struggled and aspired. I vaguely hoped for this universal comity when I stood in Stonehenge, on the Acropolis in Athens, or in the Sistine Chapel in the Vatican. But never did I so desire it as in the cathedrals of Winchester, Notre Dame, Amiens. One winter's day I traveled from Munich to Ulm because I imagined from what the art books said that the cathedral horded a medieval statement of the Positivists' final synthesis, prefiguring their conception of a "Supreme Humanity."

In this I was not altogether disappointed. The religious history carved on the choir stalls at Ulm contained Greek philosophers as well as Hebrew prophets, and among the disciples and saints stood the disoverer of music and a builder of pagan temples. Even then I was startled, forgetting for the moment the religious revolutions of south Germany, to catch sight of a window showing Luther as he affixed his thesis on the door at Wittenberg, the picture shining clear in the midst of the older glass of saint and symbol.

My smug notebook states that all this was an admission that "the saints but embodied fine action," and it proceeds at some length to set forth my hope for a "cathedral of humanity," which should be "capacious enough to house a fellowship of common purpose," and which should be "beautiful enough to persuade men to hold fast to the vision of human solidarity."

It is quite impossible for me to reproduce this experience at Ulm unless I quote pages more from the notebook in which I seem to have written half the night, in a fever of composition cast in ill-digested phrases from Comte. It doubtless reflected also something of the faith of the Old Catholics, a charming group of whom I had recently met in Stuttgart, and the same mood is easily traced in my early hopes for the Settlement that it should unite in the fellowship of the deed those of widely differing religious beliefs.

The beginning of 1887 found our little party of three in very picturesque lodgings in Rome, and settled into a certain student's routine. But my study of the Catacombs was brought to an abrupt end in a fortnight by a severe attack of sciatic rheumatism, which kept me in Rome with a trained nurse during many weeks, and later sent me to the Riviera to lead an invalid's life once more. Although my Catacomb lore thus remained hopelessly superficial, it seemed to me a sufficient basis for a course of six lectures which I timidly offered to a Deaconess's Training School during my first winter in Chicago, upon the simple ground that this early interpretation of Christianity is the one which should be presented to the poor, urging that the primitive church was composed of the poor and that it was they who took the wonderful news to the more prosperous Romans. The open-minded head of the school gladly accepted the lectures, arranging that the course should be given each spring to her graduating class of Home and Foreign Missionaries, and at the end of the third year she invited me to become one of the trustees of the school. I accepted and attended one meeting of the board, but never another, because some of the older members objected to my membership on the ground that "no religious instruction was given at Hull-House." I remember my sympathy for the embarrassment in which the head of the school was placed, but if I needed comfort, a bit of it came to me on my way home from the trustees' meeting when an Italian laborer paid my street car fare, according to the custom of our simpler neighbors. Upon my inquiry of the conductor as to whom I was indebted for the little courtesy, he replied roughly enough, "I cannot tell one dago from another when they are in a gang, but sure, any one of them would do it for you as quick as they would for the Sisters."

It is hard to tell just when the very simple plan which afterward developed into the Settlement began to form itself in my mind. It may have been even before I went to Europe for the second time, but I gradually became convinced that it would be a good thing to rent a house in a part of the city where many primitive and actual needs are found, in which young women who had been given over too exclusively to study, might restore a balance of activity along traditional lines and learn of life from life itself; where they might try out some of the things they had been taught and put truth to "the ultimate test of the conduct it dictates or inspires." I do not remember to have mentioned this plan to any one until we reached Madrid in April, 1888.

We had been to see a bull fight rendered in the most magnificent Spanish style, where greatly to my surprise and horror, I found that I had seen, with comparative indifference, five bulls and many more horses killed. The sense that this was the last survival of all the glories of the amphitheater, the illusion that the riders on the caparisoned horses might have been knights of a tournament, or the matador a slightly armed gladiator facing his martyrdom, and all the rest of the obscure yet vivid associations of an historic survival, had carried me beyond the endurance of any of the rest of the party. I finally met them in the foyer, stern and pale with disapproval of my brutal endurance, and but partially recovered from the faintness and disgust which the spectacle itself had produced upon them. I had no defense to offer to their reproaches save that I had not thought much about the bloodshed; but in the evening the natural and inevitable reaction came, and in deep chagrin I felt myself tried and condemned, not only by this disgusting experience but by the entire moral situation which it revealed. It was suddenly made quite clear to me that I was lulling my conscience by a dreamer's scheme, that a mere paper reform had become a defense for continued idleness, and that I was making it a *raison d'être* for going on indefinitely with study and travel. It is easy to become the dupe of a deferred purpose, of the promise the future can never keep, and I had fallen into the meanest type of self-deception in making myself believe that all this was in preparation for great things to come. Nothing less than the moral reaction following the experience at a bull-fight had been able to reveal to me that so far from following in the wake of a chariot of philanthropic fire, I had been tied to the tail of the veriest ox-cart of self-seeking.

I had made up my mind that next day, whatever happened, I would begin to carry out the plan, if only by talking about it. I can well recall the stumbling and uncertainty with which I finally set it forth to Miss Starr, my old-time school friend, who was one of our party. I even dared to hope that she might join in carrying out the plan, but nevertheless I told it in the fear of that disheartening experience which is so apt to afflict our most cherished plans when they are at last divulged, when we suddenly feel that there is nothing there to talk about, and as the golden dream slips through our fingers we are left to wonder at our own fatuous belief. But gradually the comfort of Miss Starr's companionship, the vigor and enthusiasm which she brought to bear upon it, told both in the growth of the plan and upon the sense of its validity, so that by the time we had reached the enchantment of the Alhambra, the scheme had become convincing and tangible although still most hazy in detail.

A month later we parted in Paris, Miss Starr to go back to Italy, and I to journey on to London to secure as many suggestions as possible from those wonderful places of which we had heard, Toynbee Hall and the People's Palace. So that it finally came about that in June, 1888, five years after my first visit in East London, I found myself at Toynbee Hall equipped not only with a letter of introduction from Canon Fremantle, but with high expectations and a certain belief that whatever perplexities and discouragement concerning the life of the poor were in store for me, I should at least know something at first hand and have the solace of daily activity. I had confidence that although life itself might contain many difficulties, the period of mere passive receptivity had come to an end, and I had at last finished with the everlasting "preparation for life," however ill-prepared I might be.

It was not until years afterward that I came upon Tolstoy's phrase "the snare of preparation," which he insists we spread before the feet of young people, hopelessly entangling them in a curious inactivity at the very period of life when they are longing to construct the world anew and to conform it to their own ideals.

4. "The Subjective Necessity for Social Settlements"

1892

In the summer of 1892, three years after the founding of Hull-House, the Ethical Culture Societies held a summer school at Plymouth, Massachusetts, on the subject of philanthropy and social progress. Jane Addams read the following lecture, which shows the connection between her entrance into settlement work and the emotional crisis from which she had just emerged. The autobiographical character of these observations will be clear to anyone who comes to them fresh from reading "The Snare of Preparation."

From Jane Addams, *Philanthropy and Social Progress* (New York: Thomas Y. Crowell & Company, 1893), pp. 1–26.

Hull House, which was Chicago's first Settlement, was established in September, 1889. It represented no association, but was opened by two women, backed by many friends, in the belief that the mere foothold of a house, easily accessible, ample in space, hospitable and tolerant in spirit, situated in the midst of the large foreign colonies which so easily isolate themselves in American cities, would be in itself a serviceable thing for Chicago. Hull House endeavors to make social intercourse express the growing sense of the economic unity of society. It is an effort to add the social function to democracy. It was opened on the theory that the dependence of classes on each other is reciprocal; and that as "the social relation is essentially a reciprocal relation, it gave a form of expression that has peculiar value."

This paper is an attempt to treat of the subjective necessity for Social Settlements, to analyze the motives which underlie a movement based not only upon conviction, but genuine emotion. Hull House of Chicago is used as an illustration, but so far as the analysis is faithful, it obtains wherever educated young people are seeking an outlet for that sentiment of universal brotherhood which the best spirit of our times is forcing from an emotion into a motive.

I have divided the motives which constitute the subjective pressure toward Social Settlements into three great lines: the first contains the desire to make the entire social organism democratic, to extend democracy beyond its political expression; the second is the impulse to share the race life, and to bring as much as possible of social energy and the accumulation of civilization to those portions of the race which have little; the third springs from a certain *renaissance* of Christianity, a movement toward its early humanitarian aspects.

It is not difficult to see that although America is pledged to the democratic ideal, the view of democracy has been partial, and that its best achievement thus far has been pushed along the line of the franchise. Democracy has made little attempt to assert itself in social affairs. We have refused to move beyond the position of its eighteenth-century leaders, who believed that political equality alone would secure all good to all men. We conscientiously followed the gift of the ballot hard upon the gift of freedom to the negro, but we are quite unmoved by the fact that he lives among us in a practical social ostracism. We hasten to give the franchise to the immigrant from a sense of justice, from a tradition that he ought to have it, while we dub him with epithets deriding his past life or present occupation, and feel no duty to invite him to our houses. We are forced to acknowledge that it is only in our local and national politics that we try very hard for the ideal so dear to those who were enthusiasts when the century was young. We have almost given it up as our ideal in social intercourse. There are city wards in which many of the votes are sold for drinks and dollars; still there is a remote pretence, at least a fiction current, that a man's vote is his own. The judgment of the voter is consulted and an opportunity for remedy given. There is not even a theory in the social order, not a shadow answering to the polls in politics. The time may come when the politician who sells one by one to the highest bidder all the offices in his grasp, will not be considered more base in his code of morals, more hardened in his practice, than the woman who constantly invites to her receptions those alone who bring her an equal social return, who shares her beautiful surroundings only with those who minister to a liking she has for successful social events. In doing this is she not just as unmindful of the common weal, as unscrupulous in her use of power, as is any city "boss" who consults only the interests of the "ring"?

In politics "bossism" arouses a scandal. It goes on in society constantly and is only beginning to be challenged. Our consciences are becoming tender in regard to the lack of democracy in social affairs. We are perhaps entering upon the second phase of democracy, as the French philosophers entered upon the first, somewhat bewildered by its logical conclusions. The social organism has broken down through large districts of our great cities. Many of the people living there are very poor, the majority of them without leisure or energy for anything but the gain of subsistence. They move often from one wretched lodging to another. They live for the moment side by side, many of them without knowledge of each other, without fellowship, without local tradition or public spirit, without social organization of any kind. Practically nothing is done to remedy this. The people who might do it, who have the social tact and training, the large houses, and the traditions and custom of hospitality, live in other parts of the city. The club-houses, libraries, galleries, and semi-public conveniences for social life are also blocks away. We find working-men organized into armies of producers because men of executive ability and business sagacity have found it to their interests thus to organize them. But these working-men are not organized socially; although living in crowded tenement-houses, they are living without a corresponding social contact. The chaos is as great as it would be were they working in huge factories without foreman or superintendent. Their ideas and resources are cramped. The desire for higher social pleasure is extinct. They have no share in the traditions and social energy which make for progress. Too often their only place of meeting is a saloon, their only host a bartender; a local demagogue forms their public opinion. Men of ability and refinement, of social power and university cultivation, stay away from them. Personally, I believe the men who lose most are those who thus stay away. But the paradox is here: when cultivated people do stay away from a certain portion of the population, when all social advantages are persistently withheld, it may be for years, the result itself is pointed at as a reason, is used as an argument, for the continued withholding.

It is constantly said that because the masses have never had social advantages they do not want them, that they are heavy and dull, and that it will take political or philanthropic machinery to change them. This divides a city into rich and poor; into the favored, who express their sense of the social obligation by gifts of money, and into the unfavored, who express it by clamoring for a "share"—both of them actuated by a vague sense of justice. This division of the city would be more justifiable, however, if the people who thus isolate themselves on certain streets and use their social ability for each other gained enough thereby and added sufficient to the sum total of social progress to justify the withholding of the pleasures and results of that progress from so many people who ought to have them. But they cannot accomplish this. "The social spirit discharges itself in many forms, and no one form is adequate to its total expression." We are all uncomfortable in regard to the sincerity of our best phrases, because we hesitate to translate our philosophy into the deed.

It is inevitable that those who feel most keenly this insincerity and partial living should be our young people, our so-called educated young people who accomplish little toward the solution of this social problem, and who bear the brunt of being cultivated into unnourished, over-sensitive lives. They have been shut off from the common labor by which they live and which is a great source of moral and physical health. They feel a fatal want of harmony between their theory and their lives, a lack of co-ordination between thought and action. I think it is hard for us to realize how seriously many of them are taking to the notion of human brotherhood, how eagerly they long to give tangible expression to the democratic ideal. These young men and women, longing to socialize their democracy, are animated by certain hopes.

These hopes may be loosely formulated thus: that if in a democratic country nothing can be permanently achieved save through the masses of the people, it will be impossible to establish a higher political life than the people themselves crave; that it is difficult to see how the notion of a higher civic life can be fostered save through common intercourse; that the blessings which we associate with a life of refinement and cultivation can be made universal and must be made universal if they are to be permanent; that the good we secure for ourselves is precarious and uncertain, is floating in mid-air, until it is secured for all of us and incorporated into our common life.

These hopes are responsible for results in various directions, pre-eminently in the extension of educational advantages. We find that all educational matters are more democratic in their political than in their social aspects. The public schools in the poorest and most crowded wards of the city are inadequate to the number of children, and many of the teachers are ill-prepared and overworked; but in each ward there is an effort to secure public education. The schoolhouse itself stands as a pledge that the city recognizes and endeavors to fulfil the duty of educating its children. But what becomes of these children when they are no longer in public schools? Many of them never come under the influence of a professional teacher nor a cultivated friend after they are twelve. Society at large does little for their intellectual development. The dream of transcendentalists that each New England village would be a university, that every child taken from the common school would be put into definite lines of study and mental development, had its unfulfilled beginning in the village lyceum and lecture courses, and has its feeble representative now in the multitude of clubs for study which are so sadly restricted to educators, to the leisure class, or only to the advanced and progressive wage-workers.

The University Extension movement—certainly when it is closely identified with Settlements—would not confine learning to those who already want it, or to those who, by making an effort, can gain it, or to those among whom professional educators are already at work, but would take it to the tailors of East London and the dock-laborers of the Thames. It requires tact and training, love of learning, and the conviction of the justice of its diffusion to give it to people whose intellectual faculties are untrained and disused. But men in England are found who do it successfully, and it is believed there are men and women in America who can do it. I also believe that the best work in University Extension can be done in Settlements, where the teaching will be further socialized, where the teacher will grapple his students, not only by formal lectures, but by every hook possible to the fuller intellectual life which he represents. This teaching requires distinct methods, for it is true of people who have been allowed to remain undeveloped and whose faculties are inert and sterile, that they cannot take their learning heavily. It has to be diffused in a social atmosphere. Information held in solution, a medium of fellowship and goodwill can be assimilated by the dullest.

If education is, as Froebel[1] defined it, "deliverance," deliverance of the forces of the body and mind, then the untrained must first be delivered from all constraint and rigidity before their faculties can be used. Possibly one of the most pitiful periods in the drama of the much-praised young American who attempts to rise in life is the time when his educational requirements seem to have locked him up and made him rigid. He fancies himself shut off from his uneducated family and misunderstood by his friends. He is bowed down by his mental accumulations and often gets no farther than to carry them through life as a great burden. Not once has he had a glimpse of the delights of knowledge. Intellectual life requires for its expansion and manifestation the influence and assimilation of the interests and affections of others. Mazzini, that greatest of all democrats, who broke his heart over the condition of the South European peasantry, said: "Education is not merely a

---

[1] Friederich Wilhelm August Froebel (1782–1852), German philosopher and educational reformer, carried on the work begun by Pestalozzi (see below, p. 37, n. 2). He was the originator of the kindergarten; and his book *The Education of Man* argued that very young children learn best by doing [Ed.].

necessity of true life by which the individual renews his vital force in the vital force of humanity; it is a Holy Communion with generations dead and living, by which he fecundates all his faculties. When he is withheld from this Communion for generations, as the Italian peasant has been, we point our finger at him and say, 'He is like a beast of the field; he must be controlled by force.' " Even to this it is sometimes added that it is absurd to educate him, immoral to disturb his content. We stupidly use again the effect as an argument for a continuance of the cause. It is needless to say that a Settlement is a protest against a restricted view of education, and makes it possible for every educated man or woman with a teaching faculty to find out those who are ready to be taught. The social and educational activities of a Settlement are but differing manifestations of the attempt to socialize democracy, as is the existence of the settlement itself.

I find it somewhat difficult to formulate the second line of motives which I believe to constitute the trend of the subjective pressure toward the Settlement. There is something primordial about these motives, but I am perhaps over-bold in designating them as a great desire to share the race life. We all bear traces of the starvation struggle which for so long made up the life of the race. Our very organism holds memories and glimpses of that long life of our ancestors which still goes on among so many of our contemporaries. Nothing so deadens the sympathies and shrivels the power of enjoyment as the persistent keeping away from the great opportunities for helpfulness and a continual ignoring of the starvation struggle which makes up the life of at least half the race. To shut one's self away from that half of the race life is to shut one's self away from the most vital part of it; it is to live out but half the humanity which we have been born heir to and to use but half our faculties. We have all had longings for a fuller life which should include the use of these faculties. These longings are the physical complement of the "Intimations of Immortality" on which no ode has yet been written. To portray these would be the work of a poet, and it is hazardous for any but a poet to attempt it.

You may remember the forlorn feeling which occasionaly seizes you when you arrive early in the morning a stranger in a great city. The stream of laboring people goes past you as you gaze through the plate-glass window of your hotel. You see hard-working men lifting great burdens; you hear the driving and jostling of huge carts. Your heart sinks with a sudden sense of futility. The door opens behind you and you turn to the man who brings you in your breakfast with a quick sense of human fellowship. You find yourself praying that you may never lose your hold on it at all. A more poetic prayer would be that the great mother breasts of our common humanity, with its labor and suffering and its homely comforts, may never be withheld from you. You turn helplessly to the waiter. You feel that it would be almost grotesque to claim from him the sympathy you crave. Civilization has placed you far apart, but you resent your position with a sudden sense of snobbery. Literature is full of portrayals of these glimpses. They come to shipwrecked men on rafts; they overcome the differences of an incongruous multitude when in the presence of a great danger or when moved by a common enthusiasm. They are not, however, confined to such moments, and if we were in the habit of telling them to each other, the recital would be as long as the tales of children are, when they sit down on the green grass and confide to each other how many times they have remembered that they lived once before. If these tales are the stirring of inherited impressions, just so surely is the other the striving of inherited powers.

"There is nothing after disease, indigence, and a sense of guilt so fatal to health and to life itself as the want of a proper outlet for active faculties." I have seen young girls suffer and grow sensibly lowered in vitality in the first years after they leave school. In our attempt then to give a girl pleasure and freedom from care we succeed, for the most part, in making her pitifully miserable. She finds "life" so different from what she expected it to be. She is besotted with innocent little ambitions, and does not understand this apparent waste of herself, this elaborate preparation, if no work is provided for her. There is a heritage of noble obligation which young people accept and long to perpetuate. The desire for action, the wish to right wrong and alleviate suffering, haunts them daily. Society smiles at it indulgently instead of making it of value to itself. The wrong to them begins even farther back, when we restrain the first childish desires for "doing good" and tell them that they must wait until they are older and better fitted. We intimate that social obligation begins at a fixed date, forgetting that it begins with birth itself. We treat them as children who, with strong-growing limbs, are allowed to use their legs but not their arms, or whose legs are daily carefully exercised that after awhile their arms may be put to high use. We do this in spite of the protest of the best educators, Locke and Pestalozzi.[2] We are fortunate in the mean time if their unused members do not weaken and disappear. They do sometimes. There are a few girls who, by the time they are "educated," forget their old childish desires to help the world and to play with poor little girls "who haven't playthings." Parents are often inconsistent. They deliberately expose their daughters to knowledge of the distress in the world. They send them to hear missionary addresses on famines in India and China; they accompany them to lectures on the suffering in Siberia; they agitate together over the forgotten region of East London. In

---

[2] Johann Heinrich Pestalozzi (1746–1827), a Swiss, may be regarded as a distant ancestor of progressive education. His books *Leonard and Gertrude* (1781) and *How Gertrude Teaches Her Children* (1801) anticipated two of the progressives' principal doctrines: (1) ideas have meaning only in relation to concrete things—hence his emphasis on drawing, singing, and physical exercise—and (2) education can be used as an agency of social reformation [Ed.].

addition to this, from babyhood the altruistic tendencies of these daughters are persistently cultivated. They are taught to be self-forgetting and self-sacrificing, to consider the good of the Whole before the good of the Ego. But when all this information and culture show results, when the daughter comes back from college and begins to recognize her social claim to the "submerged tenth," and to evince a disposition to fulfil it, the family claim is strenuously asserted; she is told that she is unjustified, ill-advised in her efforts. If she persists the family too often are injured and unhappy, unless the efforts are called missionary, and the religious zeal of the family carry them over their sense of abuse. When this zeal does not exist the result is perplexing. It is a curious violation of what we would fain believe a fundamental law—that the final return of the Deed is upon the head of the Doer. The deed is that of exclusiveness and caution, but the return instead of falling upon the head of the exclusive and cautious, falls upon a young head full of generous and unselfish plans. The girl loses something vital out of her life which she is entitled to. She is restricted and unhappy; her elders, meanwhile, are unconscious of the situation, and we have all the elements of a tragedy.

We have in America a fast-growing number of cultivated young people who have no recognized outlet for their active faculties. They hear constantly of the great social mal-adjustment, but no way is provided for them to change it, and their uselessness hangs about them heavily. Huxley declares that the sense of uselessness is the severest shock which the human system can sustain, and that, if persistently sustained, it results in atrophy of function. These young people have had advantages of college, of European travel and economic study, but they are sustaining this shock of inaction. They have pet phrases, and they tell you that the things that make us all alike are stronger than the things that make us different. They say that all men are united by needs and sympathies far more permanent and radical than anything that temporarily divides them and sets them in opposition to each other. If they affect art, they say that the decay in artistic expression is due to the decay in ethics, that art when shut away from the human interests and from the great mass of humanity is self-destructive. They tell their elders with all the bitterness of youth that if they expect success from them in business, or politics, or in whatever lines their ambition for them has run, they must let them consult all of humanity; that they must let them find out what the people want and how they want it. It is only the stronger young people, however, who formulate this. Many of them dissipate their energies in so-called enjoyment. Others, not content with that, go on studying and go back to college for their second degrees, not that they are especially fond of study, but because they want something definite to do, and their powers have been trained in the direction of mental accumulation. Many are buried beneath mere mental accumulation with lowered vitality and discontent. Walter Besant says they have had the vision that Peter had when he saw the great sheet let down from heaven, wherein was neither clean nor unclean. He calls it the sense of humanity. It is not philanthropy nor benevolence. It is a thing fuller and wider than either of these. This young life, so sincere in its emotion and good phrases and yet so undirected, seems to me as pitiful as the other great mass of destitute lives. One is supplementary to the other, and some method of communication can surely be devised. Mr. Barnett,[3] who urged the first Settlement,—Toynbee Hall, in East London,—recognized this need of outlet for the young men of Oxford and Cambridge, and hoped that the Settlement would supply the communication. It is easy to see why the Settlement movement originated in England, where the years of education are more constrained and definite than

---

[3] Samuel Augustus Barnett (1844–1913) was an Anglican clergyman who became the first warden of Toynbee Hall, founded in 1884—the first social settlement, referred to many times in Jane Addams' writings [Ed.].

they are here, where class distinctions are more rigid. The necessity of it was greater there, but we are fast feeling the pressure of the need and meeting the necessity for Settlements in America. Our young people feel nervously the need of putting theory into action, and respond quickly to the Settlement form of activity.

The third division of motives which I believe make toward the Settlement is the result of a certain *renaissance* going forward in Christianity. The impulse to share the lives of the poor, the desire to make social service, irrespective of propaganda, express the spirit of Christ, is as old as Christianity itself. We have no proof from the records themselves that the early Roman Christians, who strained their simple art to the point of grotesqueness in their eagerness to record a "good news" on the walls of the catacombs, considered this "good news" a religion. Jesus had no set of truths labelled "Religious." On the contrary, his doctrine was that all truth is one, that the appropriation of it is freedom. His teaching had no dogma to mark it off from truth and action in general. He himself called it a revelation—a life. These early Roman Christians received the Gospel message, a command to love all men, with a certain joyous simplicity. The image of the Good Shepherd is blithe and gay beyond the gentlest shepherd of Greek mythology; the hart no longer pants, but rushes to the water brooks. The Christians looked for the continuous revelation, but believed what Jesus said, that this revelation to be held and made manifest must be put into terms of action; that action is the only medium man has for receiving and appropriating truth. "If any man will do His will, he shall know of the doctrine."

That Christianity has to be revealed and embodied in the line of social progress is a corollary to the simple proposition that man's action is found in his social relationships in the way in which he connects with his fellows, that his motives for action are the zeal and affection with which he regards his fellows. By this simple process was created a deep enthusiasm for humanity, which regarded man as at once the organ and object of revelation; and by this process came about that wonderful fellowship, that true democracy of the early Church, that so captivates the imagination. The early Christians were pre-eminently non-resistant. They believed in love as a cosmic force. There was no iconoclasm during the minor peace of the Church. They did not yet denounce, nor tear down temples, nor preach the end of the world. They grew to a mighty number, but it never occurred to them, either in their weakness or their strength, to regard other men for an instant as their foes or as aliens. The spectacle of the Christians loving all men was the most astounding Rome had ever seen. They were eager to sacrifice themselves for the weak, for children and the aged. They identified themselves with slaves and did not avoid the plague. They longed to share the common lot that they might receive the constant revelation. It was a new treasure which the early Christians added to the sum of all treasures, a joy hitherto unknown in the world—the joy of finding the Christ which lieth in each man, but which no man can unfold save in fellowship. A happiness ranging from the heroic to the pastoral enveloped them. They were to possess a revelation as long as life had new meaning to unfold, new action to propose.

I believe that there is a distinct turning among many young men and women toward this simple acceptance of Christ's message. They resent the assumption that Christianity is a set of ideas which belong to the religious consciousness, whatever that may be, that it is a thing to be proclaimed and instituted apart from the social life of the community. They insist that it shall seek a simple and natural expression in the social organism itself. The Settlement movement is only one manifestation of that wider humanitarian movement which throughout Christendom, but pre-eminently in England, is endeavoring to embody itself, not in a sect, but in society itself. Tolstoi has reminded us all very forcibly of Christ's principle of non-resistance. His formulation has been startling and his expression has deviated from the general movement, but there is little doubt that he has many adherents, men and women who are philosophically convinced of the futility of opposition, who believe that evil can be overcome only with good and cannot be opposed. If love is the creative force of the universe, the principle which binds men together, and by their interdependence on each other makes them human, just so surely is anger and the spirit of opposition the destructive principle of the universe, that which tears down, thrusts men apart, and makes them isolated and brutal.

I cannot, of course, speak for other Settlements, but it would, I think, be unfair to Hull House not to emphasize the conviction with which the first residents went there, that it would be a foolish and and unwarrantable expenditure of force to oppose or to antagonize any individual or set of people in the neighborhood; that whatever of good the House had to offer should be put into positive terms; that its residents should live with opposition to no man, with recognition of the good in every man, even the meanest. I believe that this turning, this *renaissance* of the early Christian humanitarianism, is going on in America, in Chicago, if you please, without leaders who write or philosophize, without much speaking, but with a bent to express in social service, in terms of action, the spirit of Christ. Certain it is that spiritual force is found in the Settlement movement, and it is also true that this force must be evoked and must be called into play before the success of any Settlement is assured. There must be the overmastering belief that all that is noblest in life is common to men as men, in order to accentuate the likenesses and ignore the differences which are found among the people whom the Settlement constantly brings into juxtaposition. It may be true, as Frederic Harrison insists, that the very religious fervor of man can be turned into love for his race and his desire for a future life into content to live in the echo of his deeds. How far the Positivists' formula of the high ardor for humanity can carry the Settlement movement, Mrs. Humphry Ward's house in London may in course of time illustrate. Paul's formula of seeking for the Christ which lieth in each man and founding our likenesses on him seems a simpler formula to many of us.

If you have heard a thousand voices singing in the Hallelujah Chorus in Handel's "Messiah," you have found that the leading voices could still be distinguished, but that the differences of training and cultivation between them and the voices of the chorus were lost in the unity of purpose and the fact that they were all human voices lifted by a high motive. This is a weak illustration of what a Settlement attempts to do. It aims, in a measure, to lead whatever of social life its neighborhood may afford, to focus and give form to that life, to bring to bear upon it the results of cultivation and training; but it receives in exchange for the music of isolated voices the volume and strength of the chorus. It is quite impossible for me to say in what proportion or degree the subjective necessity which led to the opening of Hull House combined the three trends: first the desire to interpret democracy in social terms; secondly, the impulse beating at the very source of our lives urging us to aid in the race progress; and, thirdly, the Christian movement toward Humanitarianism. It is difficult to analyze a living thing; the analysis is at best imperfect. Many more motives may blend with the three trends; possibly the desire for a new form of social success due to the nicety of imagination, which refuses worldly pleasures unmixed with the joys of self-sacrifice; possibly a love of approbation, so vast that is it not content with the treble clapping of delicate hands, but wishes also to hear the bass notes from toughened palms, may mingle with these. . . .

PART II
THE CITY

---

5. "The Objective Value of a Social Settlement"

1 8 9 2

At the same conference at which she read her paper on "The Subjective Necessity for Social Settlements," Miss Addams offered this companion piece, which serves as a good introduction to the problems she was beginning to encounter in the working-class wards of a great industrial city. It also describes the practical activities of the Hull-House residents, concluding, characteristically, with the reminder that Hull-House, although it had "several distinct charitable departments which are conscientiously carried on," was not a "philanthropy."

In treating of the value of the Social Settlement, I shall confine myself to Hull House, and what it has been able to do for its neighborhood, only because I am most familiar with that Settlement.

Hull House stands on South Halsted Street, next door to the corner of Polk. South Halsted Street is thirty-two miles long and one of the great thoroughfares of Chicago. Polk Street crosses Halsted midway between the stock-yards to the south

---

From Jane Addams, "The Objective Value of a Social Settlement," *Philanthropy and Social Progress* (New York: Thomas Y. Crowell & Company, 1893), pp. 27–40.

and the ship-building yards on the north branch of the Chicago River. For the six miles between these two industries the street is lined with shops of butchers and grocers, with dingy and gorgeous saloons, and pretentious establishments for the sale of ready-made clothing. Polk Street, running west from Halsted Street, grows rapidly more respectable; running a mile east to State Street, it grows steadily worse, and crosses a net-work of gilded vice on the corners of Clark Street and Fourth Avenue.

Hull House is an ample old residence, well built and somewhat ornately decorated after the manner of its time, 1856. It has been used for many purposes, and although battered by its vicissitudes, is essentially sound and has responded kindly to repairs and careful furnishing. Its wide hall and open fires always insure it a gracious aspect. It once stood in the suburbs, but the city has steadily grown up around it and its site now has corners on three or four more or less distinct foreign colonies. Between Halsted Street and the river live about ten thousand Italians: Neapolitans, Sicilians, and Calabrians, with an occasional Lombard or Venetian. To the south on Twelfth Street are many Germans, and side streets are given over almost entirely to Polish and Russian Jews. Still farther south, these Jewish colonies merge into a huge Bohemian colony, so vast that Chicago ranks as the third Bohemian city in the world. To the northwest are many Canadian-French, clannish in spite of their long residence in America, and to the north are many Irish and first-generation Americans. On the streets directly west and farther north are well-to-do English-speaking families, many of whom own their houses and have lived in the neighborhood for years. I know one man who is still living in his old farm-house. This corner of Polk and Halsted Street is in the fourteenth precinct of the nineteenth ward. This ward has a population of about fifty thousand, and at the last presidential election registered 7072 voters. It has had no unusual political scandal connected with it, but its aldermen are generally saloon-keepers and its political manipulations are those to be found in the crowded wards where the activities of the petty politician are unchecked.

The policy of the public authorities of never taking an initiative, and always waiting to be urged to do their duty, is fatal in a ward where there is no initiative among the citizens. The idea underlying our self-government breaks down in such a ward. The streets are inexpressibly dirty, the number of schools inadequate, factory legislation unenforced, the street-lighting bad, the paving miserable and altogether lacking in the alleys and smaller streets, and the stables defy all laws of sanitation. Hundreds of houses are unconnected with the street sewer. The older and richer inhabitants seem anxious to move away as rapidly as they can afford it. They make room for newly arrived immigrants who are densely ignorant of civic duties. This substitution of the older inhabitants is accomplished industrially also in the south and east quarters of the ward. The Hebrews and Italians do the finishing for the great clothing-manufacturers formerly done by Americans, Irish, and Germans, who refused to submit to the extremely low prices to which the sweating system has reduced their successors. As the design of the sweating system is the elimination of rent from the manufacture of clothing, the "outside work" is begun after the clothing leaves the cutter. An unscrupulous contractor regards no basement as too dark, no stable loft too foul, no rear shanty too provisional, no tenement room too small for his workroom, as these conditions imply low rental. Hence these shops abound in the worst of the foreign districts, where the sweater easily finds his cheap basement and his home finishers. There is a constant tendency to employ school-children, as much of the home and shop work can easily be done by children.

The houses of the ward, for the most part wooden, were originally built for one family and are now occupied by several. They are after the type of the inconvenient frame cottages found in the poorer suburbs twenty years ago. Many of them were built where they now stand; others were brought thither on rollers, because their previous site had been taken for a factory. The fewer brick tenement buildings which are three or four stories high are comparatively new. There are few huge and foul tenements. The little wooden houses have a temporary aspect, and for this reason, perhaps, the tenement-house legislation in Chicago is totally inadequate. Back tenements flourish; many houses have no water supply save the faucet in the back yard; there are no fire escapes; the garbage and ashes are placed in wooden boxes which are fastened to the street pavements. One of the most discouraging features about the present system of tenement houses is that many are owned by sordid and ignorant immigrants. The theory that wealth brings responsibility, that possession entails at length education and refinement, in these cases fails utterly. The children of an Italian immigrant owner do not go to school and are no improvement on their parents. His wife picks rags from the street gutter, and laboriously sorts them in a dingy court. Wealth may do something for her self-complacency and feeling of consequence; it certainly does nothing for her comfort or her children's improvement nor for the cleanliness of any one concerned. Another thing that prevents better houses in Chicago is the tentative attitude of the real-estate men. Many unsavory conditions are allowed to continue which would be regarded with horror if they were considered permanent. Meanwhile, the wretched conditions persist until at least two generations of children have been born and reared in them.

Our ward contains two hundred and fifty-five saloons; our own precinct boasts of eight, and the one directly north of us twenty. This allows one saloon to every twenty-eight voters, and there is no doubt that the saloon is the centre of the liveliest political and social life of the ward. The leases and fixtures of these saloons are, in the majority of cases, owned by the wholesale liquor houses, and the saloon-keeper himself is often a bankrupt.

There are seven churches and two missions in the ward. All

of these are small and somewhat struggling, save the large Catholic church connected with the Jesuit College on the south boundary of the ward, and the French Catholic church on the west boundary. Out of these nine religious centres there are but three in which the service is habitually conducted in English. This enumeration of churches does not include the chevras found among the recently immigrated Jews of the Ashkenazite branch. The chevras combine the offices of public worship and the rites of mourning with the function of a sick benefit and mutual aid society. There are seven Catholic parochial schools in the ward, accommodating 6244 children; three Protestant schools care for 141 children. A fine manual-training school sustained by the Hebrews is found in the seventh ward just south of us. In the same ward is the receiving shelter for the Jewish refugees.

This site for a Settlement was selected in the first instance because of its diversity and the variety of activity for which it presented an opportunity. It has been the aim of the residents to respond to all sides of the neighborhood life: not to the poor people alone, nor to the well-to-do, nor to the young in contradistinction to the old, but to the neighborhood as a whole, "men, women, and children taken in families as the Lord mixes them." The activities of Hull House divide themselves into four, possibly more lines. They are not formally or consciously thus divided, but broadly separate according to the receptivity of the neighbors. They might be designated as the social, educational, and humanitarian, I have added civic—if indeed a Settlement of women can be said to perform civic duties. These activities spring from no preconceived notion of what a Social Settlement should be, but have increased gradually on demand. In describing these activities and their value to the neighborhood, I shall attempt to identify those people who respond to each form.

A Settlement which regards social intercourse as the terms of its expression logically brings to its aid all those adjuncts

which have been found by experience to free social life. It casts
aside nothing which the cultivated man regards as good and
suggestive of participation in the best life of the past. It ignores
none of the surroundings which one associates with a life of
simple refinement. The amount of luxury which an individual
indulges in is a thing which has to be determined by each
for himself. It must always be a relative thing. The one test
which the Settlement is bound to respect is that its particular
amount of luxury shall tend to "free" the social expression of
its neighbors, and not cumber that expression. The residents
at Hull House find that the better in quality and taste their
surroundings are, the more they contribute to the general
enjoyment.

We have distinct advantages for Settlements in America.
There are fewer poor people here than in England, there are
fewer people who expect to remain poor, and they are less
strictly confined to their own districts. It is an advantage that
our cities are diversified by foreign colonies. We go to Europe
and consider our view incomplete if we do not see something
of the present life of the little villages with their quaint customs
and suggestive habits. We can see the same thing here. There
are Bohemians, Italians, Poles, Russians, Greeks, and Arabs in
Chicago vainly trying to adjust their peasant life to the life of
a large city, and coming in contact with only the most ignorant
Americans in that city. The more of scholarship, the more of
linguistic attainment, the more of beautiful surroundings a
Settlement among them can command, the more it can do
for them.

It is much easier to deal with the first generation of crowded
city life than with the second or third, because it is more
natural and cast in a simpler mould. The Italian and Bohemian
peasants who live in Chicago still put on their bright holiday
clothes on a Sunday and go to visit their cousins. They tramp
along with at least a suggestion of having once walked over
ploughed fields and breathed country air. The second genera-

tion of city poor have no holiday clothes and consider their cousins "a bad lot." I have heard a drunken man, in a maudlin stage, babble of his good country mother and imagine he was driving the cows home, and I knew that his little son, who laughed loud at him, would be drunk earlier in life, and would have no such pastoral interlude to his ravings. Hospitality still survives among foreigners, although it is buried under false pride among the poorest Americans. One thing seemed clear in regard to entertaining these foreigners: to preserve and keep for them whatever of value their past life contained and to bring them in contact with a better type of Americans. For two years, every Saturday evening, our Italian neighbors were our guests; entire families came. These evenings were very popular during our first winter at Hull House. Many educated Italians helped us, and the house became known as a place where Italians were welcome and where national holidays were observed. They come to us with their petty lawsuits, sad relics of the *vendetta*, with their incorrigible boys, with their hospital cases, with their aspirations for Amercian clothes, and with their needs for an interpreter.

Friday evening is devoted to Germans and is similar in purpose; but owing to the superior education of our Teutonic guests and the clever leading of a cultivated German woman, we can bring out the best of that cozy social intercourse which is found in its perfection in the "Fatherland." They sing a great deal in the tender minor of the German folksong or in the rousing spirit of the Rhine, and they are slowly but persistently pursuing a course in German history and literature. The relationship by no means ends with social civilities, and the acquaintance made there has brought about radical changes in the lives of many friendless families. I recall one peasant woman, straight from the fields of Germany. Her two years in America had been spent in patiently carrying water up and down two flights of stairs, and in washing the heavy flannel suits of iron-foundry workers. For this her pay averaged

thirty-five cents a day. Three of her daughters had fallen victims to the vice of the city. The mother was bewildered and
distressed, but understood nothing. We were able to induce
the betrayer of one daughter to marry her; the second, after a
tedious lawsuit, supported his child; with the third we were
able to do nothing. This woman is now living with her family
in a little house seventeen miles from the city. She has made
two payments on her land and is a lesson to all beholders as
she pastures her cow up and down the railroad tracks and
makes money from her ten acres. She did not need charity.
She had an immense capacity for hard work, but she sadly
needed "heading." She is our most shining example, but I
think of many forlorn cases of German and Bohemian peasants
in need of neighborly help.

Perhaps of more value than to the newly arrived peasant is
the service of the Settlement to those foreigners who speak
English fairly well, and who have been so successful in material affairs that they are totally absorbed by them. Their social
life is too often reduced to a sense of comradeship. The lives
of many Germans, for instance, are law-abiding, but inexpressibly dull. They have resigned poetry and romance with
the other good things of the Fatherland. There is a strong family affection between them and their English-speaking children,
but their pleasures are not in common and they seldom go out
together. Perhaps the greatest value of the Settlement to them
is in simply placing large and pleasant rooms with musical
facilities at their disposal, and in reviving their almost forgotten enthusiasm for Körner and Schiller. I have seen sons
and daughters stand in complete surprise as their mother's
knitting-needles softly beat time to the song she was singing,
or her worn face turned rosy under the hand-clapping as she
made an old-fashioned courtesy at the end of a German poem.
It was easy to fancy a growing touch of respect in her children's manner to her, and a rising enthusiasm for German
literature and reminiscence on the part of all the family, an

effort to bring together the old life and the new, a respect for the older cultivation, and not quite so much assurance that the new was the best. I think that we have a right to expect that our foreigners will do this for us: that they will project a little of the historic and romantic into the prosaic quarters of our American cities.

But our social evenings are by no means confined to foreigners. Our most successful clubs are entirely composed of English-speaking and American-born young people. Those over sixteen meet in two clubs, one for young men and one for girls, every Monday evening. Each club dispatches various literary programs before nine o'clock, when they meet together for an hour of social amusement before going home at ten. The members of the Tuesday evening clubs are from fourteen to sixteen years old; a few of them are still in school, but most of them are working. The boys who are known as the Young Citizen's Club are supposed to inform themselves on municipal affairs, as are the Hull House Columbian Guards who report alleys and streets for the Municipal Order League. We have various other clubs of young people that meet weekly; their numbers are limited only by the amount of room. We hold the dining-room, the reception-room, and the octagon with the art-exhibit-room and the studio each evening for the College Extension classes, and can reserve only the large drawing-room and gymnasium for the clubs and receptions. The gymnasium is a somewhat pretentious name for a building next door which was formerly a saloon, but which we rented last fall, repaired, and fitted up with good apparatus. A large and well-equipped gymnasium is at present being built for Hull House. During the winter the old one sheltered some enthusiastic athletic classes. The evenings were equally divided between men and women. The children came in the afternoon. It is difficult to describe the social evenings, and there is much social life going on constantly which cannot be tabulated.

To turn to the educational effort, it will be perhaps better first to describe the people who respond to it. In every neighborhood where poorer people live, because rents are supposed to be cheaper there, is an element which, although uncertain in the individual, in the aggregate can be counted upon. It is composed of people of former education and opportunity who have cherished ambitions and prospects, but who are caricatures of what they meant to be—"hollow ghosts which blame the living men." There are times in many lives when there is a cessation of energy and loss of power. Men and women of education and refinement come to live in a cheaper neighborhood because they lack the power of making money, because of ill health, because of an unfortunate marriage, or for various other reasons which do not imply criminality or stupidity. Among them are those who, in spite of untoward circumstances, keep up some sort of an intellectual life, those who are "great for books" as their neighbors say. To such the Settlement is a genuine refuge. In addition to these there are many young women who teach in the public schools, young men who work at various occupations, but who are bent upon self-improvement and are preparing for professions. It is of these that the College Extension classes are composed. The majority of the two hundred students live within the radius of six blocks from the house, although a few of them come from other parts of the city. The educational effort of Hull House always has been held by the residents to be subordinate to its social life, and, as it were, a part of it. What is now known as the College Extension course, a series of lectures and classes held in the evening on the general plan of University Extension, had its origin in an informal club which, during the first winter, read "Romola" with the original residents. During the last term thirty-five classes a week were in existence. The work is divided into terms of twelve weeks, and circulars are issued at the beginning of each term. Many students have taken studies in each of the seven terms of work offered. . . .

. . . In addition to the neighbors who respond to the receptions and classes are found those who are too battered and oppressed to care for them. To these, however, is left that susceptibility to the bare offices of humanity which raises such offices into a bond of fellowship. These claim humanitarian efforts. Perhaps the chief value of a Settlement to its neighborhood, certainly to the newly arrived foreigner, is its office as an information and interpretation bureau. It sometimes seems as if the business of the Settlement were that of a commission merchant. Without endowment and without capital itself, it constantly acts between the various institutions of the city and the people for whose benefit these institutions were erected. The hospitals, the county agencies, and State asylums, are often but vague rumors to the people who need them most. This commission work, as I take it, is of value not only to the recipient, but to the institutions themselves. Each institution, unlike a settlement, is obliged to determine upon the line of its activity, to accept its endowment for that end and do the best it can. But each time this is accomplished it is apt to lace itself up in certain formulas, is in danger of forgetting the mystery and complexity of life, of repressing the promptings that spring from growing insight.

The residents of a Social Settlement have an opportunity of seeing institutions from the recipient's standpoint, of catching the spirit of the original impulse which founded them. This experience ought to have a certain value and ultimately find expression in institutional management. One of the residents of Hull House received this winter an appointment from the Cook County agent as a county visitor. She reported at the agency each morning, and all the cases within a radius of several blocks from Hull House were given to her for investigation. This gave her a legitimate opportunity for knowing the poorest people in the neighborhood. In no cases were her recommendations refused or her judgments reversed by the men in charge of the office. From the very nature of our existence and purpose we are bound to keep on good terms with every beneficent institution in the city. Passing by our telephone last Sunday morning, I was struck with the list of numbers hung on the wall for easy reference. They were those of the Visiting Nurses' Association; Cook County Hospital; Women's and Children's Hospital; Maxwell Street Police Station for city ambulance; Health Department, City Hall; Cook County Agent, etc. We have been on very good terms with the Hebrew Relief and Aid Society, the Children's Aid, the Humane Society, the Municipal Order League, and with the various church and national relief associations. Every summer we send out dozens of children to the country on the "Daily News" Fresh Air Fund and to the Holiday Home at Lake Geneva. Our most complete co-operation has been with the Visiting Nurses' Association. One of the nurses lives at Hull House, pays her board as a resident, and does her work from there. Friends of the house are constantly in need of her ministrations, and her cases become friends of the house. Owing to the lack of a charity organization society in Chicago we have been obliged to keep a sum of money as a relief fund. Five bath-rooms in the rear of Hull House are open to the neighborhood and are constantly in use. The number of baths taken in July was nine hundred and eighty.

The more definite humanitarian effort of Hull House has taken shape in a day nursery, which was started during the second year of our residence on Halsted Street. A frame cottage of six rooms across our yard has been fitted up as a *crèche*. At present we receive from thirty to forty children daily. A young lady who has had kindergarten training is in charge; she has the assistance of an older woman, and a kindergarten by a professional teacher is held each morning in the play-room. This nursery is not merely a convenience in the neighborhood; it is, to a certain extent, a neighborhood affair. Similar in spirit is the Hull House Diet Kitchen, in a little cottage directly back of the nursery. Food is prepared for invalids and orders are taken from physicians and visiting nurses of the district. We have lately had an outfit of Mr. Atkinson's inventions,[1] in which the women of the neighborhood have taken a most intelligent interest, especially the members of the Hull House Woman's Club. This club meets one afternoon a week. It is composed of the most able women of the neighborhood, who enjoy the formal addresses and many informal discussions. The economics of food and fuel are freely discussed. The Hull House household expenses are frankly compared with those of other households. There is little doubt that "friendly visiting," while of great value, to be complete should also include the "friendly visited." The residents at Hull House find in themselves a constantly increasing tendency to consult their neighbors on the advisability of each new undertaking. We have lately opened a boarding club for working girls near Hull House on the co-operative plan. I say advisedly that we have "opened" it; the running of it is quite in the hands of the girls themselves. The furniture, pictures, etc., belong to Hull House, and whatever experience we have is at their disposal; but it is in no sense a working-girls' "home," nor is it to be run from the outside. We hope a great deal from this little attempt at co-operative housekeeping. The club has been running three months on a self-supporting basis and has thirty-five members.

The Coffee House which is being built in connection with Hull House contains a large kitchen fitted on the New-England Kitchen plan. We hope by the sale of properly cooked foods, to make not only co-operative housekeeping but all the housekeeping of the neighborhood easier and more economical. The Coffee House itself, with its club-rooms, will be a less formal social centre than our drawing-room.

---

[1] Edward Atkinson (1827–1905) was a Boston businessman and reformer, known also for his invention of the Alladin oven, in which kerosene was substituted for coal with great savings in cost [Ed.].

Helpful recourses from the neighborhood itself constantly develop, physician benefit societies, ministers and priests are always ready to co-operate in any given case. Young girls from the neighborhood assist in the children's classes, mothers help in the nursery, young men teach in the gymnasium, or secure students for an experimental course of lectures. We constantly rely more and more on neighborhood assistance.

In summing up the objective value of Hull House, I am sorry we have not more to present in the line of civic activities. It was through the energy of a resident this spring that the fact that the public-school census recorded 6976 school-children in the nineteenth ward and that they were provided with only 2957 public-school sittings was made prominent just before the appropriations were voted for school buildings and sites. It was largely through her energy, and the energy of the people whom she interested in it, that the Board of Education was induced to purchase a site for a school building in our ward and to save and equip for immediate use a school-house about to be turned into a warehouse.

During two months of this summer the reports sent in from Hull House to the Municipal Order League, and through it to the Health Department, were one thousand and thirty-seven. The Department showed great readiness to co-operate with this volunteer inspection, and a marked improvement has taken place in the scavenger service and in the regulation of the small stables of the ward.

Hull House has had, I hope, a certain value to the women's trades unions of Chicago. It seems to me of great importance that as trades unions of women are being formed they should be kept, if possible, from falling into the self-same pits the men's unions have fallen into. Women possessing no votes, and therefore having little political value, will be both of advantage and disadvantage to their unions. Four women's unions have met regularly at Hull House: the book-binders', the shoemakers', the shirtmakers', and the cloak-makers'. The last two were organized at Hull House. It has seemed to us that the sewing trades are most in need of help. They are thoroughly disorganized, Russian and Polish tailors competing against English-speaking tailors, young girls and Italian women competing against both. An efficient union which should combine all these elements seems very difficult, unless it grow strong enough to offer a label and receive unexpected aid from the manufacturers. In that case there would be the hope of co-operation on the part of the consumers, as the fear of contagion from ready-made clothing has at last seized the imagination of the public.

That the trades unions themselves care for what we have done for them, is shown by the fact that when the committee of investigation for the sweating system was appointed by the Trades and Labor Assembly, consisting of five delegates from the unions and five from other citizens, two of the latter were residents of Hull House. It is logical that a Settlement should have a certain value in labor complications, having from its very position sympathies entangled on both sides. Last May twenty girls from a knitting factory who struck because they were docked for loss of time when they were working by the piece, came directly from the factory to Hull House. They had heard that we "stood by working people." We were able to have the strike arbitrated, and although six girls lost their places, the unjust fines were remitted, and we had the satisfaction of putting on record one more case of arbitration in the slowly growing list. We were helped in this case, as we have been in many others, by the Bureau of Justice. Its office is constantly crowded with working people who hope for redress from the law, but have no money with which to pay for it. There should be an office of this bureau in every ward; "down town" seems far away and inaccessible to the most ignorant. Hull House, in spite of itself, does a good deal of legal work. We have secured support for deserted women,

insurance for bewildered widows, damages for injured oper-
ators, furniture from the clutches of the instalment store. One
function of the Settlement to its neighborhood somewhat re-
sembles that of the big brother whose mere presence on the
play-ground protects the little one from bullies. A resident at
Hull House is at present collecting labor statistics in the
neighborhood for the Illinois State Bureau of Labor. It is a
matter of satisfaction that this work can be done from the
Settlement, and the residents receive the benefit of the information collected.

It is difficult to classify the Working People's Social Science
Club, which meets weekly at Hull House. It is social, educational, and civic in character, the latter chiefly because it
strongly connects the House with the labor problems in their
political and social aspects. This club was organized at Hull
House in the spring of 1890 by an English working-man. It
has met weekly since, save during the months of summer. At
eight o'clock every Wednesday evening the secretary calls to
order from forty to one hundred people. A chairman for the
evening is elected, and a speaker is introduced who is allowed
to talk until nine o'clock; his subject is then thrown open to
discussion and a lively debate ensues until ten o'clock, at
which hour the meeting is declared adjourned. The enthusiasm
of this club seldom lags. Its zest for discussion is unceasing,
and any attempt to turn it into a study or reading club always
meets with the strong disapprobation of the members. Chicago
is full of social theorists. It offers a cosmopolitan opportunity
for discussion. The only possible danger from this commingling of many theories is incurred when there is an attempt
at suppression; bottled up, there is danger of explosion; constantly uncorked, open to the deodorizing and freeing process
of the air, all danger is averted. Nothing so disconcerts a social
agitator as to find among his auditors men who have been
through all that, and who are quite as radical as he in another
direction.

The economic conferences which were held between business men and working-men, during the winter of 1888–89 and the two succeeding winters, doubtless did much toward relieving this state of effervescence. Many thoughtful men in Chicago are convinced that, if these conferences had been established earlier, the Haymarket riot and all its sensational results might have been avoided. The Sunset Club is at present performing much the same function. There is still need, however, for many of these clubs where men who differ widely in their social theories can meet for discussion, where representatives of the various economic schools can modify each other, and at least learn tolerance and the futility of endeavoring to convince all the world of the truth of one position. To meet in a social-science club is more educational than to meet in a single-tax club, or a socialistic chapter, or a personal-rights league, although the millennium may seem farther off after such a meeting. In addition to this modification of view there is doubtless a distinct modification of attitude. Last spring the Hull House Social Science Club heard a series of talks on municipal and county affairs by the heads of the various departments. During the discussion following the address on "The Chicago Police," a working-man had the pleasure of telling the chief of police that he had been arrested, obliged to pay two dollars and a half, and had lost three days' work, because he had come out of the wrong gate when he was working on the World's Fair grounds. The chief sighed, expressed his regret, and made no defence. The speaker sat down bewildered; evidently for the first time in his life he realized that blunders cut the heart of more than the victim.

Is it possible for men, however far apart in outward circumstances, for the capitalist and the working-man, to use the common phrase, to meet as individuals beneath a friendly roof, open their minds each to each, and not have their "class theories" insensibly modified by the kindly attrition of a personal acquaintance? In the light of our experience I should say not.

In describing Hull House and in referring so often to the "residents," I feel that I may have given a wrong impression. By far the larger amount of the teaching and formal club work is done by people living outside of the House. Between ninety and one hundred of these people meet an appointment regularly each week. Our strength lies largely in this element. The average number of people who come to the House during the week is one thousand.

I am always sorry to have Hull House regarded as philanthropy, although it doubtless has strong philanthropic tendencies, and has several distinct charitable departments which are conscientiously carried on. It is unfair, however, to apply the word philanthropic to the activities of the House as a whole. Charles Booth, in his brilliant chapter on "The Unemployed,"[2] expresses regret that the problems of the working class are so often confounded with the problems of the inefficient, the idle, and distressed. To confound thus two problems is to render the solution of both impossible. Hull House, while endeavoring to fulfil its obligations to neighbors of varying needs, will do great harm if it confounds distinct problems. Working people live in the same streets with those in need of charity, but they themselves, so long as they have health and good wages, require and want none of it. As one of their number has said, they require only that their aspirations be recognized and stimulated, and the means of attaining them put at their disposal. Hull House makes a constant effort to secure these means for its neighbors, but to call that effort philanthropy is to use the word unfairly and to underestimate the duties of good citizenship.

---

[2] Jane Addams refers to Charles Booth's classic survey of poverty in London (a forerunner of similar studies in the United States), *Life and Labour of the People in London (1892–1903)* [Ed.].

6. *Democracy and Social Ethics*

1902

Democracy and Social Ethics was Jane Addams' first book. It struck some of her contemporaries with the force of revelation. William James called it "one of the great books of our time." "The religion of democracy," he told her, "needs nothing so much as sympathetic interpretation to one another of the different classes of which society consists; and you have made your contribution in a masterly manner."[1] Fremont Older, the California reformer and editor of the San Francisco *Bulletin*, declared,

It was not until I read your "Democracy and Social Ethics" that I was able to understand how wrong I had always been in condemning the masses of the people for what I deemed to be a low moral standard. Your psychology of the minds of the poor has been by far the most helpful aid I have ever known. Formerly I sat in my office after an election where the poor had voted crooks into office, and raged at them. I did not understand them as you do, and as you have taught me to understand them.[2]

One has only to read the chapter deceptively titled "Charitable Effort" to understand what it was about this book that elicited such enthusiasm. What Jane Addams had done was to make it clear, perhaps for the first time, that the working class represented not merely a class but a culture—a culture quite alien to that of the middle class. She accomplished this by drawing a vivid contrast between the social worker's own values and those of her clients. The social worker, with her bourgeois habits of temperance and thrift, was at first baffled and even outraged by a culture in which

---

[1] William James to Jane Addams, September 17, 1902; Jane Addams MSS (Swarthmore College Peace Collection, Swarthmore, Pennsylvania).

[2] Fremont Older to Jane Addams, April 2, 1910; *ibid.*

these virtues were not highly esteemed. She was tempted to conclude that poor people were simply lazy and vicious. But once she realized that differences in behavior reflected differences in values, such a view of things became untenable. Just as the cultural anthropologists were undermining the old assumption that primitive peoples lived in a state of moral anarchy, Jane Addams was attempting to show that poor people could not be regarded as failures and misfits because they did not act like solid middle-class citizens. They had to be seen, rather, as conforming to customs peculiar to their own culture.

Democracy and Social Ethics was, in effect, an exercise in anthropology, though it dealt not with distant tribes but with Americans. That these Americans were in many ways as far removed from American culture as the inhabitants of the South Sea Islands provided a measure of the social disintegration which industrialism everywhere induced. Like all anthropological studies, it also called into question the universality of bourgeois ethics. It is no wonder that people found it both exhilarating and disturbing.

CHARITABLE EFFORT

All those hints and glimpses of a larger and more satisfying democracy, which literature and our own hopes supply, have a tendency to slip away from us and to leave us sadly unguided and perplexed when we attempt to act upon them.

Our conceptions of morality, as all our other ideas, pass through a course of development; the difficulty comes in adjusting our conduct, which has become hardened into customs and habits, to these changing moral conceptions. When this adjustment is not made, we suffer from the strain and indecision of believing one hypothesis and acting upon another.

Probably there is no relation in life which our democracy is changing more rapidly than the charitable relation—that

---

From Jane Addams, *Democracy and Social Ethics* (New York: The Macmillan Company, 1902), pp. 13–25, 30–41, 44–51, 58–70.

relation which obtains between benefactor and beneficiary; at the same time there is no point of contact in our modern experience which reveals so clearly the lack of that equality which democracy implies. We have reached the moment when democracy has made such inroads upon this relationship, that the complacency of the old-fashioned charitable man is gone forever; while, at the same time, the very need and existence of charity, denies us the consolation and freedom which democracy will at last give.

It is quite obvious that the ethics of none of us are clearly defined, and we are continually obliged to act in circles of habit, based upon convictions which we no longer hold. Thus our estimate of the effect of environment and social conditions has doubtless shifted faster than our methods of administering charity have changed. Formerly when it was believed that poverty was synonymous with vice and laziness, and that the prosperous man was the righteous man, charity was administered harshly with a good conscience; for the charitable agent really blamed the individual for his poverty, and the very fact of his own superior prosperity gave him a certain consciousness of superior morality. We have learned since that time to measure by other standards, and have ceased to accord to the money-earning capacity exclusive respect; while it is still rewarded out of all proportion to any other, its possession is by no means assumed to imply the possession of the highest moral qualities. We have learned to judge men by their social virtues as well as by their business capacity, by their devotion to intellectual and disinterested aims, and by their public spirit, and we naturally resent being obliged to judge poor people so solely upon the industrial side. Our democratic instinct instantly takes alarm. It is largely in this modern tendency to judge all men by one democratic standard, while the old charitable attitude commonly allowed the use of two standards, that much of the difficulty adheres. We know that unceasing bodily toil becomes wearing and brutalizing, and our position is totally untenable if we judge large numbers of our fellows solely upon their success in maintaining it.

The daintily clad charitable visitor who steps into the little house made untidy by the vigorous efforts of her hostess, the washerwoman, is no longer sure of her superiority to the latter; she recognizes that her hostess after all represents social value and industrial use, as over against her own parasitic cleanliness and a social standing attained only through status.

The only families who apply for aid to the charitable agencies are those who have come to grief on the industrial side; it may be through sickness, through loss of work, or for other guiltless and inevitable reasons; but the fact remains that they are industrially ailing, and must be bolstered and helped into industrial health. The charity visitor, let us assume, is a young college woman, well-bred and open-minded; when she visits the family assigned to her, she is often embarrassed to find herself obliged to lay all the stress of her teaching and advice upon the industrial virtues, and to treat the members of the family almost exclusively as factors in the industrial system. She insists that they must work and be self-supporting, that the most dangerous of all situations is idleness, that seeking one's own pleasure, while ignoring claims and responsibilities, is the most ignoble of actions. The members of her assigned family may have other charms and virtues—they may possibly be kind and considerate of each other, generous to their friends, but it is her business to stick to the industrial side. As she daily holds up these standards, it often occurs to the mind of the sensitive visitor, whose conscience has been made tender by much talk of brotherhood and equality, that she has no right to say these things; that her untrained hands are no more fitted to cope with actual conditions than those of her brokendown family.

The grandmother of the charity visitor could have done the industrial preaching very well, because she did have the industrial virtues and housewifely training. In a generation our experiences have changed, and our views with them; but we still keep on in the old methods, which could be applied when our consciences were in line with them, but which are daily becoming more difficult as we divide up into people who work with their hands and those who do not. The charity visitor belonging to the latter class is perplexed by recognitions and suggestions which the situation forces upon her. Our democracy has taught us to apply our moral teaching all around, and the moralist is rapidly becoming so sensitive that when his life does not exemplify his ethical convictions, he finds it difficult to preach.

Added to this is a consciousness, in the mind of the visitor, of a genuine misunderstanding of her motives by the recipients of her charity, and by their neighbors. Let us take a neighborhood of poor people, and test their ethical standards by those of the charity visitor, who comes with the best desire in the world to help them out of their distress. A most striking incongruity, at once apparent, is the difference between the emotional kindness with which relief is given by one poor neighbor to another poor neighbor, and the guarded care with which relief is given by a charity visitor to a charity recipient. The neighborhood mind is at once confronted not only by the difference of method, but by an absolute clashing of two ethical standards.

A very little familiarity with the poor districts of any city is sufficient to show how primitive and genuine are the neighborly relations. There is the greatest willingness to lend or borrow anything, and all the residents of the given tenement know the most intimate family affairs of all the others. The fact that the economic condition of all alike is on a most precarious level makes the ready outflow of sympathy and material assistance the most natural thing in the world. There are numberless instances of self-sacrifice quite unknown in the circles where greater economic advantages make that kind of intimate knowledge of one's neighbors impossible. An Irish family in

which the man has lost his place, and the woman is struggling
to eke out the scanty savings by day's work, will take in the
widow and her five children who have been turned into the
street, without a moment's reflection upon the physical dis-
comforts involved. The most maligned landlady who lives in
the house with her tenants is usually ready to lend a scuttle
full of coal to one of them who may be out of work, or to
share her supper. A woman for whom the writer had long tried
in vain to find work failed to appear at the appointed time
when employment was secured at last. Upon investigation it
transpired that a neighbor further down the street was taken
ill, that the children ran for the family friend, who went of
course, saying simply when reasons for her non-appearance
were demanded, "It broke my heart to leave the place, but
what could I do?" A woman whose husband was sent up to
the city prison for the maximum term, just three months,
before the birth of her child found herself penniless at the
end of that time, having gradually sold her supply of household furniture. She took refuge with a friend whom she supposed to be living in three rooms in another part of town.
When she arrived, however, she discovered that her friend's
husband had been out of work so long that they had been
reduced to living in one room. The friend, however, took her
in, and the friend's husband was obliged to sleep upon a
bench in the park every night for a week, which he did uncomplainingly if not cheerfully. Fortunately it was summer,
"and it only rained one night." The writer could not discover
from the young mother that she had any special claim upon
the "friend" beyond the fact that they had formerly worked
together in the same factory. The husband she had never seen
until the night of her arrival, when he at once went forth in
search of a midwife who would consent to come upon his
promise of future payment.

The evolutionists tell us that the instinct to pity, the impulse
to aid his fellows, served man at a very early period, as a rude

rule of right and wrong. There is no doubt that this rude rule still holds among many people with whom charitable agencies are brought into contact, and that their ideas of right and wrong are quite honestly outraged by the methods of these agencies. When they see the delay and caution with which relief is given, it does not appear to them a conscientious scruple, but as the cold and calculating action of a selfish man. It is not the aid that they are accustomed to receive from their neighbors, and they do not understand why the impulse which drives people to "be good to the poor" should be so severely supervised. They feel, remotely, that the charity visitor is moved by motives that are alien and unreal. They may be superior motives, but they are different, and they are "agin nature." They cannot comprehend why a person whose intellectual perceptions are stronger than his natural impulses, should go into charity work at all. The only man they are accustomed to see whose intellectual perceptions are stronger than his tenderness of heart, is the selfish and avaricious man who is frankly "on the make." If the charity visitor is such a person, why does she pretend to like the poor? Why does she not go into business at once?

We may say, of course, that it is a primitive view of life, which thus confuses intellectuality and business ability; but it is a view quite honestly held by many poor people who are obliged to receive charity from time to time. In moments of indignation the poor have been known to say: "What do you want, anyway? If you have nothing to give us, why not let us alone and stop your questionings and investigations?" "They investigated me for three weeks, and in the end gave me nothing but a black character," a little woman has been heard to assert. This indignation, which is for the most part taciturn, and a certain kindly contempt for her abilities, often puzzles the charity visitor. The latter may be explained by the standard of worldly success which the visited families hold. Success does not ordinarily go, in the minds of the poor, with charity and kind-heartedness, but rather with the opposite qualities.

The rich landlord is he who collects with sternness, who accepts no excuse, and will have his own. There are moments of irritation and of real bitterness against him, but there is still admiration, because he is rich and successful. The good-natured landlord, he who pities and spares his poverty-pressed tenants, is seldom rich. He often lives in the back of his house, which he has owned for a long time, perhaps has inherited; but he has been able to accumulate little. He commands the genuine love and devotion of many a poor soul, but he is treated with a certain lack of respect. In one sense he is a failure. The charity visitor, just because she is a person who concerns herself with the poor, receives a certain amount of this good-natured and kindly contempt, sometimes real affection, but little genuine respect. The poor are accustomed to help each other and to respond according to their kindliness; but when it comes to worldly judgment, they use industrial success as the sole standard. In the case of the charity visitor who has neither natural kindness nor dazzling riches, they are deprived of both standards, and they find it of course utterly impossible to judge of the motive of organized charity. . . .

The neighborhood understands the selfish rich people who stay in their own part of town, where all their associates have shoes and other things. Such people don't bother themselves about the poor; they are like the rich landlords of the neighborhood experience. But this lady visitor, who pretends to be good to the poor, and certainly does talk as though she were kind-hearted, what does she come for, if she does not intend to give them things which are so plainly needed?

The visitor says, sometimes, that in holding her poor family so hard to a standard of thrift she is really breaking down a rule of higher living which they formerly possessed; that saving, which seems quite commendable in a comfortable part of town, appears almost criminal in a poorer quarter where the next-door neighbor needs food, even if the children of the family do not.

She feels the sordidness of constantly being obliged to urge the industrial view of life. The benevolent individual of fifty years ago honestly believed that industry and self-denial in youth would result in comfortable possessions for old age. It was, indeed, the method he had practised in his own youth, and by which he had probably obtained whatever fortune he possessed. He therefore reproved the poor family for indulging their children, urged them to work long hours, and was utterly untouched by many scruples which afflict the contemporary charity visitor. She says sometimes, "Why must I talk always of getting work and saving money, the things I know nothing about? If it were anything else I had to urge, I could do it; anything like Latin prose, which I had worried through myself, it would not be so hard." But she finds it difficult to connect the experiences of her youth with the experiences of the visited family.

Because of this diversity in experience, the visitor is continually surprised to find that the safest platitude may be challenged. She refers quite naturally to the "horrors of the saloon," and discovers that the head of her visited family does not connect them with "horrors" at all. He remembers all the kindnesses he has received there, the free lunch and treating which goes on, even when a man is out of work and not able to pay up; the loan of five dollars he got there when the charity visitor was miles away and he was threatened with eviction. He may listen politely to her reference to "horrors," but considers it only "temperance talk."

The charity visitor may blame the women for lack of gentleness toward their children, for being hasty and rude to them, until she learns that the standard of breeding is not that of gentleness toward the children so much as the observance of certain conventions, such as the punctilious wearing of mourning garments after the death of a child. The standard of gentleness each mother has to work out largely by herself, assisted only by the occasional shame-faced remark of a neighbor, "That they do better when you are not too hard on them";

but the wearing of mourning garments is sustained by the definitely expressed sentiment of every woman in the street. The mother would have to bear social blame, a certain social ostracism, if she failed to comply with that requirement. It is not comfortable to outrage the conventions of those among whom we live, and, if our social life be a narrow one, it is still more difficult. The visitor may choke a little when she sees the lessened supply of food and the scanty clothing provided for the remaining children in order that one may be conventionally mourned, but she doesn't talk so strongly against it as she would have done during her first month of experience with the family since bereaved.

The subject of clothes indeed perplexes the visitor constantly, and the result of her reflections may be summed up somewhat in this wise: The girl who has a definite social standing, who has been to a fashionable school or to a college, whose family live in a house seen and known by all her friends and associates, may afford to be very simple, or even shabby as to her clothes, if she likes. But the working girl, whose family lives in a tenement, or moves from one small apartment to another, who has little social standing and has to make her own place, knows full well how much habit and style of dress has to do with her position. Her income goes into her clothing, out of all proportion to the amount which she spends upon other things. But, if social advancement is her aim, it is the most sensible thing she can do. She is judged largely by her clothes. Her house furnishing, with its pitiful little decorations, her scanty supply of books, are never seen by the people whose social opinions she most values. Her clothes are her background, and from them she is largely judged. It is due to this fact that girls' clubs succeed best in the business part of town, where "working girls" and "young ladies" meet upon an equal footing, and where the clothes superficially look very much alike. Bright and ambitious girls will come to these downtown clubs to eat lunch and rest at noon, to study all sorts of subjects and listen to lectures, when they might hesitate a long time before joining a club identified with their own neighborhood, where they would be judged not solely on their own merits and the unconscious social standing afforded by good clothes, but by other surroundings which are not nearly up to these. For the same reason, girls' clubs are infinitely more difficult to organize in little towns and villages, where every one knows every one else, just how the front parlor is furnished, and the amount of mortgage there is upon the house. These facts get in the way of a clear and unbiased judgment; they impede the democratic relationship and add to the self-consciousness of all concerned. Every one who has had to do with down-town girls' clubs has had the experience of going into the home of some bright, well-dressed girl, to discover it uncomfortable and perhaps wretched, and to find the girl afterward carefully avoiding her, although the working girl may not have been at home when the call was made, and the visitor may have carried herself with the utmost courtesy throughout. In some very successful down-town clubs the home address is not given at all, and only the "business address" is required. Have we worked out our democracy further in regard to clothes than anything else?

The charity visitor has been rightly brought up to consider it vulgar to spend much money upon clothes, to care so much for "appearances." She realizes dimly that the care for personal decoration over that for one's home or habitat is in some way primitive and undeveloped; but she is silenced by its obvious need. She also catches a glimpse of the fact that the disproportionate expenditure of the poor in the matter of clothes is largely due to the exclusiveness of the rich who hide from them the interior of their houses, and their more subtle pleasures, while of necessity exhibiting their street clothes and their street manners. Every one who goes shopping at the same time may see the clothes of the richest women in town, but only those invited to her receptions see the Corot on her walls or the bindings in her library. The poor naturally try to bridge the difference by reproducing the street clothes which they have seen. They are striving to conform to a common standard which their democratic training presupposes belongs to all of us. The charity visitor may regret that the Italian peasant woman has laid aside her picturesque kerchief and substituted a cheap street hat. But it is easy to recognize the first attempt toward democratic expression.

The charity visitor finds herself still more perplexed when she comes to consider such problems as those of early marriage and child labor; for she cannot deal with them according to economic theories, or according to the conventions which have regulated her own life. She finds both of these fairly upset by her intimate knowledge of the situation, and her sympathy for those into whose lives she has gained a curious insight. She discovers how incorrigibly bourgeois her standards have been, and it takes but a little time to reach the conclusion that she cannot insist so strenuously upon the conventions of her own class, which fail to fit the bigger, more emotional, and freer lives of working people. The charity visitor holds well-grounded views upon the imprudence of early marriages, quite naturally because she comes from a family and circle of professional and business people. A professional man is scarcely equipped and started in his profession before he is thirty. A business man, if he is on the road to success, is much nearer prosperity at thirty-five than twenty-five, and it is therefore wise for these men not to marry in the twenties; but this does not apply to the workingman. In many trades he is laid upon the shelf at thirty-five, and in nearly all trades he receives the largest wages in his life between twenty and thirty. If the young workingman has all his wages to himself, he will probably establish habits of personal comfort, which he cannot keep up when he has to divide with a family—habits which he can, perhaps, never overcome.

The sense of prudence, the necessity for saving, can never

come to a primitive, emotional man with the force of a conviction; but the necessity of providing for his children is a powerful incentive. He naturally regards his children as his savings-bank; he expects them to care for him when he gets old, and in some trades old age comes very early. A Jewish tailor was quite lately sent to the Cook County poorhouse, paralyzed beyond recovery at the age of thirty-five. Had his little boy of nine been but a few years older, he might have been spared this sorrow of public charity. He was, in fact, better able to well support a family when he was twenty than when he was thirty-five, for his wages had steadily grown less as the years went on. Another tailor whom I know, who is also a Socialist, always speaks of saving as a bourgeois virtue, one quite impossible to the genuine workingman. He supports a family consisting of himself, a wife and three children, and his two parents on eight dollars a week. He insists it would be criminal not to expend every penny of this amount upon food and shelter, and he expects his children later to care for him.

This economic pressure also accounts for the tendency to put children to work overyoung and thus cripple their chances for individual development and usefulness, and with the avaricious parent also leads to exploitation. "I have fed her for fourteen years, now she can help me pay my mortgage" is not an unusual reply when a hard-working father is expostulated with because he would take his bright daughter out of school and put her into a factory. . . .

. . . The struggle for existence, which is so much harsher among people near the edge of pauperism, sometimes leaves ugly marks on character, and the charity visitor finds these indirect results most mystifying. Parents who work hard and anticipate an old age when they can no longer earn, take care that their children shall expect to divide their wages with them from the very first. Such a parent, when successful, impresses the immature nervous system of the child thus tyrannically establishing habits of obedience, so that the nerves and will may not depart from this control when the child is older. The charity visitor, whose family relation is lifted quite out of this, does not in the least understand the industrial foundation for this family tyranny.

The head of a kindergarten training-class once addressed a club of working women, and spoke of the despotism which is often established over little children. She said that the so-called determination to break a child's will many times arose from a lust of dominion, and she urged the ideal relationship founded upon love and confidence. But many of the women were puzzled. One of them remarked to the writer as she came out of the club room, "If you did not keep control over them from the time they were little, you would never get their wages when they are grown up." Another one said, "Ah, of course she (meaning the speaker) doesn't have to depend upon her children's wages. She can afford to be lax with them, because even if they don't give money to her, she can get along without it."

There are an impressive number of children who uncomplainingly and constantly hand over their weekly wages to their parents, sometimes receiving back ten cents or a quarter for spending-money, but quite as often nothing at all; and the writer knows one girl of twenty-five who for six years has received two cents a week from the constantly falling wages which she earns in a large factory. Is it habit or virtue which holds her steady in this course? If love and tenderness had been substituted for parental despotism, would the mother have had enough affection, enough power of expression to hold her daughter's sense of money obligation through all these years? This girl who spends her paltry two cents on chewing-gum and goes plainly clad in clothes of her mother's choosing, while many of her friends spend their entire wages on those clothes which factory girls love so well, must be held by some powerful force.

The charity visitor finds these subtle and elusive problems most harrowing. The head of a family she is visiting is a man who has become black-listed in a strike. He is not a very good workman, and this, added to his agitator's reputation, keeps him out of work for a long time. The fatal result of being long out of work follows: he becomes less and less eager for it, and gets a "job" less and less frequently. In order to keep up his self-respect, and still more to keep his wife's respect for him, he yields to the little self-deception that this prolonged idleness follows because he was once black-listed, and he gradually becomes a martyr. Deep down in his heart perhaps—but who knows what may be deep down in his heart? Whatever may be in his wife's, she does not show for an instant that she thinks he has grown lazy, and accustomed to see her earn, by sewing and cleaning, most of the scanty income for the family. The charity visitor, however, does see this, and she also sees that the other men who were in the strike have gone back to work. She further knows by inquiry and a little experience that the man is not skillful. She cannot, however, call him lazy and good-for-nothing, and denounce him as worthless as her grandmother might have done, because of certain intellectual conceptions at which she has arrived. She sees other workmen come to him for shrewd advice; she knows that he spends many more hours in the public library reading good books than the average workman has time to do. He has formed no bad habits and has yielded only to those subtle temptations toward a life of leisure which come to the intellectual man. He lacks the qualifications which would induce his union to engage him as a secretary or organizer, but he is a constant speaker at workingmen's meetings, and takes a high moral attitude on the questions discussed there. He contributes a certain intellectuality to his friends, and he has undoubted social value. The neighboring women confide to the charity visitor their sympathy with his wife, because she has to work so hard, and because her husband does not "provide." Their remarks are sharpened by a certain resentment toward the superiority of the husband's education and gentle manners. The charity visitor is ashamed to take this point of view, for she knows that it is not altogether fair. She is reminded of a college friend of hers, who told her that she was not going to allow her literary husband to write unworthy potboilers for the sake of earning a living. "I insist that we shall live within my own income; that he shall not publish until he is ready, and can give his genuine message." The charity visitor recalls what she has heard of another acquaintance, who urged her husband to decline a lucrative position as a railroad attorney, because she wished him to be free to take municipal positions, and handle public questions without the inevitable suspicion which unaccountably attaches itself in a corrupt city to a corporation attorney. The action of these two women seemed noble to her, but in their cases they merely lived on a lesser income. In the case of the workingman's wife, she faced living on no income at all, or on the precarious one which she might be able to get together.

She sees that this third woman has made the greatest sacrifice, and she is utterly unwilling to condemn her while praising the friends of her own social position. She realizes, of course, that the situation is changed by the fact that the third family needs charity, while the other two do not; but, after all, they have not asked for it, and their plight was only discovered through an accident to one of the children. The charity visitor has been taught that her mission is to preserve the finest traits to be found in her visited family, and she shrinks from the thought of convincing the wife that her husband is worthless and she suspects that she might turn all this beautiful devotion into complaining drudgery. To be sure, she could give up visiting the family altogether, but she has become much interested in the progress of the crippled child who eagerly anticipates her visits, and she also suspects that she will never know many finer women than the mother. She is unwilling, therefore, to give up the friendship, and goes on bearing her perplexities as best she may. . . .

. . . The greatest difficulty is experienced when the two standards come sharply together, and when both sides make an attempt at understanding and explanation. The difficulty of making clear one's own ethical standpoint is at times insurmountable. A woman who had bought and sold school books stolen from the school fund,—books which are all plainly marked with a red stamp,—came to Hull House one morning in great distress because she had been arrested, and begged a resident "to speak to the judge." She gave as a reason the fact that the House had known her for six years, and had once been very good to her when her little girl was buried. The resident more than suspected that her visitor knew the school books were stolen when buying them, and any attempt to talk upon that subject was evidently considered very rude. The visitor wished to get out of her trial, and evidently saw no reason why the House should not help her. The alderman was out of town, so she could not go to him. After a long conversation the visitor entirely failed to get another point of view and went away grieved and disappointed at a refusal, thinking the resident simply disobliging; wondering, no doubt, why such a mean woman had once been good to her; leaving the resident, on the other hand, utterly baffled and in the state of mind she would have been in, had she brutally insisted that a little child should lift weights too heavy for its undeveloped muscles.

Such a situation brings out the impossibility of substituting a higher ethical standard for a lower one without similarity of experience, but it is not as painful as that illustrated by the following example, in which the highest ethical standard yet attained by the charity recipient is broken down, and the substituted one not in the least understood:—

A certain charity visitor is peculiarly appealed to by the weakness and pathos of forlorn old age. She is responsible for the well-being of perhaps a dozen old women to whom she sustains a sincerely affectionate and almost filial relation. Some of them learn to take her benefactions quite as if they came from their own relatives, grumbling at all she does, and scolding her with a family freedom. One of these poor old women was injured in a fire years ago. She has but the fragment of a hand left, and is grievously crippled in her feet. Through years of pain she had become addicted to opium, and when she first came under the visitor's care, was only held from the poorhouse by the awful thought that she would there perish without her drug. Five years of tender care have done wonders for her. She lives in two neat little rooms, where with her thumb and two fingers she makes innumerable quilts, which she sells and gives away with the greatest delight. Her opium is regulated to a set amount taken each day, and she has drawn away from much drinking. She is a voracious reader, and has her head full of strange tales made up from books and her own imagination. At one time it seemed impossible to do anything for her in Chicago, and she was kept for two years in a suburb, where the family of the charity visitor lived, and where she was nursed through several hazardous illnesses. She now lives a better life than she did, but she is still far from being a model old woman. The neighbors are constantly shocked by the fact that she is supported and comforted by a "charity lady," while at the same time she occasionally "rushes the growler,"[1] scolding at the boys lest they jar her in her tottering walk. The care of her has broken through even that second standard, which the neighborhood had learned to recognize as the standard of charitable societies, that only the "worthy poor" are to be helped; that temperance and thrift are the virtues which receive the plums of benevolence. The old lady herself is conscious of this criticism. Indeed, irate neighbors tell her to her face that she doesn't in the least deserve what she gets. In order to disarm them, and at the same time

---

[1] Gets drunk on beer. "Growler" is a beer container [Ed.].

to explain what would otherwise seem loving-kindness so colossal as to be abnormal, she tells them that during her sojourn in the suburb she discovered an awful family secret,—a horrible scandal connected with the long-suffering charity visitor; that it is in order to prevent the divulgence of this that she constantly receives her ministrations. Some of her perplexed neighbors accept this explanation as simple and offering a solution of this vexed problem. Doubtless many of them have a glimpse of the real state of affairs, of the love and patience which ministers to need irrespective of worth. But the standard is too high for most of them, and it sometimes seems unfortunate to break down the second standard, which holds that people who "rush the growler" are not worthy of charity, and that there is a certain justice attained when they go to the poorhouse. It is certainly dangerous to break down the lower, unless the higher is made clear.

Just when our affection becomes large enough to care for the unworthy among the poor as we would care for the unworthy among our own kin, is certainly a perplexing question. To say that it should never be so, is a comment upon our democratic relations to them which few of us would be willing to make.

Of what use is all this striving and perplexity? Has the experience any value? It is certainly genuine, for it induces an occasional charity visitor to live in a tenement house as simply as the other tenants do. It drives others to give up visiting the poor altogether, because, they claim, it is quite impossible unless the individual becomes a member of a sisterhood, which requires, as some of the Roman Catholic sisterhoods do, that the member first take the vows of obedience and poverty, so that she can have nothing to give save as it is first given to her, and thus she is not harassed by a constant attempt at adjustment.

Both the tenement-house resident and the sister assume to have put themselves upon the industrial level of their neighbors, although they have left out the most awful element of poverty, that of imminent fear of starvation and a neglected old age.

The young charity visitor who goes from a family living upon a most precarious industrial level to her own home in a prosperous part of the city, if she is sensitive at all, is never free from perplexities which our growing democracy forces upon her.

We sometimes say that our charity is too scientific, but we would doubtless be much more correct in our estimate if we said that it is not scientific enough. We dislike the entire arrangement of cards alphabetically classified according to streets and names of families, with the unrelated and meaningless details attached to them. Our feeling of revolt is probably not unlike that which afflicted the students of botany and geology in the middle of the last century, when flowers were tabulated in alphabetical order, when geology was taught by colored charts and thin books. No doubt the students, wearied to death, many times said that it was all too scientific, and were much perplexed and worried when they found traces of structure and physiology which their so-called scientific principles were totally unable to account for. But all this happened before science had become evolutionary and scientific at all, before it had a principle of life from within. The very indications and discoveries which formerly perplexed, later illumined and made the study absorbing and vital.

We are singularly slow to apply this evolutionary principle to human affairs in general, although it is fast being applied to the education of children. We are at last learning to follow the development of the child; to expect certain traits under certain conditions; to adapt methods and matter to his growing mind. No "advanced educator" can allow himself to be so absorbed in the question of what a child ought to be as to exclude the discovery of what he is. But in our charitable efforts we think much more of what a man ought to be than of what he is or of what he may become; and we ruthlessly force our conventions and standards upon him, with a sternness which we would consider stupid indeed did an educator use it in forcing his mature intellectual convictions upon an undeveloped mind.

Let us take the example of a timid child, who cries when he is put to bed because he is afraid of the dark. The "softhearted" parent stays with him, simply because he is sorry for him and wants to comfort him. The scientifically trained parent stays with him, because he realizes that the child is in a stage of development in which his imagination has the best of him, and in which it is impossible to reason him out of a belief in ghosts. These two parents, wide apart in point of view, after all act much alike, and both very differently from the pseudo-scientific parent, who acts from dogmatic conviction and is sure he is right. He talks of developing his child's self-respect and good sense, and leaves him to cry himself to sleep, demanding powers of self-control and development which the child does not possess. There is no doubt that our development of charity methods has reached this pseudo-scientific and stilted stage. We have learned to condemn unthinking, ill-regulated kind-heartedness, and we take pride in mere repression much as the stern parent tells the visitor below how admirably he is rearing the child, who is hysterically crying upstairs and laying the foundation for future nervous disorders. The pseudo-scientific spirit, or rather, the undeveloped stage of our philanthropy, is perhaps most clearly revealed in our tendency to lay constant stress on negative action. "Don't give!" "don't break down self-respect," we are constantly told. We distrust the human impulse as well as the teachings of our own experience, and in their stead substitute dogmatic rules for conduct. We forget that the accumulation of knowledge and the holding of convictions must finally result in the application of that knowledge and those convictions to life itself; that the necessity for activity and a pull upon the sympathies is so severe, that all the knowledge in the possession of the visitor is constantly applied, and she has a reasonable chance for an ultimate intellectual comprehension. Indeed, part of the perplexity in the administration of charity comes from the fact that the type of person drawn to it is the one who insists that her convictions shall not be unrelated to action. Her moral concepts constantly tend to float away from her, unless they have a basis in the concrete relation of life. She is confronted with the task of reducing her scruples to action, and of converging many wills, so as to unite the strength of all of them into one accomplishment, the value of which no one can foresee.

On the other hand, the young woman who has succeeded in expressing her social compunction through charitable effort finds that the wider social activity, and the contact with the larger experience, not only increases her sense of social obligation but at the same time recasts her social ideals. She is chagrined to discover that in the actual task of reducing her social scruples to action, her humble beneficiaries are far in advance of her, not in charity or singleness of purpose, but in self-sacrificing action. She reaches the old-time virtue of humility by a social process, not in the old way, as the man who sits by the side of the road and puts dust upon his head, calling himself a contrite sinner, but she gets the dust upon her head because she has stumbled and fallen in the road through her efforts to push forward the mass, to march with her fellows. She has socialized her virtues not only through a social aim but by a social process.

The Hebrew prophet made three requirements from those who would join the great forward-moving procession led by Jehovah. "To love mercy" and at the same time "to do justly" is the difficult task; to fulfil the first requirement alone is to fall into the error of indiscriminate giving with all its disastrous results; to fulfil the second solely is to obtain the stern policy of withholding, and it results in such a dreary lack of sympathy and understanding that the establishment of justice is impossible. It may be that the combination of the two can never be attained save as we fulfil still the third requirement— "to walk humbly with God," which may mean to walk for many dreary miles beside the lowliest of His creatures, not even in that peace of mind which the company of the humble is popularly supposed to afford, but rather with the pangs and throes to which the poor human understanding is subjected whenever it attempts to comprehend the meaning of life.

7. *The Spirit of Youth and the City Streets*

1909

It was this book that called forth William James's celebrated tribute to its author: "The fact is, Madam, that you are not like the rest of us, who *seek* the truth and try to express it. You *inhabit* reality."[1]

Her long struggle, as a young woman, to find herself left Jane Addams with a keen understanding of the youth's search for identity. *The Spirit of Youth* combines a lyrical evocation of youth with an indignation somewhat unusual in Jane Addams' work. The social arrangements in which young people were expected to grow up appeared to her so "stupid" that she could not conceal her impatience with them. The writing here, accordingly, is more highly charged than the writing in *Democracy and Social Ethics;* but the underlying point is essentially the same: young people constitute what amounts to a subculture of their own. "Never before," Miss Addams writes, "have the pleasures of the young and mature be-

---

[1] William James to Jane Addams, December 13, 1909; Jane Addams MSS (Swarthmore College Peace Collection, Swarthmore, Pennsylvania).

come so definitely separated as in the modern city." Not only does industrialism tend to segregate social classes; within the same class, it segregates the generations. *The Spirit of Youth*, like *Democracy and Social Ethics*, is a study of the break-up of the sense of community, a study in social disintegration.

YOUTH IN THE CITY

Nothing is more certain than that each generation longs for a reassurance as to the value and charm of life, and is secretly afraid lest it lose its sense of the youth of the earth. This is doubtless one reason why it so passionately cherishes its poets and artists who have been able to explore for themselves and to reveal to others the perpetual springs of life's self-renewal.

And yet the average man cannot obtain this desired reassurance through literature, nor yet through glimpses of earth and sky. It can come to him only through the chance embodiment of joy and youth which life itself may throw in his way. It is doubtless true that for the mass of men the message is never so unchallenged and so invincible as when embodied in youth itself. One generation after another has depended upon its young to equip it with gaiety and enthusiasm, to persuade it that living is a pleasure, until men everywhere have anxiously provided channels through which this wine of life might flow, and be preserved for their delight. The classical city promoted play with careful solicitude, building the theater and stadium as it built the market place and the temple. The Greeks held their games so integral a part of religion and patriotism that they came to expect from their poets the highest utterances at the very moments when the sense of pleasure released the national life. In the medieval city the knights held their tourneys, the guilds their pageants, the people their dances, and

From Jane Addams, *The Spirit of Youth and the City Streets* (New York: The Macmillan Company, 1909), pages 3–21.

the church made festival for its most cherished saints with gay street processions, and presented a drama in which no less a theme than the history of creation became a matter of thrilling interest. Only in the modern city have men concluded that it is no longer necessary for the municipality to provide for the insatiable desire for play. In so far as they have acted upon this conclusion, they have entered upon a most difficult and dangerous experiment; and this at the very moment when the city has become distinctly industrial, and daily labor is continually more monotonous and subdivided. We forget how new the modern city is, and how short the span of time in which we have assumed that we can eliminate public provision for recreation.

A further difficulty lies in the fact that this industrialism has gathered together multitudes of eager young creatures from all quarters of the earth as a labor supply for the countless factories and workshops, upon which the present industrial city is based. Never before in civilization have such numbers of young girls been suddenly released from the protection of the home and permitted to walk unattended upon city streets and to work under alien roofs; for the first time they are being prized more for their labor power than for their innocence, their tender beauty, their ephemeral gaiety. Society cares more for the products they manufacture than for their immemorial ability to reaffirm the charm of existence. Never before have such numbers of young boys earned money independently of the family life, and felt themselves free to spend it as they choose in the midst of vice deliberately disguised as pleasure.

This stupid experiment of organizing work and failing to organize play has, of course, brought about a fine revenge. The love of pleasure will not be denied, and when it has turned into all sorts of malignant and vicious appetites, then we, the middle aged, grow quite distracted and resort to all sorts of restrictive measures. We even try to dam up the sweet fountain itself because we are affrighted by these neglected streams; but almost worse than the restrictive measures is our apparent belief that the city itself has no obligation in the matter, an assumption upon which the modern city turns over to commercialism practically all the provisions for public recreation.

Quite as one set of men has organized the young people into industrial enterprises in order to profit from their toil, so another set of men and also of women, I am sorry to say, have entered the neglected field of recreation and have organized enterprises which make profit out of this invincible love of pleasure.

In every city arise so-called "places"—"gin-palaces," they are called in fiction; in Chicago we euphemistically say merely "places,"—in which alcohol is dispensed, not to allay thrist, but, ostensibly to stimulate gaiety, it is sold really in order to empty pockets. Huge dance halls are opened to which hundreds of young people are attracted, many of whom stand wistfully outside a roped circle, for it requires five cents to procure within it for five minutes the sense of allurement and intoxication which is sold in lieu of innocent pleasure. These coarse and illicit merrymakings remind one of the unrestrained jollities of Restoration London, and they are indeed their direct descendants, properly commercialized, still confusing joy with lust, and gaiety with debauchery. Since the soldiers of Cromwell shut up the people's playhouses and destroyed their pleasure fields, the Anglo-Saxon city has turned over the provision for public recreation to the most evil-minded and the most unscrupulous members of the community. We see thousands of girls walking up and down the streets on a pleasant evening with no chance to catch a sight of pleasure even through a lighted window, save as those lurid places provide it. Apparently the modern city sees in these girls only two possibilities, both of them commercial: first, a chance to utilize by day their new and tender labor power in its factories and shops, and then another chance in the evening to extract from them their petty wages by pandering to their love of pleasure.

As these overworked girls stream along the street, the rest of us see only the self-conscious walk, the giggling speech, the preposterous clothing. And yet through the huge hat, with its wilderness of bedraggled feathers, the girl announces to the world that she is here. She demands attention to the fact of her existence, she states that she is ready to live, to take her place in the world. The most precious moment in human development is the young creature's assertion that he is unlike any other human being, and has an individual contribution to make to the world. The variation from the established type is at the root of all change, the only possible basis for progress, all that keeps life from growing unprofitably stale and repetitious.

Is it only the artists who really see these young creatures as they are—the artists who are themselves endowed with immortal youth? Is it our disregard of the artist's message which makes us so blind and so stupid, or are we so under the influence of our *Zeitgeist* that we can detect only commercial values in the young as well as in the old? It is as if our eyes were holden to the mystic beauty, the redemptive joy, the civic pride which these multitudes of young people might supply to our dingy towns.

The young creatures themselves piteously look all about them in order to find an adequate means of expression for their most precious message. One day a serious young man came to Hull-House with his pretty young sister who, he explained, wanted to go somewhere every single evening, "although she could only give the flimsy excuse that the flat was too little and too stuffy to stay in." In the difficult rôle of elder brother, he had done his best, stating that he had taken her "to all the missions in the neighborhood, that she had had a chance to listen to some awful good sermons and to some elegant hymns, but that some way she did not seem to care for the society of the best Christian people." The little sister reddened painfully under this cruel indictment and could offer no word of excuse, but a curious thing happened to me. Perhaps it was the phrase "the best Christian people," perhaps it was the delicate color of her flushing cheeks and her swimming eyes, but certain it is, that instantly and vividly there appeared to my mind the delicately tinted piece of wall in a Roman catacomb where the early Christians, through a dozen devices of spring flowers, skipping lambs and a shepherd tenderly guiding the young, had indelibly written down that the Christian message is one of inexpressible joy. Who is responsible for forgetting this message delivered by the "best Christian people" two thousand years ago? Who is to blame that the lambs, the little ewe lambs, have been so caught upon the brambles?

But quite as the modern city wastes this most valuable moment in the life of the girl, and drives into all sorts of absurd and obscure expressions her love and yearning towards the world in which she forecasts her destiny, so it often drives the boy into gambling and drinking in order to find his adventure.

Of Lincoln's enlistment of two and a half million soldiers, a very large number were under twenty-one, some of them under eighteen, and still others were mere children under fifteen. Even in those stirring times when patriotism and high resolve were at the flood, no one responded as did "the boys," and the great soul who yearned over them, who refused to shoot the sentinels who slept the sleep of childhood, knew, as no one else knew, the precious glowing stuff of which his army was made. But what of the millions of boys who are now searching for adventurous action, longing to fulfil the same high purpose?

One of the most pathetic sights in the public dance halls in Chicago is the number of young men, obviously honest young fellows from the country, who stand about vainly hoping to make the acquaintance of some "nice girl." They look eagerly up and down the rows of girls, many of whom are drawn to the hall by the same keen desire for pleasure and social intercourse which the lonely young men themselves feel.

One Sunday night at twelve o'clock I had occasion to go into a large public dance hall. As I was standing by the rail looking for the girl I had come to find, a young man approached me and quite simply asked me to introduce him to some "nice girl," saying that he did not know any one there. On my replying that a public dance hall was not the best place in which to look for a nice girl, he said: "But I don't know any other place where there is a chance to meet any kind of a girl. I'm awfully lonesome since I came to Chicago." And then he added rather defiantly: "Some nice girls do come here! It's one of the best halls in town." He was voicing the "bitter loneliness" that many city men remember to have experienced during the first years after they had "come up to town." Occasionally the right sort of man and girl meet each other in these dance halls and the romance with such a tawdry beginning ends happily and respectably. But, unfortunately, mingled with the respectable young men seeking to form the acquaintance of young women through the only channel which is available to them, are many young fellows of evil purpose, and among the girls who have left their lonely boarding houses or rigid homes for a "little fling" are likewise women who openly desire to make money from the young men whom they meet, and back of it all is the desire to profit by the sale of intoxicating and "doctored" drinks.

Perhaps never before have the pleasures of the young and mature become so definitely separated as in the modern city. The public dance halls filled with frivolous and irresponsible young people in a feverish search for pleasure, are but a sorry substitute for the old dances on the village green in which all of the older people of the village participated. Chaperonage was not then a social duty but natural and inevitable, and the whole courtship period was guarded by the conventions and restraint which were taken as a matter of course and had developed through years of publicity and simple propriety.

The only marvel is that the stupid attempt to put the fine old wine of traditional country life into the new bottles of the modern town does not lead to disaster oftener than it does, and that the wine so long remains pure and sparkling.

We cannot afford to be ungenerous to the city in which we live without suffering the penalty which lack of fair interpretation always entails. Let us know the modern city in its weakness and wickedness, and then seek to rectify and purify it until it shall be free at least from the grosser temptations which now beset the young people who are living in its tenement houses and working in its factories. The mass of these young people are possessed of good intentions and they are equipped with a certain understanding of city life. This itself could be made a most valuable social instrument toward securing innocent recreation and better social organization. They are already serving the city in so far as it is honeycombed with mutual benefit societies, with "pleasure clubs," with organizations connected with churches and factories which are filling a genuine social need. And yet the whole apparatus for supplying pleasure is wretchedly inadequate and full of danger to whomsoever may approach it. Who is responsible for its inadequacy and dangers? We certainly cannot expect the fathers and mothers who have come to the city from farms or who have emigrated from other lands to appreciate or rectify these dangers. We cannot expect the young people themselves to cling to conventions which are totally unsuited to modern city conditions, nor yet to be equal to the task of forming new conventions through which this more agglomerate social life may express itself. Above all we cannot hope that they will understand the emotional force which seizes them and which, when it does not find the traditional line of domesticity, serves as a cancer in the very tissues of society and as a disrupter of the securest social bonds. No attempt is made to treat the manifestations of this fundamental instinct with dignity or to give it possible social utility. The spontaneous joy, the clamor for pleasure, the desire of the young people to appear finer and better and altogether more lovely than they really are, the idealization not only of each other but of the whole earth which they regard but as a theater for their noble exploits, the unworldly ambitions, the romantic hopes, the make-believe world in which they live, if properly utilized, what might they not do to make our sordid cities more beautiful, more companionable? And yet at the present moment every city is full of young people who are utterly bewildered and uninstructed in regard to the basic experience which must inevitably come to them, and which has varied, remote, and indirect expressions.

Even those who may not agree with the authorities who claim that it is this fundamental sex susceptibility which suffuses the world with its deepest meaning and beauty, and furnishes the momentum towards all art, will perhaps permit me to quote the classical expression of this view as set forth in that ancient and wonderful conversation between Socrates and the wise woman Diotima. Socrates asks: "What are they doing who show all this eagerness and heat which is called love? And what is the object they have in view? Answer me." Diotima replies: "I will teach you. The object which they have in view is birth in beauty, whether of body or soul. . . . For love, Socrates, is not as you imagine the love of the beautiful only . . . but the love of birth in beauty, because to the mortal creature generation is a sort of eternity and immortality."

To emphasize the eternal aspects of love is not of course an easy undertaking, even if we follow the clue afforded by the heart of every generous lover. His experience at least in certain moments tends to pull him on and out from the passion for one to an enthusiasm for that highest beauty and excellence of which the most perfect form is but an inadequate expression. Even the most loutish tenement-house youth vaguely feels this, and at least at rare intervals reveals it in his talk to his "girl." His memory unexpectedly brings hidden treasures to the surface of consciousness and he recalls the more delicate and tender experiences of his childhood and earlier youth. "I remember the time when my little sister died, that I rode out to the cemetery feeling that everybody in Chicago had moved away from the town to make room for that kid's funeral, everything was so darned lonesome and yet it was kind of peaceful too." Or, "I never had a chance to go into the country when I was a kid, but I remember one day when I had to deliver a package way out on the West Side, that I saw a flock of sheep in Douglas Park. I had never thought that a sheep could be anywhere but in a picture, and when I saw those big white spots on the green grass beginning to move and to turn into sheep, I felt exactly as if Saint Cecilia had come out of her frame over the organ and was walking in the park." Such moments come into the life of the most prosaic youth living in the most crowded quarters of the cities. What do we do to encourage and to solidify those moments, to make them come true in our dingy towns, to give them expression in forms of art?

We not only fail in this undertaking but even debase existing forms of art. We are informed by high authority that there is nothing in the environment to which youth so keenly responds as to music, and yet the streets, the vaudeville shows, the five-cent theaters are full of the most blatant and vulgar songs. The trivial and obscene words, the meaningless and flippant airs run through the heads of hundreds of young people for hours at a time while they are engaged in monotonous factory work. We totally ignore that ancient connection between music and morals which was so long insisted upon by philosophers as well poets. The street music has quite broken away from all control, both of the educator and the patriot, and we have grown singularly careless in regard to its influence upon young people. Although we legislate against it in saloons because of its dangerous influence there, we constantly permit music on the street to incite that which should be controlled, to degrade that which should be exalted, to make sensuous that which might be lifted into the realm of the higher imagination.

Our attitude towards music is typical of our carelessness towards all those things which make for common joy and for the restraints of higher civilization on the streets. It is as if our cities had not yet developed a sense of responsibility in regard to the life of the streets, and continually forget that recreation is stronger than vice, and that recreation alone can stifle the lust for vice.

Perhaps we need to take a page from the philosophy of the Greeks to whom the world of fact was also the world of the ideal, and to whom the realization of what ought to be, involved not the destruction of what was, but merely its perfecting upon its own lines. To the Greeks virtue was not a hard conformity to a law felt as alien to the natural character, but a free expression of the inner life. To treat thus the fundamental susceptibility of sex which now so bewilders the street life and drives young people themselves into all sort of difficulties, would mean to loosen it from the things of sense and to link it to the affairs of the imagination. It would mean to fit to this gross and heavy stuff the wings of the mind, to scatter from it "the clinging mud of banality and vulgarity," and to speed it on through our city streets amid spontaneous laughter, snatches of lyric song, the recovered forms of old dances, and the traditional rondels of merry games. It would thus bring charm and beauty to the prosaic city and connect it subtly with the arts of the past as well as with the vigor and renewed life of the future.

8. "Immigrants and Their Children"

1910

This chapter from *Twenty Years at Hull-House* is a more systematic examination of the generational segregation touched upon in the preceding selection. It is one of the first studies, and one of the most lucid, of what is now recognized as a classic sociological phenomenon—the conflict between first- and second-generation immigrants.

. . . An overmastering desire to reveal the humbler immigrant parents to their own children lay at the base of what has come to be called the Hull-House Labor Museum. This was first suggested to my mind one early spring day when I saw an old Italian woman, her distaff against her homesick face, patiently spinning a thread by the simple stick spindle so reminiscent of all southern Europe. I was walking down Polk Street, perturbed in spirit, because it seemed so difficult to come into genuine relations with the Italian women and because they themselves so often lost their hold upon their Americanized children. It seemed to me that Hull-House ought to be able to devise some educational enterprise, which should build a bridge between European and American experiences in such wise as to give them both more meaning and a sense of relation. I meditated that perhaps the power to see life as a whole, is more needed in the immigrant quarter of a large

From Jane Addams, *Twenty Years at Hull-House* (The Macmillan Company, 1910), pp. 231–250, 252–253.

city than anywhere else, and that the lack of this power is the most fruitful source of misunderstanding between European immigrants and their children, as it is between them and their American neighbors; and why should that chasm between fathers and sons, yawning at the feet of each generation, be made so unnecessarily cruel and impassable to these bewildered immigrants? Suddenly I looked up and saw the old woman with her distaff, sitting in the sun on the steps of a tenement house. She might have served as a model for one of Michael Angelo's Fates, but her face brightened as I passed and, holding up her spindle for me to see, she called out that when she had spun a little more yarn, she would knit a pair of stockings for her goddaughter. The occupation of the old woman gave me the clew that was needed. Could we not interest the young people working in the neighboring factories, in these older forms of industry, so that, through their own parents and grandparents, they would find a dramatic representation of the inherited resources of their daily occupation. If these young people could actually see that the complicated machinery of the factory had been evolved from simple tools, they might at least make a beginning towards that education which Dr. Dewey defines as "a continuing reconstruction of experience." They might also lay a foundation for reverence of the past which Goethe declares to be the basis of all sound progress.

My exciting walk on Polk Street was followed by many talks with Dr. Dewey and with one of the teachers in his school who was a resident at Hull-House. Within a month a room was fitted up to which we might invite those of our neighbors who were possessed of old crafts and who were eager to use them.

We found in the immediate neighborhood, at least four varieties of these most primitive methods of spinning and three distinct variations of the same spindle in connection with wheels. It was possible to put these seven into historic sequence and order and to connect the whole with the present method of factory spinning. The same thing was done for weaving, and on every Saturday evening a little exhibit was made of these various forms of labor in the textile industry. Within one room a Syrian woman, a Greek, an Italian, a Russian, and an Irish-woman enabled even the most casual observer to see that there is no break in orderly evolution if we look at history from the industrial standpoint; that industry develops similarly and peacefully year by year among the workers of each nation, heedless of differences in language, religion, and political experiences.

And then we grew ambitious and arranged lectures upon industrial history. I remember that after an interesting lecture upon the industrial revolution in England and a portrayal of the appalling conditions throughout the weaving districts of the north, which resulted from the hasty gathering of the weavers into the new towns, a Russian tailor in the audience was moved to make a speech. He suggested that whereas time had done much to alleviate the first difficulties in the transition of weaving from hand work to steam power, that in the application of steam to sewing we are still in the first stages, illustrated by the isolated woman who tries to support herself by hand needlework at home until driven out by starvation, as many of the hand weavers had been.

The historical analogy seemed to bring a certain comfort to the tailor as did a chart upon the wall, showing the infinitesimal amount of time that steam had been applied to manufacturing processes compared to the centuries of hand labor. Human progress is slow and perhaps never more cruel than in the advance of industry, but is not the worker comforted by knowing that other historical periods have existed similiar to the one in which he finds himself, and that the readjustment may be shortened and alleviated by judicious action; and is he not entitled to the solace which an artistic portrayal of the situation might give him? I remember the evening of the tailor's speech that I felt reproached because no poet or artist has endeared the sweaters' victim to us as George Eliot has made us love the belated weaver, Silas Marner. The textile museum is connected directly with the basket weaving, sewing, millinery, embroidery, and dressmaking constantly being taught at Hull-House, and so far as possible with the other educational departments; we have also been able to make a collection of products, of early implements, and of photographs which are full of suggestion. Yet far beyond its direct educational value, we prize it because it so often puts the immigrants into the position of teachers, and we imagine that it affords them a pleasant change from the tutelage in which all Americans, including their own children, are so apt to hold them. I recall a number of Russian women working in a sewing-room near Hull-House, who heard one Christmas week that the House was going to give a party to which they might come. They arrived one afternoon when, unfortunately, there was no party on hand and, although the residents did their best to entertain them with impromptu music and refreshments, it was quite evident that they were greatly disappointed. Finally it was suggested that they be shown the Labor Museum—where gradually the thirty sodden, tired women were transformed. They knew how to use the spindles and were delighted to find the Russian spinning frame. Many of them had never seen the spinning wheel, which has not penetrated to certain parts of Russia, and they regarded it as a new and wonderful invention. They turned up their dresses to show their homespun petticoats; they tried the looms; they explained the difficulty of the old patterns; in short, from having been stupidly entertained, they themselves did the entertaining. Because of a direct appeal to former experiences, the immigrant visitors were able for the moment to instruct their American hostesses in an old and honored craft, as was indeed becoming to their age and experience.

In some such ways as these have the Labor Museum and

the shops pointed out the possibilities which Hull-House has scarcely begun to develop, of demonstrating that culture is an understanding of the long-established occupations and thoughts of men, of the arts with which they have solaced their toil. A yearning to recover for the household arts something of their early sanctity and meaning, arose strongly within me one evening when I was attending a Passover Feast to which I had been invited by a Jewish family in the neighborhood, where the traditional and religious significance of woman's daily activity was still retained. The kosher food the Jewish mother spread before her family had been prepared according to traditional knowledge and with constant care in the use of utensils; upon her had fallen the responsibility to make all ready according to Mosaic instructions that the great crisis in a religious history might be fittingly set forth by her husband and son. Aside from the grave religious significance in the ceremony, my mind was filled with shifting pictures of woman's labor with which travel makes one familiar; the Indian women grinding grain outside of their huts as they sing praises to the sun and rain; a file of white-clad Moorish women whom I had once seen waiting their turn at a well in Tangiers; south Italian women kneeling in a row along the stream and beating their wet clothes against the smooth white stones; the milking, the gardening, the marketing in thousands of hamlets, which are such direct expressions of the solicitude and affection at the basis of all family life.

There has been some testimony that the Labor Museum has revealed the charm of woman's primitive activities. I recall a certain Italian girl who came every Saturday evening to a cooking class in the same building in which her mother spun in the Labor Museum exhibit; and yet Angelina always left her mother at the front door while she herself went around to a side door because she did not wish to be too closely identified in the eyes of the rest of the cooking class with an Italian woman who wore a kerchief over her head, uncouth boots, and short petticoats. One evening, however, Angelina saw her mother surrounded by a group of visitors from the School of Education, who much admired the spinning, and she concluded from their conversation that her mother was "the best stick-spindle spinner in America." When she inquired from me as to the truth of this deduction, I took occasion to describe the Italian village in which her mother had lived, something of her free life, and how, because of the opportunity she and the other women of the village had to drop their spindles over the edge of a precipice, they had developed a skill in spinning beyond that of the neighboring towns. I dilated somewhat on the freedom and beauty of that life—how hard it must be to exchange it all for a two-room tenement, and to give up a beautiful homespun kerchief for an ugly department store hat. I intimated it was most unfair to judge her by these things alone, and that while she must depend on her daughter to learn the new ways, she also had a right to expect her daughter to know something of the old ways.

That which I could not convey to the child but upon which my own mind persistently dwelt, was that her mother's whole life had been spent in a secluded spot under the rule of traditional and narrowly localized observances, until her very religion clung to local sanctities,—to the shrine before which she had always prayed, to the pavement and walls of the low vaulted church,—and then suddenly she was torn from it all and literally put out to sea, straight away from the solid habits of her religious and domestic life, and she now walked timidly but with poignant sensibility upon a new and strange shore.

It was easy to see that the thought of her mother with any other background than that of the tenement was new to Angelina and at least two things resulted; she allowed her mother to pull out of the big box under the bed the beautiful homespun garments which had been previously hidden away as uncouth; and she openly came into the Labor Museum by the same door as did her mother, proud at least of the mastery of the craft which had been so much admired.

A club of necktie workers formerly meeting at Hull-House, persistently resented any attempt on the part of their director to improve their minds. The president once said that she "wouldn't be caught dead at a lecture," that she came to the club "to get some fun out of it," and indeed it was most natural that she should crave recreation after a hard days' work. One evening I saw the entire club listening to quite a stiff lecture in the Labor Museum and to my rather wicked remark to the president that I was surprised to see her enjoying a lecture, she replied, that she did not call this a lecture, she called this "getting next to the stuff you work with all the time." It was perhaps the sincerest tribute we have ever received as to the success of the undertaking.

The Labor Museum continually demanded more space as it was enriched by a fine textile exhibit lent by the Field Museum, and later by carefully selected specimens of basketry from the Philippines. The shops have finally included a group of three or four women, Irish, Italian, Danish, who have become a permanent working force in the textile department which has developed into a self-supporting industry through the sale of its homespun products.

These women and a few men, who come to the museum to utilize their European skill in pottery, metal, and wood, demonstrate that immigrant colonies might yield to our American life something very valuable, if their resources were intelligently studied and developed. I recall an Italian, who had decorated the doorposts of his tenement with a beautiful pattern he had previously used in carving the reredos of a Neapolitan church, who was "fired" by his landlord on the ground of destroying property. His feelings were hurt, not so much that he had been put out of his house, as that his work had been so disregarded; and he said that when people traveled in Italy they liked to look at wood carvings but that in America "they only made money out of you."

Sometimes the suppression of the instinct of workmanship is followed by more disastrous results. A Bohemian whose little girl attended classes at Hull-House, in one of his periodic drunken spells had literally almost choked her to death, and later had committed suicide when in delirium tremens. His poor wife, who stayed a week at Hull-House after the disaster until a new tenement could be arranged for her, one day showed me a gold ring which her husband had made for their betrothal. It exhibited the most exquisite workmanship, and she said that although in the old country he had been a gold-smith, in America he had for twenty years shoveled coal in a furnace room of a large manufacturing plant; that whenever she saw one of his "restless fits," which preceded his drunken periods, "coming on," if she could provide him with a bit of metal and persuade him to stay at home and work at it, he was all right and the time passed without disaster, but that "nothing else would do it." This story threw a flood of light upon the dead man's struggle and on the stupid maladjust-ment which had broken him down. Why had we never been told? Why had our interest in the remarkable musical ability of his child, blinded us to the hidden artistic ability of the father? We had forgotten that a long-established occupation may form the very foundations of the moral life, that the art with which a man has solaced his toil may be the salvation of his uncertain temperament.

There are many examples of touching fidelity to immigrant parents on the part of their grown children; a young man, who day after day, attends ceremonies which no longer express his religious convictions and who makes his vain effort to interest his Russian Jewish father in social problems; a daughter who might earn much more money as a stenographer could she work from Monday morning till Saturday night, but who quietly and docilely makes neckties for low wages because she can thus abstain from work Saturdays to please her father; these young people, like poor Maggie Tulliver, through many painful experiences have reached the conclusion that pity, memory, and faithfulness are natural ties with paramount claims.

This faithfulness, however, is sometimes ruthlessly imposed upon by immigrant parents who, eager for money and accustomed to the patriarchal authority of peasant households, hold their children in a stern bondage which requires a surrender of all their wages and concedes no time or money for pleasures.

There are many convincing illustrations that this parental harshness often results in juvenile delinquency. A Polish boy of seventeen came to Hull-House one day to ask a contribution of fifty cents "towards a flower piece for the funeral of an old Hull-House club boy." A few questions made it clear that the object was fictitious, whereupon the boy broke down and half defiantly stated that he wanted to buy two twenty-five cent tickets, one for his girl and one for himself, to a dance of the Benevolent Social Twos; that he hadn't a penny of his own although he had worked in a brass foundry for three years and had been advanced twice, because he always had to give his pay envelope unopened to his father; "just look at the clothes he buys me" was his concluding remark.

Perhaps the girls are held even more rigidly. In a recent investigation of two hundred working girls it was found that only five per cent had the use of their own money and that sixty-two per cent turned in all they earned, literally every penny, to their mothers. It was through this little investigation that we first knew Marcella, the pretty young German girl who helped her widowed mother year after year to care for a large family of younger children. She was content for the most part although her mother's old-country notions of dress gave her but an infinitesimal amount of her own wages to spend on her clothes, and she was quite sophisticated as to proper dressing because she sold silk in a neighborhood department store. Her mother approved of the young man who was showing her various attentions and agreed that Marcella should accept his invitation to a ball, but would allow her not a penny towards a new gown to replace one impossibly plain and shabby. Marcella spent a sleepless night and wept bitterly, although she well knew that the doctor's bill for the children's scarlet fever was not yet paid. The next day as she was cutting off three yards of shining pink silk, the thought came to her that it would make her a fine new waist to wear to the ball. She wistfully saw it wrapped in paper and carelessly stuffed into the muff of the purchaser, when suddenly the parcel fell upon the floor. No one was looking and quick as a flash the girl picked it up and pushed it into her blouse. The theft was discovered by the relentless department store detective who, for "the sake of the example," insisted upon taking the case into court. The poor mother wept bitter tears over this downfall of her "frommes Mädchen" and no one had the heart to tell her of her own blindness. . . .

. . . Many of these children have come to grief through their premature fling into city life, having thrown off parental control as they have impatiently discarded foreign ways. Boys of ten and twelve will refuse to sleep at home, preferring the freedom of an old brewery vault or an empty warehouse to the obedience required by their parents, and for days these boys will live on the milk and bread which they steal from the back porches after the early morning delivery. Such children complain that there is "no fun" at home. One little chap who was given a vacant lot to cultivate by the City Garden Association, insisted upon raising only popcorn and tried to present the entire crop to Hull-House "to be used for the parties," with the stipulation that he would have "to be invited every single time." Then there are little groups of dissipated young men who pride themselves upon their ability to live without working, and who despise all the honest and sober ways of their immigrant parents. They are at once a menace and a center of demoralization. Certainly the bewildered parents, unable to speak English and ignorant of the city, whose children have disappeared for days or weeks, have often come to Hull-House, evincing that agony which fairly separates the marrow from the bone, as if they had discovered a new type of suffering, devoid of the healing in familiar sorrows. It is as if they did not know how to search for the children without the assistance of the children themselves. Perhaps the most pathetic aspect of such cases is their revelation of the premature dependence of the older and wiser upon the young and foolish, which is in itself often responsible for the situation because it has given the children an undue sense of their own importance and a false security that they can take care of themselves. . . .

9. "A Modern Lear"

1894

In 1894 Chicago witnessed a characteristic industrial upheaval, the famous Pullman strike. The strike began at the Pullman Palace Car Company in the suburb of Pullman, Illinois, and eventually involved the entire railroad system west of Chicago. After five successive wage reductions, the Pullman workers struck; whereupon Eugene Debs's American Railway Union, organized the year before and fresh from a recent victory over the Great Northern Railroad, declared a sympathetic boycott of all Pullman cars. The railroads thus affected dismissed workers who refused to handle Pullman cars; the union replied by striking the railroads; railroad traffic came to a standstill; and rioting broke out at Blue Island, Illinois. President Cleveland, ignoring the protest of Governor Altgeld of Illinois, sent in federal troops, and this show of force, together with a federal injunction against the strikers, completely defeated both the Pullman workers and the American Railway Union.

Meanwhile the respectable citizenry of Chicago trembled at this disclosure of the implacable resentments that lay so near the surface of American life. The strike was doubly disturbing because George M. Pullman had been regarded as a model employer and Pullman, Illinois, as a model town, from which, as one admirer wrote, "all that is ugly, discordant, and demoralizing is eliminated." It was built "as a solution of the industrial problem based upon the idea of mutual recognition."[1] It was precisely the collapse of this "solution," this dream of a benevolent paternalism, that unnerved the middle class. That Pullman's men hated not only his arbitrary reduction of wages but his benevolence itself revealed the extent of their alienation from the norms of middle-class society. The strike raised the terrifying spectacle of class war.

Jane Addams' essay on this affair treats the obsolescence of paternalism in the industrial order. She used the Pullman strike as an object lesson in one of her favorite texts: the conflict between individual and social ethics—Pullman representing the former; his workers, the latter. Her attack upon Pullman, however, was so vehement—so it seemed to her contemporaries—that she was advised that the essay could not be published as she had written it. Henry Demarest Lloyd thought that it might be possible "to depersonalize the paper, and yet retain its dramatic quality,"[2] but Miss Addams rejected that alternative and withheld the paper altogether. Therefore, although read to the Chicago Woman's Club and the Twentieth Century Club of Boston, it was not published until 1912, when it finally appeared in *Survey*.

From Jane Addams, "A Modern Lear," *Survey*, XXIX (November 2, 1912) 131–137.

[1] Quoted in Thomas G. Manning, ed., *The Chicago Strike of 1894* (New York: Holt, Rinehart and Winston, 1960), p. 2. See also Almont Lindsey, *The Pullman Strike* (Chicago: University of Chicago Press, 1942).

[2] Henry Demarest Lloyd to Jane Addams, February 23, 1896; Jane Addams MSS (Swarthmore College Peace Collection, Swarthmore, Pennsylvania).

Those of us who lived in Chicago during the summer of 1894 were confronted by a drama which epitomized and, at the same time, challenged the code of social ethics under which we live, for a quick series of unusual events had dispelled the good nature which in happier times envelopes the ugliness of the industrial situation. It sometimes seems as if the shocking experiences of that summer, the barbaric instinct to kill, roused on both sides, the sharp division into class lines, with the resultant distrust and bitterness, can only be endured if we learn from it all a great ethical lesson. To endure is all we can hope for. It is impossible to justify such a course of rage and riot in a civilized community to whom the methods of conciliation and control were open. Every public-spirited citizen in Chicago during that summer felt the stress and perplexity of the situation and asked himself, "How far am I responsible for this social disorder? What can be done to prevent such outrageous manifestations of ill-will?"

If the responsibility of tolerance lies with those of the widest vision, it behooves us to consider this great social disaster, not alone in its legal aspect nor in its sociological bearings, but from those deep human motives, which, after all, determine events.

During the discussions which followed the Pullman strike, the defenders of the situation were broadly divided between the people pleading for individual benevolence and those insisting upon social righteousness; between those who held that the philanthropy of the president of the Pullman company had been most ungratefully received and those who maintained that the situation was the inevitable outcome of the social consciousness developing among working people.

In the midst of these discussions the writer found her mind dwelling upon a comparison which modified and softened all her judgments. Her attention was caught by the similarity of ingratitude suffered by an indulgent employer and an indulgent parent. King Lear came often to her mind. We have all shared the family relationship and our code of ethics concerning it is somewhat settled. We also bear a part in the industrial relationship, but our ethics concerning that are still uncertain. A comparative study of these two relationships presents an advantage, in that it enables us to consider the situation from the known experience toward the unknown. The minds of all of us reach back to our early struggles, as we emerged from the state of self-willed childhood to a recognition of the family claim.

We have all had glimpses of what it might be to blaspheme against family ties; to ignore the elemental claim they make upon us, but on the whole we have recognized them, and it does not occur to us to throw them over. The industrial claim is so difficult; the ties are so intangible that we are constantly ignoring them and shirking the duties which they impose. It will probably be easier to treat of the tragedy of the Pullman strike as if it were already long past when we compare it to the family tragedy of Lear which has already become historic to our minds and which we discuss without personal feeling.

Historically considered, the relation of Lear to his children was archaic and barbaric, holding in it merely the beginnings of a family life, since developed. We may in later years learn to look back upon the industrial relationships in which we are now placed as quite as incomprehensible and selfish, quite as barbaric and undeveloped, as was the family relationship between Lear and his daughters. We may then take the relationship of this unusually generous employer at Pullman to his own townful of employes as at least a fair one, because so exceptionally liberal in many of its aspects. King Lear doubtless held the same notion of a father's duty that was held by the other fathers of his time; but he alone was a king and had kingdoms to bestow upon his children. He was unique, therefore, in the magnitude of his indulgence, and in the magnitude of the disaster which followed it. The sense of duty held by the president of the Pullman company doubtless represents the ideal in the minds of the best of the present employers as to their obligations toward their employes, but he projected this ideal more magnificently than the others. He alone gave his men so model a town, such perfect surroundings. The magnitude of his indulgence and failure corresponded and we are forced to challenge the ideal itself: the same deal which, more or less clearly defined, is floating in the minds of all philanthropic employers.

This older tragedy implied mal-adjustment between individuals; the forces of the tragedy were personal and passionate. This modern tragedy in its inception is a mal-adjustment between two large bodies of men, an employing company and a mass of employes. It deals not with personal relationships, but with industrial relationships.

Owing, however, to the unusual part played in it by the will of one man, we find that it closely approaches Lear in motif. The relation of the British King to his family is very like the relation of the president of the Pullman company to his town; the denouement of a daughter's break with her father suggests the break of the employes with their benefactor. If we call one an example of the domestic tragedy, the other of the industrial tragedy, it is possible to make them illuminate each other.

It is easy to discover striking points of similarity in the tragedies of the royal father and the philanthropic president of the Pullman company. The like quality of ingratitude they both suffered is at once apparent. It may be said that the ingratitude which Lear received was poignant and bitter to him in proportion as he recalled the extraordinary benefits he had heaped upon his daughters, and that he found his fate harder to bear because he had so far exceeded the measure of a father's duty, as he himself says. What, then, would be the bitterness of a man who had heaped extraordinary benefits upon those toward whom he had no duty recognized by common consent; who had not only exceeded the righteousness of the employer, but who had worked out original and striking methods for lavishing goodness and generosity? More than that, the president had been almost persecuted for this goodness by the more utilitarian members of his company and had at one time imperilled his business reputation for the sake of the benefactions to his town, and he had thus reached the height of sacrifice for it. This model town embodied not only his hopes and ambitions, but stood for the peculiar effort which a man makes for that which is misunderstood.[3]

It is easy to see that although the heart of Lear was cut by ingratitude and by misfortune, it was cut deepest of all by the public pity of his people, in that they should remember him no longer as a king and benefactor, but as a defeated man who had blundered through oversoftness. So the heart of the Chicago man was cut by the unparalleled publicity which brought him to the minds of thousands as a type of oppression and injustice, and to many others as an example of the evil of an irregulated sympathy for the "lower classes." He who had been dined and feted throughout Europe as the creator of a model town, as the friend and benefactor of workingmen, was now execrated by workingmen throughout the entire country. He had not only been good to those who were now basely ungrateful to him, but he felt himself deserted by the admiration of his people.

In shops such as those at Pullman, indeed, in all manufacturing affairs since the industrial revolution, industry is organized into a vast social operation. The shops are managed, however, not for the development of the workman thus socialized, but for the interests of the company owning the capital. The divergence between the social form and the individual aim becomes greater as the employes are more highly socialized and dependent, just as the clash in a family is more vital in

---

[3] While the town of Pullman was in process of construction the Pullman stock was sometimes called out on the New York Exchange: "How much for flower-beds and fountains?" To which the company naturally objected [Ed.].

proportion to the development and closeness of the family tie. The president of the Pullman company went further than the usual employer does. He socialized not only the factory but the form in which his workmen were living. He built and, in a great measure, regulated an entire town. This again might have worked out into a successful associated effort, if he had had in view the sole good of the inhabitants thus socialized, if he had called upon them for self-expression and had made the town a growth and manifestation of their wants and needs. But, unfortunately, the end to be obtained became ultimately commercial and not social, having in view the payment to the company of at least 4 per cent on the money invested, so that with this rigid requirement there could be no adaptation of rent to wages, much less to needs. The rents became statical and the wages competitive, shifting inevitably with the demands of trade. The president assumed that he himself knew the needs of his men, and so far from wishing them to express their needs he denied to them the simple rights of trade organization, which would have been, of course, the merest preliminary to an attempt at associated expression. If we may take the dictatorial relation of Lear to Cordelia as a typical and most dramatic example of the distinctively family tragedy, one will asserting its authority through all the entanglement of wounded affection, and insisting upon its selfish ends at all costs, may we not consider the absolute authority of this employer over his town as a typical and dramatic example of the industrial tragedy? One will directing the energies of many others, without regard to their desires, and having in view in the last analysis only commercial results?

It shocks our ideal of family life that a man should fail to know his daughter's heart because she awkwardly expressed her love, that he should refuse to comfort and advise her through all difference of opinion and clashing of will. That a man should be so absorbed in his own indignation as to fail to apprehend his child's thought; that he should lose his affection in his anger, is really no more unnatural than that the man who spent a million of dollars on a swamp to make it sanitary for his employes, should refuse to speak to them for ten minutes, whether they were in the right or wrong; or that a man who had given them his time and thought for twenty years should withdraw from them his guidance when he believed them misled by ill-advisers and wandering in a mental fog; or that he should grow hard and angry when they needed tenderness and help.

Lear ignored the common ancestry of Cordelia and himself. He forgot her royal inheritance of magnanimity, and also the power of obstinacy which he shared with her. So long had he thought of himself as the noble and indulgent father that he had lost the faculty by which he might perceive himself in the wrong. Even when his spirit was broken by the storm he declared himself more sinned against than sinning. He could believe any amount of kindness and goodness of himself, but could imagine no fidelity on the part of Cordelia unless she gave him the sign he demanded.

The president of the Pullman company doubtless began to build his town from an honest desire to give his employes the best surroundings. As it developed it became a source of pride and an exponent of power, that he cared most for when it gave him a glow of benevolence. Gradually, what the outside world thought of it became of importance to him and he ceased to measure its usefulness by the standard of the men's needs. The theater was complete in equipment and beautiful in design, but too costly for a troupe who depended upon the patronage of mechanics, as the church was too expensive to be rented continuously. We can imagine the founder of the town slowly darkening his glints of memory and forgetting the common stock of experience which he held with his men. He cultivated the great and noble impulses of the benefactor, until the power of attaining a simple human relationship with his employes, that of frank equality with them, was gone from him. He, too, lost the faculty of affectionate interpretation, and demanded a sign. He and his employes had no mutual interest in a common cause.

Was not the grotesque situation of the royal father and the philanthropic employer to perform so many good deeds that they lost the power of recognizing good in beneficiaries? Were not both so absorbed in carrying out a personal plan of improvement that they failed to catch the great moral lesson which their times offered them? This is the crucial point to the tragedies and may be further elucidated.

Lear had doubtless swung a bauble before Cordelia's baby eyes that he might have the pleasure of seeing the little pink and tender hands stretched for it. A few years later he had given jewels to the young princess, and felt an exquisite pleasure when she stood before him, delighted with her gaud and grateful to her father. He demanded the same kind of response for his gift of the kingdom, but the gratitude must be larger and more carefully expressed, as befitted such a gift. At the opening of the drama he sat upon his throne ready for this enjoyment, but instead of delight and gratitude he found the first dawn of character. His daughter made the awkward attempt of an untrained soul to be honest, to be scrupulous in the expressions of its feelings. It was new to him that his child should be moved by a principle outside of himself, which even his imagination could not follow; that she had caught the notion of an existence so vast that her relationship as a daughter was but part of it.

Perhaps her suitors, the King of France or the Duke of Burgundy, had first hinted to the young Cordelia that there was a fuller life beyond the seas. Certain it is that someone had shaken her from the quiet measure of her insular existence and that she had at last felt the thrill of the world's life. She was transformed by a dignity which recast her speech and made it self-contained, as is becoming a citizen of the world. She found herself in the sweep of a notion of justice so large that the immediate loss of a kingdom seemed of little consequence to her. Even an act which might be construed as disrespect to her father was justified in her eyes because she was vainly striving to fill out this larger conception of duty.

The test which comes sooner or later to many parents had come to Lear, to maintain the tenderness of the relation between father and child, after that relation had become one between adults; to be contented with the responses which this adult made to the family claim, while, at the same time, she felt the tug upon her emotions and faculties of the larger life, the life which surrounds and completes the individual and family life, and which shares and widens her attention. He was not sufficiently wise to see that only that child can fulfill the family claim in its sweetness and strength who also fulfills the larger claim, that the adjustment of the lesser and larger implies no conflict. The mind of Lear was not big enough for this test. He failed to see anything but the personal slight involved; the ingratitude alone reached him. It was impossible for him to calmly watch his child developing beyond the strength of his own mind and sympathy.

Without pressing the analogy too hard may we not compare the indulgent relation of this employer to his town to the relation which existed between Lear and Cordelia? He fostered his employees for many years, gave them sanitary houses and beautiful parks, but in their extreme need, when they were struggling with the most difficult question which the times could present to them, when, if ever, they required the assistance of a trained mind and a comprehensive outlook, he lost his touch and had nothing wherewith to help them. He did not see the situation. He had been ignorant of their gropings toward justice. His conception of goodness for them had been cleanliness, decency of living, and above all, thrift and temperance. He had provided them means for all this; had gone further, and given them opportunities for enjoyment and comradeship. But he suddenly found his town in the sweep of a world-wide moral impulse. A movement had been going on about him and through the souls of his workingmen of which he had been unconscious. He had only heard of this movement by rumor. The men who consorted with him at his club and in his business had spoken but little of it, and when they had discussed it had contemptuously called it the "Labor Movement," headed by deadbeats and agitators. Of the force and power of this movement, of all the vitality within it, of that conception of duty which induces men to go without food and to see their wives and children suffer for the sake of securing better wages for fellow-workmen whom they have never seen, this president had dreamed absolutely nothing. But his town had at last become swept into this larger movement, so that the giving up of comfortable homes, of beautiful surroundings, seemed as naught to the men within its grasp.

Outside the ken of this philanthropist, the proletariat had learned to say in many languages that "the injury of one is the concern of all." Their watchwords were brotherhood, sacrifice, the subordination of individual and trade interests to the good of the working class; and their persistent strivings were toward the ultimate freedom of that class from the conditions under which they now labor.

Compared to these watchwords the old ones which the philanthropic employer had given his town were negative and inadequate.

When this movement finally swept in his own town, or, to speak more fairly, when in their distress and perplexity his own employees appealed to the organized manifestation of this movement, they were quite sure that simply because they were workmen in distress they would not be deserted by it. This loyalty on the part of a widely ramified and well organized union toward the workmen in a "scab shop," who had contributed nothing to its cause, was certainly a manifestation of moral power.

That the movement was ill-directed, that it was ill-timed and disastrous in results, that it stirred up and became confused in the minds of the public with the elements of riot and bloodshed, can never touch the fact that it started from an unselfish impulse.

In none of his utterances or correspondence did the president of the company for an instant recognize this touch of nobility, although one would imagine that he would gladly point out this bit of virtue, in what he must have considered the moral ruin about him. He stood throughout pleading for the individual virtues, those which had distinguished the model workman of his youth, those which had enabled him and so many of his contemporaries to rise in life, when "rising in life" was urged upon every promising boy as the goal of his efforts. Of the new code of ethics he had caught absolutely nothing. The morals he had taught his men did not fail them in their hour of confusion. They were self-controlled and destroyed no property.[4] They were sober and exhibited no drunkenness, even though obliged to hold their meetings in the saloon hall of a neighboring town. They repaid their employer in kind, but he had given them no rule for the higher fellowship and life of association into which they were plunged.

The virtues of one generation are not sufficient for the next, any more than the accumulations of knowledge possessed by one age are adequate to the needs of another.

Of the virtues received from our fathers we can afford to lose none. We accept as a precious trust those principles and precepts which the race has worked out for its highest safeguard and protection. But merely to preserve those is not enough. A task is laid upon each generation to enlarge their application, to ennoble their conception, and, above all, to apply and adapt them to the peculiar problems presented to it for solution.

---

[4] The bill presented to the city of Chicago by the Pullman company for damages received during the strike was $26—the result only of petty accidents [Ed.].

The president of this company desired that his employes should possess the individual and family virtues, but did nothing to cherish in them those social virtues which his own age demanded. He rather substituted for that sense of responsibility to the community, a feeling of gratitude to himself, who had provided them with public buildings, and had laid out for them a simulacrum of public life.

Is it strange that when the genuine feeling of the age struck his town this belated and almost feudal virtue of personal gratitude fell before it?

Day after day during that horrible suspense, when the wires constantly reported the same message, "The president of the company holds that there is nothing to arbitrate," one longed to find out what was in the mind of this man, to unfold his ultimate motive. One concludes that he must have been sustained by the consciousness of being in the right. Only that could have held him against the great desire for fair play which swept over the country. Only the training which an arbitrary will receives by years of consulting first its own personal and commercial ends could have made it strong enough to withstand the demands for social adjustment. He felt himself right from the *commercial* standpoint, and could not see the situation from the *social* standpoint. For years he had gradually accustomed himself to the thought that his motive was beyond reproach; that his attitude to his town was always righteous and philanthropic. Habit held him persistent in this view of the case through all the changing conditions.

The diffused and subtle notion of dignity held by the modern philanthropist bears a curious analogy to the personal barbaric notion of dignity held by Lear. The man who persistently paced the seashore, while the interior of his country was racked with a strife which he alone might have arbitrated, lived out within himself the tragedy of King Lear. The shock of disaster upon egotism is apt to produce self-pity. It is possible that his self-pity and loneliness may have been so great and absorbing as to completely shut out from his mind a compunction of derelict duty. He may have been unconscious that men were charging him with a shirking of the issue.

Lack of perception is the besetting danger of the egoist, from whatever cause his egoism arises and envelopes him. But, doubtless, philanthropists are more exposed to this danger than any other class of people within the community. Partly because their efforts are overestimated, as no standard of attainment has yet been established, and partly because they are the exponents of a large amount of altruistic feeling with which the community has become equipped and which has not yet found adequate expression, they are therefore easily idealized.

Long ago Hawthorne called our attention to the fact that "philanthropy ruins, or is fearfully apt to ruin, the heart, the rich juices of which God never meant should be pressed violently out, and distilled into alcoholic liquor by an unnatural process; but it should render life sweet, bland and gently beneficent."

One might add to this observation that the muscles of this same heart may be stretched and strained until they lose the rhythm of the common heart-beat of the rest of the world.

Modern philanthropists need to remind themselves of the old definition of greatness: that it consists in the possession of the largest share of the common human qualities and experiences, not in the acquirements of peculiarities and excessive virtues. Popular opinion calls him the greatest of Americans who gathered to himself the largest amount of American experience, and who never forgot when he was in Washington how the "crackers" in Kentucky and the pioneers of Illinois thought and felt, striving to retain their thoughts and feelings, and to embody only the mighty will of the "common people." The danger of professionally attaining to the power of the righteous man, of yielding to the ambition "for doing good," compared to which the ambitions for political position, learning, or wealth are vulgar and commonplace, ramifies throughout our modern life, and is a constant and settled danger of philanthropy.

In so far as philanthropists are cut off from the influence of the *Zeit-Geist*, from the code of ethics which rule the body of men, from the great moral life springing from our common experiences, so long as they are "good to people," rather than "with them," they are bound to accomplish a large amount of harm. They are outside of the influence of that great faith which perennially springs up in the hearts of the people, and re-creates the world.

In spite of the danger of overloading the tragedies with moral reflections, a point ought to be made on the other side. It is the weakness in the relation of the employes to the employer, the fatal lack of generosity in the attitude of workmen toward the company under whose exactions they feel themselves wronged.

In reading the tragedy of King Lear, Cordelia does not escape our censure. Her first words are cold, and we are shocked by her lack of tenderness. Why should she ignore her father's need for indulgence, and be so unwilling to give him what he so obviously craved? We see in the old king "the overmastering desire of being beloved, which is selfish, and yet characteristic of the selfishness of a loving and kindly nature alone." His eagerness produces in us a strange pity for him, and we are impatient that his youngest and best-beloved child cannot feel this, even in the midst of her search for truth and her newly acquired sense of a higher duty. It seems to us a narrow conception that would break thus abruptly with the past, and would assume that her father had no part in her new life. We want to remind her that "pity, memory and faithfulness are natural ties," and surely as much to be prized as is the development of her own soul. We do not admire the Cordelia "who loves according to her bond" as we later admire the same Cordelia who comes back from France that she may include in her happiness and freer life the father whom she had deserted through her self-absorption. She is aroused to her affection through her pity, but when the floodgates are once open she acknowledges all. It sometimes seems as if only hardship and sorrow could arouse our tenderness, whether in our personal or social relations; that the king, the prosperous man, was the last to receive the justice which can come only through affectionate interpretation. We feel less pity for Lear on his throne than in the storm, although he is the same man, bound up in the same self-righteousness, and exhibiting the same lack of self-control.

As the vision of the life of Europe caught the sight and quickened the pulses of Cordelia, so a vision of the wider life has caught the sight of workingmen. After the vision has once been seen it is impossible to do aught but to press toward its fulfillment. We have all seen it. We are all practically agreed that the social passion of the age is directed toward the emancipation of the wage-worker; that a great accumulation of moral force is overmastering men and making for this emancipation as in another time it has made for the emancipation of the slave; that nothing will satisfy the aroused conscience of men short of the complete participation of the working classes in the spiritual, intellectual and material inheritance of the human race. But just as Cordelia failed to include her father in the scope of her salvation and selfishly took it for herself alone, so workingmen in the dawn of the vision are inclined to claim it for themselves, putting out of their thoughts the old relationships; and just as surely as Cordelia's conscience developed in the new life and later drove her back to her father, where she perished, drawn into the cruelty and wrath which had now become objective and tragic, so the emancipation of working people will have to be inclusive of the employer from the first or it will encounter many failures, cruelties and reactions. It will result not in the position of the repentant Cordelia but in that of King Lear's two older daughters.

If the workingmen's narrow conception of emancipation was

fully acted upon, they would hold much the same relationship to their expropriated employer that the two older daughters held to their abdicated father. When the kingdom was given to them they received it as altogether their own, and were dominated by a sense of possession; "it is ours not yours" was never absent from their consciousness. When Lear ruled the kingdom he had never been without this sense of possession, although he expressed it in indulgence and condescending kindness. His older daughters expressed it in cruelty, but the motive of father and children was not unlike. They did not wish to be reminded by the state and retinue of the old King that he had been the former possessor. Finally, his mere presence alone reminded them too much of that and they banished him from the palace. That a newly acquired sense of possession should result in the barbaric, the incredible scenes of bitterness and murder, which were King Lear's portion, is not without a reminder of the barbaric scenes in our political and industrial relationships, when the sense of possession, to obtain and to hold, is aroused on both sides. The scenes in Paris during the political revolution or the more familiar scenes at the mouths of the mines and the terminals of railways occur to all of us.

The doctrine of emancipation preached to the wage-workers alone runs an awful risk of being accepted for what it offers them, for the sake of fleshpots, rather than for the human affection and social justice which it involves. This doctrine must be strong enough in its fusing power to touch those who think they lose, as well as those who think they gain. Only thus can it become the doctrine of a universal movement.

The new claim on the part of the toiling multitude, the new sense of responsibility on the part of the well-to-do, arise in reality from the same source. They are in fact the same "social compunction," and, in spite of their widely varying manifestations, logically converge into the same movement. Mazzini once preached, "the consent of men and your own conscience are two wings given you whereby you may rise to God." It is so easy for the good and powerful to think that they can rise by following the dictates of conscience by pursuing their own ideals, leaving those ideals unconnected with the consent of their fellow-men. The president of the Pullman company thought out within his own mind a beautiful town. He had power with which to build this town, but he did not appeal to nor obtain the consent of the men who were living in it. The most unambitious reform, recognizing the necessity for this consent, makes for slow but sane and strenuous progress, while the most ambitious of social plans and experiments, ignoring this, is prone to the failure of the model town of Pullman.

The man who insists upon consent, who moves with the people, is bound to consult the feasible right as well as the absolute right. He is often obliged to attain only Mr. Lincoln's "best possible," and often have the sickening sense of compromising with his best convictions. He has to move along with those whom he rules toward a goal that neither he nor they see very clearly till they come to it. He has to discover what people really want, and then "provide the channels in which the growing moral force of their lives shall flow." What he does attain, however, is not the result of his individual striving, as a solitary mountain climber beyond the sight of the valley multitude, but it is underpinned and upheld by the sentiments and aspirations of many others. Progress has been slower perpendicularly, but incomparably greater because lateral.

He has not taught his contemporaries to climb mountains, but he has persuaded the villagers to move up a few feet higher. It is doubtful if personal ambition, whatever may have been its commercial results, has ever been of any value as a motive power in social reform. But whatever it may have done in the past, it is certainly too archaic to accomplish anything now. Our thoughts, at least for this generation, cannot be too much directed from mutual relationships and responsibilities. They will be warped, unless we look all men in the face, as if a community of interests lay between, unless we hold the mind open, to take strength and cheer from a hundred connections.

To touch to vibrating response the noble fibre in each man, to pull these many fibres, fragile, impalpable and constantly breaking, as they are, into one impulse, to develop that mere impulse through its feeble and tentative stages into action, is no easy task, but lateral progress is impossible without it.

If only a few families of the English speaking race had profited by the dramatic failure of Lear, much heart-breaking and domestic friction might have been spared. Is it too much to hope that some of us will carefully consider this modern tragedy, if perchance it may contain a warning for the troublous times in which we live? By considering the dramatic failure of the liberal employer's plans for his employes we may possibly be spared useless industrial tragedies in the uncertain future which lies ahead of us.

PART III

REFORM, POLITICAL
AND SOCIAL

---

10. "Why the Ward Boss Rules"

1898

Jane Addams threw herself into so many reforms that it would be impossible without swelling this anthology to ungainly proportions to give a comprehensive survey of her activities. The selections that follow touch on only a few of her varied interests, but they illustrate very clearly her method of approaching political and social questions; and it was her method, rather than the range of her activities, that distinguished Jane Addams from earlier reformers. Whereas they attacked immorality, she tried to understand the sources of immorality—if, indeed, immorality was the issue in the first place. Like other progressives, she wanted to substitute explanation and analysis for moral exhortation. Therein lay her originality and the originality of her generation.

The question of political corruption is a case in point. No other question had been so incessantly agitated in the years between Grant and McKinley, and yet on no other question had the discussion remained so superficial. The civil-service reformers of the 1870's and 1880's too often saw the problem as a problem simply of public morality. If corruption flourished in high places, they reasoned, it was because officeholders were too easily corrupted. Those who went beyond corruption itself to the more important question of the control of government by the "interests"—the question, as Charles Francis Adams, Jr., and Henry Adams put it, of *imperium in imperio*—nevertheless kept coming back to corruption as the key to the problem; to that, and to the public apathy and indifference that were presumed to underlie it. For as the Adams brothers had tried to show in their *Chapters of Erie*, the rise of monopolists like Jay Gould seemed to depend, in the last analysis, on the success with which such men were able to bribe the courts and the legislatures to do their bidding.[1] The restoration of economic competition, therefore, appeared to turn on the purification of the instruments of government.

How inadequate this was as an explanation of monopoly is shown by the fact that the eventual adoption of the merit system, though it eliminated the grosser forms of political corruption, did not do away with monopoly. It merely regularized the relations between business and politics. If anything, it made matters worse than before, because it deprived the political parties of their means of subsistence—corruption—and thereby rendered them directly dependent on corporations for support. Corruption gave way to subsidy—a far more effective form of corporate domination than old-fashioned bribery.[2]

The weak point in the older analysis was the assumption that politicians took bribes purely from motives of personal greed. The civil-service reformers of the Gilded Age failed to see that political corruption was a *system*—as Lincoln Steffens later put it—whereby the political parties raised funds that in turn they dispensed among the urban masses who sustained them in office.[3] The reformers knew that the machines rested on immigrant votes, but they took this as merely another reflection of the immigrants' ignorance and venality. In fact, however, the machine performed indispensable services for its constituents. Above all, it often gave them jobs. From this point of view, the spoils system was not so much a form

---

[1] See Charles Francis Adams, Jr., and Henry Adams, *Chapters of Erie* (Ithaca: Great Seal Books, 1956 [1870, 1871]), especially pp. 95–100.

[2] Matthew Josephson, *The Politicos* (New York: Harcourt, Brace and Company, 1938), is the definitive study of this process.

[3] See Lincoln Steffens, *The Struggle for Self-Government* (New York: McClure, Phillips & Company, 1906), pp. 4–5.

of organized greed as a crude sort of welfare agency that arose to fill a need almost totally neglected by government itself.

These things could be seen only when one looked at the political process from the point of view of the immigrants themselves. Such a vantage point was precisely the one that Jane Addams had cultivated. The following essay, an analysis of what might be called the charitable functions of the political machine—with which, incidentally, Hull-House was in direct competition—shows how rich were the rewards of her new perspective.

Primitive people, such as the South Italian peasants who live in the Nineteenth Ward, deep down in their hearts admire nothing so much as the good man. The successful candidate must be a good man according to the standards of his constituents. He must not attempt to hold up a morality beyond them, nor must he attempt to reform or change the standard. If he believes what they believe, and does what they are all cherishing a secret ambition to do, he will dazzle them by his success and win their confidence. Any one who has lived among poorer people cannot fail to be impressed with their constant kindness to each other; that unfailing response to the needs and distresses of their neighbors, even when in danger of bankruptcy themselves. This is their reward for living in the midst of poverty. They have constant opportunities for self-sacrifice and generosity, to which, as a rule, they respond. A man stands by his friend when he gets too drunk to take care of himself, when he loses his wife or child, when he is evicted for non-payment of rent, when he is arrested for a petty crime. It seems to such a man entirely fitting that his Alderman should do the same thing on a larger scale—that he should help a constituent out of trouble just because he is in trouble, irrespective of the justice involved.

The Alderman, therefore, bails out his constituents when

From Jane Addams, "Why the Ward Boss Rules," *Outlook*, LVIII (April 2, 1898), 879–882.

they are arrested, or says a good word to the police justice when they appear before him for trial; uses his "pull" with the magistrate when they are likely to be fined for a civil misdemeanor, or sees what he can do to "fix up matters" with the State's attorney when the charge is really a serious one.

Because of simple friendliness, the Alderman is expected to pay rent for the hard-pressed tenant when no rent is forthcoming, to find jobs when work is hard to get, to procure and divide among his constituents all the places he can seize from the City Hall. The Alderman of the Nineteenth Ward at one time made the proud boast that he had two thousand six hundred people in his ward upon the public pay-roll. This, of course, included day-laborers, but each one felt under distinct obligations to him for getting the job.

If we recollect, further, that the franchise-seeking companies pay respectful heed to the applicants backed by the Alderman, the question of voting for the successful man becomes as much an industrial as a political one. An Italian laborer wants a job more than anything else, and quite simply votes for the man who promises him one.

The Alderman may himself be quite sincere in his acts of kindness. In certain stages of moral evolution, a man is incapable of unselfish action the results of which will not benefit some one of his acquaintances; still more, of conduct that does not aim to assist any individual whatsoever; and it is a long step in moral progress to appreciate the work done by the individual for the community.

The Alderman gives presents at weddings and christenings. He seizes these days of family festivities for making friends. It is easiest to reach people in the holiday mood of expansive good will, but on their side it seems natural and kindly that he should do it. The Alderman procures passes from the railroads when his constituents wish to visit friends or to attend the funerals of distant relatives; he buys tickets galore for benefit entertainments given for a widow or a consumptive in peculiar distress; he contributes to prizes which are awarded to the handsomest lady or the most popular man. At a church bazaar, for instance, the Alderman finds the stage all set for his dramatic performance. When others are spending pennies he is spending dollars. Where anxious relatives are canvassing to secure votes for the two most beautiful children who are being voted upon, he recklessly buys votes from both sides, and laughingly declines to say which one he likes best, buying off the young lady who is persistently determined to find out, with five dollars for the flower bazaar, the posies, of course, to be sent to the sick of the parish. The moral atmosphere of a bazaar suits him exactly. He murmurs many times, "Never mind; the money all goes to the poor," or, "It is all straight enough if the church gets it."

There is something archaic in a community of simple people in their attitude towards death and burial. Nothing so easy to collect money for as a funeral. If the Alderman seizes upon festivities for expressions of his good will, much more does he seize upon periods of sorrow. At a funeral he has the double advantage of ministering to a genuine craving for comfort and solace, and at the same time of assisting at an important social function.

In addition to this, there is among the poor, who have few social occasions, a great desire for a well-arranged funeral. the grade of which almost determines their social standing in the neighborhood. The Alderman saves the very poorest of his constituents from that awful horror of burial by the county; he provides carriages for the poor, who otherwise could not have them; for the more prosperous he sends extra carriages, so that they may invite more friends and have a longer procession; for the most prosperous of all there will be probably only a large "flower-piece." It may be too much to say that all the relatives and friends who ride in the carriages provided by the Alderman's bounty vote for him, but they are certainly influenced by his kindness, and talk of his virtues during the long hours of the ride back and forth from the suburban cemetery. A man who would ask at such a time where all this money comes from would be considered sinister. Many a man at such a time has formulated a lenient judgment of political corruption and has heard kindly speeches which he has remembered on election day. "Ah, well, he has a big Irish heart. He is good to the widow and the fatherless." "He knows the poor better than the big guns who are always about talking civil service and reform."

Indeed, what headway can the notion of civic purity, of honesty of administration, make against this big manifestation of human friendliness, this stalking survival of village kindness? The notions of the civic reformer are negative and impotent before it. The reformers give themselves over largely to criticisms of the present state of affairs, to writing and talking of what the future must be; but their goodness is not dramatic; it is not even concrete and human.

Such an Alderman will keep a standing account with an undertaker, and telephone every week, and sometimes more than once, the kind of outfit he wishes provided for a bereaved constituent, until the sum may roll up into hundreds a year. Such a man understands what the people want, and ministers just as truly to a great human need as the musician or the artist does. I recall an attempt to substitute what we might call a later standard.

A delicate little child was deserted in the Hull House nursery. An investigation showed that it had been born ten days previously in the Cook County Hospital, but no trace could be found of the unfortunate mother. The little thing lived for several weeks, and then, in spite of every care, died. We decided to have it buried by the county, and the wagon was to arrive by eleven o'clock. About nine o'clock in the morning the rumor of this awful deed reached the neighbors. A half-dozen of them came, in a very excited state of mind, to protest. They took up a collection out of their poverty with which to defray a funeral. We were then comparatively new in the neighborhood. We did not realize that we were really shocking a genuine moral sentiment of the community. In our crudeness, we instanced the care and tenderness which had been expended upon the little creature while it was alive; that it had had every attention from a skilled physician and trained nurse; we even intimated that the excited members of the group had not taken part in this, and that it now lay with us to decide that the child should be buried, as it had been born, at the county's expense. It is doubtful whether Hull House has ever done anything which injured it so deeply in the minds of some of its neighbors. We were only forgiven by the most indulgent on the ground that we were spinsters and could not know a mother's heart. No one born and reared in the community could possibly have made a mistake like that. No one who had studied the ethical standards with any care could have bungled so completely.

Last Christmas our Alderman distributed six tons of turkeys, and four or more tons of ducks and geese; but each luckless biped was handed out either by himself or one of his friends with a "Merry Christmas." Inevitably, some families got three or four apiece, but what of that? He had none of the nagging rules of the charitable societies, nor was he ready to declare that, because a man wanted two turkeys for Christmas, he was a scoundrel, who should never be allowed to eat turkey again.

The Alderman's wisdom was again displayed in procuring from down-town friends the sum of three thousand dollars wherewith to uniform and equip a boys' temperance brigade which had been formed in the ward a few months before his campaign. Is it strange that the good leader, whose heart was filled with innocent pride as he looked upon these promising young scions of virtue, should decline to enter into a reform campaign?

The question does, of course, occur to many minds, Where does the money come from with which to dramatize so suc-

cessfully? The more primitive people accept the truthful statement of its sources without any shock to their moral sense. To
their simple minds he gets it "from the rich," and so long as
he again gives it out to the poor, as a true Robin Hood, with
open hand, they have no objections to offer. Their ethics are
quite honestly those of the merry-making foresters. The next
less primitive people of the vicinage are quite willing to admit
that he leads "the gang" in the City Council, and sells out the
city franchises; that he makes deals with the franchise-seeking
companies; that he guarantees to steer dubious measures
through the Council, for which he demands liberal pay; that
he is, in short, a successful boodler. But when there is intellect
enough to get this point of view, there is also enough to make
the contention that this is universally done; that all the Aldermen do it more or less successfully, but that the Alderman of
the Nineteenth Ward is unique in being so generous; that
such a state of affairs is to be deplored, of course, but that that
is the way business is run, and we are fortunate when a kind-
hearted man who is close to the people gets a large share of
the boodle; that he serves these franchised companies who
employ men in the building and construction of their enterprises, and that they are bound in return to give jobs to his
constituency. Even when they are intelligent enough to complete the circle, and to see that the money comes, not from the
pockets of the companies' agents, but from the street-car fares
of people like themselves, it almost seems as if they would
rather pay two cents more each time they ride than give up
the consciousness that they have a big, warm-hearted friend
at court who will stand by them in an emergency. The sense
of just dealing comes apparently much later than the desire
for protection and kindness. The Alderman is really elected
because he is a good friend and neighbor.

During a campaign a year and a half ago, when a reform
league put up a candidate against our corrupt Alderman, and
when Hull House worked hard to rally the moral sentiment

of the ward in favor of the new man, we encountered another and unexpected difficulty. Finding that it was hard to secure enough local speakers of the moral tone which we desired, we imported orators from other parts of the town, from the "better element," so to speak. Suddenly we heard it rumored on all sides that, while the money and speakers for the reform candidate were coming from the swells, the money which was backing our corrupt Alderman also came from a swell source; it was rumored that the president of a street-car combination, for whom he performed constant offices at the City Council, was ready to back him to the extent of fifty thousand dollars; that he, too, was a good man, and sat in high places; that he had recently given a large sum of money to an educational institution, and was, therefore, as philanthropic, not to say good and upright, as any man in town; that our Alderman had the sanction of the highest authorities, and that the lecturers who were talking against corruption, and the selling and buying of franchises, were only the cranks, and not the solid business men who had developed and built up Chicago.

All parts of the community are bound together in ethical development. If the so-called more enlightened members of the community accept public gifts from the man who buys up the Council, and the so-called less enlightened members accept individual gifts from the man who sells out the Council, we surely must take our punishment together.

Another curious experience during that campaign was the difference of standards between the imported speakers and the audience. One man, high in the council of the "better element," one evening used as an example of the philanthropic politician an Alderman of the vicinity, recently dead, who was devotedly loved and mourned by his constituents. When the audience caught the familiar name in the midst of the platitudes, they brightened up wonderfully. But, as the speaker went on, they first looked puzzled, then astounded, and gradually their astonishment turned to indignation. The speaker, all unconscious of the situation, went on, imagining, perhaps, that he was addressing his usual audience, and totally unaware that he was perpetrating an outrage upon the finest feelings of the people who were sitting before him. He certainly succeeded in irrevocably injuring the chances of the candidate for whom he was speaking. The speaker's standard of ethics was upright dealing in positions of public trust. The standard of ethics held by his audience was, being good to the poor and speaking gently of the dead. If he considered them corrupt and illiterate voters, they quite honestly held him a blackguard.

If we would hold to our political democracy, some pains must be taken to keep on common ground in our human experiences, and to some solidarity in our ethical conceptions. And if we discover that men of low ideals and corrupt practice are forming popular political standards simply because such men stand by and for and with the people, then nothing remains but to obtain a like sense of identification before we can hope to modify ethical standards.

11. *A New Conscience and an Ancient Evil*

1913

Prostitution—the "ancient evil" of Miss Addams' title—was doubtless the most sordid aspect of urban life to which the social workers exposed themselves. But to understand the intensity of their feelings about it, it is necessary to remember that what they attacked was not so much prostitution itself as the "white-slave traffic" —the impressment of young girls into the service, as it were, by deception and bribery. It was precisely this concern with white slavery, in my opinion, that accounts for the defects of Jane Addams' book on prostitution—its insistence that the prostitute was an innocent victim of economic exploitation; its equation of white slavery with the Negro slavery that Jane Addams' father, years earlier, had so passionately opposed.

The equation was much too simple. It ignored the fact that many prostitutes—unlike slaves—entered the profession quite willingly, not out of ignorance or even out of pecuniary need, but because the rewards—short hours and good wages—seemed to outweigh the disadvantages of such a life. Jane Addams assumed that the loss of one's virtue was so horrible that no woman would willingly suffer it, but there is no reason to suppose that all women took so severe a view of the matter. The real explanation of prostitution seems to lie in a consideration Jane Addams mentioned only to brush aside—a "dangerous cynicism regarding the value of virtue, a cynicism never so unlovely as in the young." This cynicism, not only about virtue but about all the most cherished ideals of bourgeois society—in particular, the sanctity of the sexual relation—was too disturbing, perhaps, for middle-class reformers to confront; and one suspects that the white-slave trade was largely a myth that enabled them to evade the full implications of the "social evil."

The attack upon white slavery was closely related, historically, both to the temperance movement and to the movement for women's rights. The present work helps to make the connection clear. Since they assumed that women would not voluntarily sell their bodies, reformers like Jane Addams believed that these women had to be tempted while under the influence of alcohol. Prohibition would thus eliminate the solvent of the white-slave trade. Moreover, Jane Addams believed that "women with political power," as she argued elsewhere in her book, "would not brook that men should live upon the wages of captured victims." It hardly needs to be pointed out that experience has refuted both her assumptions. Neither national prohibition nor women's suffrage put an end to the "ancient evil."

. . . A surprising number of country girls have been either brought to Chicago under false pretenses, or have been de-

Reprinted with the permission of The Macmillan Co. from *A New Conscience and an Ancient Evil* by Jane Addams, pp. 145–160. Copyright 1910 and 1911 by The S. S. McClure Company and The McClure Publications, Inc., copyright 1912, renewed 1940 by The Macmillan Co.

coyed into an evil life very soon after their arrival in the city. Mr. Clifford Roe estimates that more than half of the girls who have been recruited into a disreputable life in Chicago have come from the farms and smaller towns in Illinois and from neighboring states. This estimate is borne out by the records of Paris and other metropolitan cities in which it is universally estimated that a little less than one-third of the prostitutes found in them, at any given moment, are city born.

The experience of a pretty girl who came to the office of the Juvenile Protective Association, a year ago, is fairly typical of the argument many of these country girls offer in their own defense. This girl had been a hotel chambermaid in an Iowa town where many of the traveling patrons of the hotel had made love to her, one of them occasionally offering her protection if she would leave with him. At first she indignantly refused, but was at length convinced that the acceptance of such offers must be a very general practice and that, whatever might be the custom in the country, no one in a city made personal inquiries. She finally consented to accompany a young man to Seattle, both because she wanted to travel and because she was discouraged in her attempts to "be good." A few weeks later, when in Chicago, she had left the young man, acting from what she considered a point of honor, as his invitation had been limited to the journey which was now completed. Feeling too disgraced to go home and under the glamour of the life of idleness she had been leading, she had gone voluntarily into a disreputable house, in which the police had found her and sent her to the Association. She could not be persuaded to give up her plan, but consented to wait for a few days to "think it over." As she was leaving the office in company with a representative of the Association, they met the young man, who had been distractedly searching for her and had just discovered her whereabouts. She was married the very same day and of course the Association never saw her again.

From the point of view of the traffickers in white slaves, it is much cheaper and safer to procure country girls after they have reached the city. Such girls are in constant danger because they are much more easily secreted than girls procured from the city. A country girl entering a vicious life quickly feels the disgrace and soon becomes too broken-spirited and discouraged to make any effort to escape into the unknown city which she believes to be full of horrors similar to those she has already encountered. She desires above all things to deceive her family at home, often sending money to them regularly and writing letters describing a fictitious life of hard work. Perhaps the most flagrant case with which the Association ever dealt, was that of two young girls who had come to Chicago from a village in West Virginia, hoping to earn large wages in order to help their families. They arrived in the city penniless, having been robbed en route of their one slender purse. As they stood in the railway station, utterly bewildered, they were accosted by a young man who presented the advertising card of a boarding-house and offered to take them there. They quite innocently accepted his invitation, but an hour later, finding themselves in a locked room, they became frightened and realized they had been duped. Fortunately the two agile country girls had no difficulty in jumping from a second-story window, but upon the street they were of course much too frightened to speak to anyone again and wandered about for hours. The house from which they had escaped bore the sign "rooms for rent," and they therefore carefully avoided all houses whose placards offered shelter. Finally, when they were desperate with hunger, they went into a saloon for a "free lunch," not in the least realizing that they were expected to take a drink in order to receive it. A policeman, seeing two young girls in a saloon "without escort," arrested them and took them to the nearest station where they spent the night in a wretched cell.

At the hearing the next morning, where, much frightened, they gave a very incoherent account of their adventures, the judge fined them each fifteen dollars and costs, and as they were unable to pay the fine, they were ordered sent to the city prison. When they were escorted from the court room, another man approached them and offered to pay their fines if they would go with him. Frightened by their former experience, they stoutly declined his help, but were overpersuaded by his graphic portrayal of prison horrors and the disgrace that their imprisonment would bring upon "the folks at home." He also made clear that when they came out of prison, thirty days later, they would be no better off than they were now, save that they would have the added stigma of being jail-birds. The girls at last reluctantly consented to go with him, when a representative of the Juvenile Protective Association, who had followed them from the court room and had listened to the conversation, insisted upon the prompt arrest of the white slave trader. When the entire story, finally secured from the girls, was related to the judge, he reversed his decision, fined the man $100.00, which he was abundantly able to pay, and insisted that the girls be sent back to their mothers in Virginia. They were farmers' daughters, strong and capable of taking care of themselves in an environment that they understood, but in constant danger because of their ignorance of city life.

The methods employed to secure city girls must be much more subtle and complicated than those employed with the less sophisticated country girl. Although the city girl, once procured, is later allowed more freedom than is accorded either to a country girl or to an immigrant girl, every effort is made to demoralize her completely before she enters the life. Because she may, at any moment, escape into the city which she knows so well, it is necessary to obtain her inner consent. Those whose profession it is to procure girls for white slave trade apparently find it possible to decoy and demoralize most easily that city girl whose need for recreation has led her to the disreputable public dance hall or other questionable places of amusement.

Gradually those philanthropic agencies that are endeavoring to be of service to the girls learn to know the dangers in these places. Many parents are utterly indifferent or ignorant of the pleasures that their children find for themselves. From the time these children were five years old, such parents were accustomed to see them take care of themselves on the street and at school, and it seems but natural that when the children are old enough to earn money, they should be able to find their own amusements.

The girls are attracted to the unregulated dance halls not only by a love of pleasure but by a sense of adventure, and it is in these places that they are most easily recruited for a vicious life. Unfortunately there are three hundred and twenty-eight public dance halls in Chicago, one hundred and ninety of them connect directly with saloons, while liquor is openly sold in most of the others. This consumption of liquor enormously increases the danger to young people. A girl after a long day's work is easily induced to believe that a drink will dispel her lassitude. There is plenty of time between the dances to persuade her, as the intermissions are long, fifteen to twenty minutes, and the dances short, occupying but four or five minutes; moreover the halls are hot and dusty and it is almost impossible to obtain a drink of water. Often the entire purpose of the dance hall, with its carefully arranged intermissions, is the selling of liquor to the people it has brought together. After the girl has begun to drink, the way of the procurer, who is often in league with the "spieler" who frequents the dance hall, is comparatively easy. He assumes one of two rôles, that of the sympathetic older man or that of the eager young lover. In the character of the former, he tells "the down-trodden working girl" that her wages are a mere pittance and that he can procure a better place for her with higher wages if she will trust him. He often makes allusions to the shabbiness or cheapness of her clothing and considers it "a shame that such a pretty girl cannot dress better." In the second rôle he apparently falls in love with her, tells of his rich parents, complaining that they want him to marry, "a society swell," but that he really prefers a working girl like herself. In either case he establishes friendly relations, exalted in the girl's mind, through the excitement of the liquor and the dance, into a new sense of intimate understanding and protection.

Later in the evening, she leaves the hall with him for a restaurant because, as he truthfully says, she is exhausted and in need of food. At the supper, however, she drinks much more, and it is not surprising that she is at last persuaded that it is too late to go home and in the end consents to spend the rest of the night in a nearby lodging house. Six young girls, each accompanied by a "spieler" from a dance hall, were recently followed to a chop suey restaurant and then to a lodging-house, which the police were instigated to raid and where the six girls, more or less intoxicated, were found. If no one rescues the girl after such an experience, she sometimes does not return home at all, or if she does, feels herself initiated into a new world where it is possible to obtain money at will, to easily secure the pleasures it brings, and she comes at length to consider herself superior to her less sophisticated companions. Of course this latter state of mind is untenable for any length of time and the girl is soon found openly leading a disreputable life.

The girls attending the cheap theatres and the vaudeville shows are most commonly approached through their vanity. They readily listen to the triumphs of a stage career, sure to be attained by such a "good looker," and a large number of them follow a young man to the woman with whom he is in partnership, under the promise of being introduced to a theatrical manager. There are also theatrical agencies in league with disreputable places, who advertise for pretty girls, promising large salaries. Such an agency operating with a well-known "near theatre" in the state capital was recently prosecuted in Chicago and its license revoked. In this connection the experience of two young English girls is not unusual. They were sisters possessed of an extraordinary skill in juggling, who were brought to this country by a relative acting as their manager. Although he exploited them for his own benefit for three years, paying them the most meager salaries and supplying them with the simplest living in the towns which they "toured," he had protected them from all immorality, and they had preserved the clean living of the family of acrobats to which they belonged. Last October, when appearing in San Francisco, the girls, then sixteen and seventeen years of age, demanded more pay than the dollar and twenty cents a week each had been receiving, representing the five shillings with which they had started from home. The manager, who had become discouraged with his American experience, refused to accede to their demands, gave them each a ticket for Chicago, and heartlessly turned them adrift. Arriving in the city, they quite naturally at once applied to a theatrical agency, through which they were sent to a disreputable house where a vaudeville program was given each night. Delighted that they had found work so quickly, they took the position in good faith. During the very first performance, however, they became frightened by the conduct of the girls who preceded them on the program and by the hilarity of the audience. They managed to escape from the dressing-room, where they were waiting their turn, and on the street appealed to the first policeman, who brought them to the Juvenile Protective Association. They were detained for several days as witnesses against the theatrical agency, entering into the legal prosecution with that characteristic British spirit which is ever ready to protest against an imposition, before they left the city with a travelling company, each on a weekly salary of twenty dollars.

The methods pursued on excursion boats are similar to those of the dance halls, in that decent girls are induced to drink quantities of liquor to which they are unaccustomed. On the high seas, liquor is sold usually in original packages, which enormously increases the amount consumed. It is not unusual to see a boy or girl drinking between them an entire bottle of whiskey. Some of these excursion boats carry five thousand people and in the easy breakdown of propriety which holiday-making often implies, and the absence of police, to which city young people are unaccustomed, the utmost freedom and license is often indulged in. Thus the lake excursions, one of the most delightful possibilities for recreation in Chicago, through lack of proper policing and through the sale of liquor, are made a menace to thousands of young people to whom they should be a great resource.

When a philanthropic association, with a knowledge of the commercial exploitation of youth's natural response to gay surroundings, attempts to substitute innocent recreation, it finds the undertaking most difficult. In Chicago the Juvenile Protective Association, after a thorough investigation of public dance halls, amusement parks, five-cent theatres, and excursion boats, is insisting upon more vigorous enforcement of the existing legislation, and is also urging further legal regulation; Kansas City has instituted a Department of Public Welfare with power to regulate places of amusement; a New York committee has established model dance halls; Milwaukee is urging the appointment of commissions on public recreation, while New York and Columbus have already created them.

Perhaps nothing in actual operation is more valuable than the small parks of Chicago in which the large halls are used every evening for dancing and where outdoor sports, swimming pools and gymnasiums daily attract thousands of young people. Unless cities make some such provision for their youth, those who sell the facilities for amusement in order to make a profit will continue to exploit the normal desire of all young people for recreation and pleasure. The city of Chicago contains at present eight hundred and fourteen thousand minors, all eager for pleasure. It is not surprising that commercial enterprise undertakes to supply this demand and that penny arcades, slot machines, candy stores, ice-cream parlors, moving-picture shows, skating rinks, cheap theatres and dance halls are trying to attract young people with every device known to modern advertising. Their promoters are, of course, careless of the moral effect upon their young customers if they can but secure their money. Until municipal provisions adequately meet this need, philanthropic and social organizations must be committed to the establishment of more adequate recreational facilities.

Although many dangers are encountered by the pleasure-loving girl who demands that each evening shall bring her some measure of recreation, a large number of girls meet with difficulties and temptations while soberly at work. Many of these tempted girls are newly-arrived immigrant girls between the ages of sixteen and twenty, who find their first work in hotels. Polish girls especially are utilized in hotel kitchens and laundries, and for the interminable scrubbing of halls and lobbies where a knowledge of the English language is not necessary, but where their peasant strength is in demand. The work is very heavy and fatiguing and until the Illinois law limited the work of women to ten hours a day, it often lasted late into the night. Even now the girls report themselves so tired that at the end of the day, they crowd into dormitories and fall upon their beds undressed. When food and shelter is given them, their wages are from $14.00 to $18.00 a month, most of which is usually sent back to the old country, that the remaining members of the family may be brought to America. Such positions are surrounded by temptations of every sort. Even the hotel housekeepers, who are honestly trying to protect the girls, admit that it is impossible to do it adequately. One of these housekeepers recently said "that it takes a girl who knows the world to work in any hotel," and regretted that the sophisticated English-speaking girl who might protect herself, was unable to endure the hard work. She added that as soon as a girl learned English she promoted her from the laundry to the halls and from there to the position of chamber-maid, but that the latter position was the most dangerous of all, as the girls were constantly exposed to insults from the guests. In the less respectable hotels these newly-arrived immigrant girls, inevitably seeing a great deal of the life of the underworld and the apparent ease with which money may be earned in illicit ways, find their first impression of the moral standards of life in America most bewildering. One young Polish girl had worked for two years in a downtown hotel, and had steadfastly resisted all improper advances even sometimes by the aid of her own powerful fist. She yielded at last to the suggestions of the life about her when she received a telegram from Ellis Island stating that her mother had arrived in New York, but was too ill to be sent to Chicago. All of her money had gone for the steamer ticket and as the thought of her old country mother, ill and alone among strangers, was too much for her long fortitude, she made the best bargain possible with the head waiter whose importunities she had hitherto resisted, accepted the little purse the other Polish girls in the hotel collected for her and arrived in New York only to find that her mother had died the night before. . . .

12. "Why Women Should Vote"

1 9 1 0

One of Jane Addams' arguments for women's suffrage, advanced in *A New Conscience*, was that women voters would not tolerate the traffic in white slaves. It could also be argued that they would not tolerate child labor, sweatshops, political corruption, or any of the other abuses against which the progressives were trying to

direct public indignation. Such is the polemical strategy of the following article, one of many Jane Addams wrote on the subject of
women's suffrage. Like other feminists, she combined this line of
reasoning with the ingenious argument that in concerning themselves with public questions women were, after all, only pursuing
their traditional activities in a larger context, society having taken
over many functions formerly exercised by the family.

For many generations it has been believed that woman's
place is within the walls of her own home, and it is indeed
impossible to imagine the time when her duty there shall be
ended or to forecast any social change which shall release her
from that paramount obligation.

This paper is an attempt to show that many women today
are failing to discharge their duties to their own households
properly simply because they do not perceive that as society
grows more complicated it is necessary that woman shall extend her sense of responsibility to many things outside of her
own home if she would continue to preserve the home in its
entirety. One could illustrate in many ways. A woman's simplest duty, one would say, is to keep her house clean and
wholesome and to feed her children properly. Yet if she lives
in a tenement house, as so many of my neighbors do, she cannot fulfill these simple obligations by her own efforts because
she is utterly dependent upon the city administration for the
conditions which render decent living possible. Her basement
will not be dry, her stairways will not be fireproof, her house
will not be provided with sufficient windows to give light and
air, nor will it be equipped with sanitary plumbing, unless the
Public Works Department sends inspectors who constantly
insist that these elementary decencies be provided. Women
who live in the country sweep their own dooryards and may
either feed the refuse of the table to a flock of chickens or

allow it innocently to decay in the open air and sunshine. In a crowded city quarter, however, if the street is not cleaned by the city authorities no amount of private sweeping will keep the tenement free from grime; if the garbage is not properly collected and destroyed a tenement-house mother may see her children sicken and die of diseases from which she alone is powerless to shield them, although her tenderness and devotion are unbounded. She cannot even secure untainted meat for her household, she cannot provide fresh fruit, unless the meat has been inspected by city officials and [unless] the decayed fruit, which is so often placed upon sale in the tenement districts, has been destroyed in the interests of public health. In short, if woman would keep on with her old business of caring for her house and rearing her children she will have to have some conscience in regard to public affairs lying quite outside of her immediate household. The individual conscience and devotion are no longer effective. . . .

. . . If women follow only the lines of their traditional activities here are certain primary duties which belong to even the most conservative women, and which no one woman or group of women can adequately discharge unless they join the more general movements looking toward social amelioration through legal enactment.

The first of these, of which this article has already treated, is woman's responsibility for the members of her own household that they may be properly fed and clothed and surrounded by hygienic conditions. The second is a responsibility for the education of children: (*a*) that they may be provided with good schools; (*b*) that they may be kept free from vicious influences on the street; (*c*) that when working they may be protected by adequate child-labor legislation.

(*a*) The duty of a woman toward the schools which her children attend is so obvious that it is not necessary to dwell upon it. But even this simple obligation cannot be effectively carried out without some form of social organization as the mothers' school clubs and mothers' congresses testify, and to which the most conservative women belong because they feel the need of wider reading and discussion concerning the many problems of childhood. It is, therefore, perhaps natural that the public should have been more willing to accord a vote to women in school matters than in any other, and yet women have never been members of a Board of Education in sufficient numbers to influence largely actual school curriculi. If they had been kindergartens, domestic science courses and school playgrounds would be far more numerous than they are. More than once woman has been convinced of the need of the ballot by the futility of her efforts in persuading a business man that young children need nurture in something besides the three r's. Perhaps, too, only women realize the influence which the school might exert upon the home if a proper adaptation to actual needs were considered. An Italian girl who has had lessons in cooking at the public school will help her mother to connect the entire family with American food and household habits. That the mother has never baked bread in Italy—only mixed it in her own house and then taken it out to the village oven—makes it all the more necessary that her daughter should understand the complications of a cooking-stove. The same thing is true of the girl who learns to sew in the public school, and more than anything else, perhaps, of the girl who receives the first simple instruction in the care of little children, that skillful care which every tenement-house baby requires if he is to be pulled through his second summer. The only time, to my knowledge, that lessons in the care of children were given in the public schools of Chicago was one summer when the vacation schools were being managed by a volunteer body of women. The instruction was eagerly received by the Italian girls, who had been "little mothers" to younger children ever since they could remember.

As a result of this teaching I recall a young girl who carefully explained to her Italian mother that the reason the babies in Italy were so healthy and the babies in Chicago were so sickly was not, as her mother had always firmly insisted, because her babies in Italy had goat's milk and her babies in America had cow's milk, but because the milk in Italy was clean and the milk in Chicago was dirty. She said that when you milked your own goat before the door you knew that the milk was clean, but when you bought milk from the grocery store after it had been carried for many miles in the country "you couldn't tell whether or not it was fit for the baby to drink until the men from the City Hall, who had watched it all the way, said that it was all right." She also informed her mother that the "City Hall wanted to fix up the milk so that it couldn't make the baby sick, but that they hadn't quite enough votes for it yet." The Italian mother believed what her child had been taught in the big school; it seemed to her quite as natural that the city should be concerned in providing pure milk for her younger children as that it should provide big schools and teachers for her older children. She reached this naïve conclusion because she had never heard those arguments which make it seem reasonable that a woman should be given the school franchise, but no other.

(*b*) But women are also beginning to realize that children need attention outside of school hours; that much of the petty vice in cities is merely the love of pleasure gone wrong, the overrestrained boy or girl seeking improper recreation and excitement. It is obvious that a little study of the needs of children, a sympathetic understanding of the conditions under which they go astray, might save hundreds of them. Women traditionally have had an opportunity to observe the plays of children and the needs of youth, and yet in Chicago, at least, they had done singularly little in this vexed problem of juvenile delinquency until they helped to inaugurate the Juvenile Court movement a dozen years ago. The Juvenile Court Committee, made up largely of women, paid the salaries of the probation officers connected with the court for the first six years of its existence, and after the salaries were cared for by the county the same organization turned itself into a Juvenile Protective League, and through a score of paid officers are doing valiant service in minimizing some of the dangers of city life which boys and girls encounter. . . .

. . . (c) As the education of her children has been more and more transferred to the school, so that even children four years old go to the kindergarten, the woman has been left in a household of constantly-narrowing interests, not only because the children are away, but also because one industry after another is slipping from the household into the factory. Ever since steam power has been applied to the processes of weaving and spinning woman's traditional work has been carried on largely outside of the home. The clothing and household linen are not only spun and woven, but also usually sewed, by machinery; the preparation of many foods has also passed into the factory and necessarily a certain number of women have been obliged to followed their work there, although it is doubtful, in spite of the large number of factory girls, whether women now are doing as large a proportion of the world's work as they used to do. Because many thousands of those working in factories and shops are girls between the ages of fourteen and twenty-two there is a necessity that older women should be interested in the conditions of industry. The very fact that these girls are not going to remain in industry permanently makes it more important that some one should see to it that they shall not be incapacitated for their future family life because they work for exhausting hours and under insanitary conditions.

If woman's sense of obligation had enlarged as the industrial conditions changed she might naturally and almost imperceptibly have inaugurated the movements for social amelioration in the line of factory legislation and shop sanitation. That she has not done so is doubtless due to the fact that her conscience is slow to recognize any obligation outside of her own family circle, and because she was so absorbed in her own household that she failed to see what the conditions outside actually were. It would be interesting to know how far the consciousness that she had no vote and could not change matters operated in this direction. After all, we see only those things to which our attention has been drawn, we feel responsibility for those things which are brought to us as matters of responsibility. If conscientious women were convinced that it was a civic duty to be informed in regard to these grave industrial affairs, and then to express the conclusions which they had reached by depositing a piece of paper in a ballot-box, one cannot imagine that they would shirk simply because the action ran counter to old traditions.

To those of my readers who would admit that although woman has no right to shirk her old obligations, that all of these measures could be secured more easily through her influence upon the men of her family than through the direct use of the ballot, I should like to tell a little story. I have a friend in Chicago who is the mother of four sons and the grandmother of twelve grandsons who are voters. She is a woman of wealth, of secured social position, of sterling character and clear intelligence, and may, therefore, quite fairly be cited as a "woman of influence." Upon one of her recent birthdays, when she was asked how she had kept so young, she promptly replied: "Because I have always advocated at least one unpopular cause." It may have been in pursuance of this policy that for many years she has been an ardent advocate of free silver, although her manufacturing family are all Republicans! I happened to call at her house on the day that Mr. McKinley was elected President against Mr. Bryan for the first time. I found my friend much disturbed. She said somewhat bitterly that she had at last discovered what the much-vaunted influence of woman was worth; that she had implored each one of her sons and grandsons, had entered into endless arguments and moral appeals to induce one of them to represent her convictions by voting for Bryan! That, although sincerely devoted to her, each one had assured her that his convictions forced him to vote the Republican ticket. She said that all she had been able to secure was the promise from one of the grandsons, for whom she had an especial tenderness because he bore her husband's name, that he would not vote at all. He could not vote for Bryan, but out of respect for her feeling he would refrain from voting for McKinley. My friend said that for many years she had suspected that women could influence men only in regard to those things in which men were not deeply concerned, but when it came to persuading a man to a woman's view in affairs of politics or business it was absolutely useless. I contended that a woman had no right to persuade a man to vote against his own convictions; that I respected the men of her family for following their own judgment regardless of the appeal which the honored head of the house had made to their chivalric devotion. To this she replied that she would agree with that point of view when a woman had the same opportunity as a man to register her convictions by vote. I believed then as I do now, that nothing is gained when independence of judgment is assailed by "influence," sentimental or otherwise, and that we test advancing civilization somewhat by our power to respect differences and by our tolerance of another's honest conviction. . . .

. . . In a complex community like the modern city all points of view need to be represented; the resultants of diverse experiences need to be pooled if the community would make for sane and balanced progress. If it would meet fairly each problem as it arises, whether it be connected with a freight tunnel having to do largely with business men, or with the increasing death rate among children under five years of age, a problem in which women are vitally concerned, or with the question of more adequate street-car transfers, in which both men and women might be said to be equally interested, it must not ignore the judgments of its entire adult population.

To turn the administration of our civic affairs wholly over to men may mean that the American city will continue to push forward in its commercial and industrial development, and continue to lag behind in those things which make a city healthful and beautiful. After all, woman's traditional function has been to make her dwelling-place both clean and fair. Is that dreariness in city life, that lack of domesticity which the humblest farm dwelling presents, due to a withdrawal of one of the naturally coöperating forces? If women have in any sense been responsible for the gentler side of life which softens and blurs some of its harsher conditions, may they not have a duty to perform in our American cities?

In closing, may I recapitulate that if woman would fulfill her traditional responsibility to her own children; if she would educate and protect from danger factory children who must find their recreation on the street; if she would bring the cultural forces to bear upon our materialistic civilization; and if she would do it all with the dignity and directness fitting one who carries on her immemorial duties, then she must bring herself to the use of the ballot—that latest implement for self-government. May we not fairly say that American women need this implement in order to preserve the home?

13. "The Larger Aspects of the Women's Movement"

1 9 1 4

This piece repeats the arguments of the previous one in a somewhat larger context. The historical parallels that it draws make clear that Jane Addams, like most feminists of her time, conceived of women as a social class in their own right, and of their struggle for political representation as analogous to the earlier struggles of the middle class and the proletariat. She imagined women to have a set of distinctive interests of their own, which could no more be served by men than the interests of the proletariat could be served by the *bourgeosie*. The excitements attending the controversy over women's suffrage—the heroism of the suffragists, the implacable opposition of so many men—tended to obscure the fact that women's social position was ambiguous in a way that the proletariat's was not; that class lines, rather than coinciding with sexual distinctions, confusingly cut across them. Half a century of women's suffrage has shown that women do not vote as a class or interest. The argument that their enfranchisement would revolutionize politics no longer seems convincing. A stronger argument for the feminist position was that ideas of what was properly masculine and what was feminine were themselves misleading, being culturally rather than biologically determined. Some feminists have stood on this ground.[1] Jane Addams notably did not. Her kind of feminism, far from breaking down the myth that temperament is a function of sex, tended to perpetuate it.

Perhaps no presentation of history is so difficult as that which treats of the growth of a new consciousness; but assuming that the historic review, now so universal in the field of social judgment and investigation, is applicable to any current development, I have ventured to apply it to that disturbing manifestation called the "votes-for-women" movement, which at the present moment is not only the centre of hot debate but, unhappily, also of conduct which in the minds of many is most unseemly.

Because I shall need the indulgence of the reader who may

From Jane Addams, "The Larger Aspects of the Woman's Movement," *Annals of the American Academy of Political and Social Science*, LVI (November 1914), 1–8.

[1] See Margaret Mead, *Sex and Temperament in Three Primitive Societies* (New York: William Morrow, 1935).

kindly follow this review, I will at once recall to his mind the statement of an ironic Englishman that it would be better to be convicted of petty larceny than to be found wanting in historic mindedness.

To begin then with the world-wide aspect of the votes-for-women movement—that there may be nothing more petty about us than the theme itself imposes—it is possible to make certain classifications of underlying trends, which, while not always clear, and sometimes overlapping, are yet international in their manifestations.

First: the movement is obviously a part of that evolutionary conception of self-government which has been slowly developing through the centuries. For the simple reason that self-government must ever be built up anew in relation to changing experiences its history is largely a record of new human interests which have become the object of governmental action, and of the incorporation into the body politic of the classes representing those interests. As the governing classes have been enlarged by the enfranchisement of one body of men after another, government itself has not only become enriched through new human interests, but at the same time it has become further democratized through the accession of the new classes representing those interests. The two propositions are complementary.

When the middle classes in every country in Europe struggled to wrest governmental power from the exclusive grasp of the nobles, the existing governments were already concerned with levying tariffs and embargoes, and the merchants insisted, not only that the problems of a rising commerce could not be settled by self interested nobles, but that they themselves must have direct representation before those problems could even be stated intelligently.

When the working men of the nineteenth century, the chartist in England and the "men of forty-eight" in Germany, vigorously demanded the franchise, national parliaments had already begun to regulate the condition of mines and the labor of little children. The working men insisted that they themselves could best represent their own interests, but, at the same time, their very entrance into government increased in volume the pressure of those interests.

In certain aspects, the entrance of women into government differs from former efforts in the extension of the franchise. We recall that the final entrance of the middle class into government was characterized by two dramatic revolutions, one in America and one in France, neither of them without bloodshed. This world-wide entrance into government on the part of women is happily a bloodless one and has been without a semblance of violence save in England where its manifestations are not unlike those of the earlier movement among English workingmen. Throughout those efforts so to change political institutions that they might effectively give expression to the growth of new experiences, the dependence of the political machine for its driving force upon the many varieties of social fuel constantly was made clear. It was, after all, rather an astute statesman who remarked that "What liberty and prosperity depend upon are the souls of men." Certain it is that the phenomenal entrance of woman into governmental responsibilities in the dawn of the twentieth century is co-incident with the consideration by governmental bodies of the basic human interests with which women have traditionally been concerned, quite as the membership of the middle class and that of the working class each in turn followed its own interests and became a part of representative government.

The new demand of women for political enfranchisement comes at a time when unsatisfactory and degraded social conditions are held responsible for so much wretchedness and when the fate of all the unfortunate, the suffering, and the criminal, is daily forced upon woman's attention in painful and intimate ways. At the same moment, governments all over the world are insisting that it is their function, and theirs alone, so to regulate social and industrial conditions that a desirable citizenship may be secured.

In certain respects the insistence of women for political expression, which characterizes the opening years of the twentieth century, bears an analogy to their industrial experiences in the early part of the nineteenth century, when the textile industries were taken out of private houses and organized as factory enterprises. If women had not followed those old industries into factories, thousands of them would have sat idly at home in empty houses, losing not only the money they had formerly earned but their old occupation as well. It was often considered "unwomanly" for these spinsters to go outside the home in order to use a spindle driven by steam power, possibly because all the queens of polite history, since the days of Penelope, when interrupted by their amours were always languidly engaged with textiles. It is hard to see now how the basic industry of England could have been developed without the thousands of women and girls who in spite of public opprobrium followed their old occupations.

But is it not obvious that, as industrial changes took spinning out of private houses, so political changes are taking out of the home humanitarian activities, not to mention the teaching of children? The aged poor of a community who were formerly cared for in the houses of distant relatives or old neighbors, the sick who were nursed night and day by kindly friends and acquaintances taking turn and turn about, are now housed in large infirmaries and in hospitals built and supported by the tax payers' money. The woman who wishes to be a teacher or a nurse takes her training in public institutions, as she formerly went to the factory to spin, not because she wishes primarily to leave home but because her work has been transferred. As she was helpless, without the franchise, to keep little children from working all night in the early textile mills of Yorkshire, so she is powerless now to regulate the administration of schoolhouse or hospital. A college woman who was recently appointed dietitian for the institutions of Cook County found that the menu in essential respects had not been changed in thirty-two years because it was easier for the county commissioners to copy the old forms upon which the food contracts had been awarded than to make new ones.

Studied from a second aspect, the "votes-for-women" movement is doubtless one result of the fundamental change which is taking place in the conception of politics analogous to the changes in the basic notions in education, criminology, and political economy. Graham Wallas,[2] in his very interesting book *Human Nature in Politics,* points out that, while educators have learned to study child psychology so that teachers understand children rather than manage schools, and that while jurists are ceasing to classify offenders solely on the basis of their crimes and are beginning to regard them as human beings, politicians have not yet learned to apply social psychology to the field of political action. The individual voter is still regarded as a party adjunct, a useful unit for party organization exactly as the old economist long considered the "economic man" as a sort of lone wolf impelled by no other motive than the desire for food. Quite as the science of political economy made little progress until it got rid of that fiction and looked at men as they really exist, each a bundle of complicated and overlapping motives, so politicians are making many blunders because their action is not founded upon the genuine facts of human existence. They have failed to observe how rapidly the materials and methods of political life are changing, that the law courts and legislature are struggling desperately to meet modern demands with conceptions of property and authority and duty founded upon the rude compromises made centuries ago, that there is obvious need for bolder arrangements and

---

[2] Graham Wallas (1858–1932), English Fabian socialist, wrote *The Great Society* (1914) and through this and other writings had a considerable influence on American radicals [Ed.].

interactions in the distribution of employment, education, invention. Such changes can only come about if they are carried on with that same spirit of free thinking and outspoken publication that has won in the field of natural science.

An able man long ago pointed out that the qualities most valuable in an electorate are social sympathies and a sense of justice, then openness and plainness of character, lastly habits of action and a practical knowledge of social misery. Woman's value to the modern states, which constantly are forced to consider social reforms, lies in the fact that statesmen at the present moment are attempting to translate the new social sympathy into political action.

The contemporary efforts to extend the principles of social insurance to illness in several European states, and to control unemployment through national labor exchanges, are not so much social reforms as titanic pieces of social engineering in which the judgment of women is most necessary. Governmental commissions everywhere take woman's testimony as to legislation for better housing, for public health and education, for the care of dependents, and many other remedial measures, because it is obviously a perilous business to turn over delicate social experiments to men who have remained quite untouched by social compunctions and who have been elected to their legislative position solely upon the old political issues. Certainly under this new conception of politics it is much easier to legislate for those human beings of whose condition the electorate are "vividly aware," to use a favorite phrase of Professor James.

It is not difficult to find instances in which legislators have made themselves a little absurd by ignoring this philosophic postulate. A most advanced German statesman in the reichstag declared recently that it was a reproach to the imperial government that out of two million children born annually in Germany four hundred thousand died during the first twelve months of their existence. He proceeded to instance various reforms which might remedy this, such as better housing, the increase of park areas, the erection of municipal hospitals, the provision for adequate milk supply and many another, but he did not make the very obvious suggestion that the advice of women might be valuable in the care of children less than two years old. Nor did the English Parliament see the connection when they spent an entire evening discussing the propriety of prohibiting the use of a popular brand of flannelette for children's night gowns because so many tenement house babies had been burned to death when lighted candles held by weary mothers came in contact with the inflammable material whose smooth finish had been superinduced by an industrial process in which turpentine was used. The House was hotly divided as to whether the use of wool was absolutely necessary to the health of young children, although the members of the party, advocating "cottonette" as a substitute, were somewhat chagrined when upon consulting their wives at breakfast the next morning they found that the word had been coined in the heat of argument and that there was no such material on the market. During the last presidential election in the United States, when measures of social reform suddenly became the basis of party pledges, many women were pushed into the stream of party politics with a momentum almost as instinctive as that of a mother who springs into the water to rescue her child. Naturally when women see their social causes, some of them tiny things and new born, about to be turned over to governmental officials, they insist upon an opportunity to help select the men who are to become the protagonists of their most cherished reforms.

Women have discovered that the unrepresented are always liable to be given what they do not need by legislators who wish merely to placate them; a child labor law exempts street trades, the most dangerous of all trades to a child's morals; a law releasing mothers from petty industry that they may rear worthy children provides a pension so inadequate that overburdened women must continue to neglect their young in order to feed them.

More than one woman, while waiting in the lobby for an opportunity to persuade recalcitrant law-makers in regard to a legislative measure, has had ample time to regret that she had no vote by which to select the men upon whom her social reform had become so absolutely dependent. Such a woman can even recall some cherished project which has been so modified by uninformed legislators during the process of legal enactment that the law finally passed injured the very people it was meant to protect.

The community, for instance, will never be made "vividly aware" of the effects of chronic fatigue upon young working girls or upon children who divert their energy from growth to pasting labels on a box by men whose minds are fixed upon factory management from the point of view of profits. The cultural outlook on life must become as aggressive as the commercial if it hopes to be effective.

The third trend in the feminist movement might be called evolutionary rather than historic, if indeed the two may be separated. In this trend the very earliest stage is doubtless represented by those women of Asia who are making their first struggle against the traditional bondages and customs whose roots creep back into primitive times, and whose efforts are yet in that incipient and unorganized stage which characterized the efforts of western women a hundred years ago. As a whole, this trend is connected with contemporary revolutions carried on by men demanding a direct representation in governments which at present ignore them. The most striking example, perhaps, is Russia, where women have taken an active part in the recently established constitutional government. Twenty-one of them at the present moment are sitting as members in the Finnish Parliament. Due to that inveterate tendency of revolutionists to incorporate into their program the most advanced features of existing governments, the demand for woman's political representation has reached even Mohammedan countries, such as Persia and Turkey, where it is directly opposed to their religious teaching. Both China and Siam, in spite of eastern customs, have given woman a political status in their new constitutions by extending to certain classes of them the right of suffrage.

In contrast to these contemporary revolutions in which women have been recognized are the European revolutions of the nineteenth century in which women also worked side by side with men for a larger democracy, but where they were ignored when the constitutions were finally written. This is clearly seen in such states as Bohemia, Silesia, and Hungary, where women with certain property qualifications are still sending members to Parliament who directly represent their interests. This right of women to vote has survived from the days when the ownership of property was the only basis upon which either men or women were given the franchise. When the vote for men was based upon a broader qualification than that of property, the vote, although it was not extended to other women, was not taken away from the women previously qualified. It was upon such a basis that women a few centuries ago sat in the English Parliament and at this moment are voting upon the same terms as men in the municipal governments of Rangoon and other Indian cities. These surviving votes, representing a stage long past, are a reproach to existing governments which at the present moment are making a greater disparity between the political status of men and women than that which existed three hundred years ago. Whatever the result, in the final adjustment, so long as the revolutions both of the nineteenth and the twentieth century were purely inspirational and doctrinaire, the revolutionists recognized the equality of women. The aftermath was obvious, during the recent election in Chicago, that the women of those nations recently stirred by revolution were the women most eager to utilize the franchise—Bohemian, Polish, and Irish women, and the Italian women whose families had been committed to a new Italy.

The generous moral feeling evoked in a time of revolution, reducing life to its first principles as it were, tends to restore women to their earlier place in society, somewhat as women regain much of their original social importance in pioneer countries where there is little division of labor. Because good government is not a matter of sex when it means a method of identifying cattle which have become mixed with the neighboring herd or of defending little children from the dangers incident to frontier life, it has evidently been difficult for the pioneer man to withhold political rights from women when government has become more conventional. Such a condition is represented by all of the Australian states, one following another in the granting of the franchise to women until the entire seven are included; by Wyoming which gave suffrage to women in 1869, and by others of the western states in America, and last of all by Alaska. Even the conservative Boers of the early Dutch republics in South Africa had given the right of franchise to the women who had trekked and fought and ploughed by their sides in the spirit of the early German woman who evoked the admiration of Tacitus. And although the Dutch women had never used the vote, being inhibited by some notion that it was not ladylike, there it was ready at hand until the English inaugurated a more sophisticated rule.

The final impression of a review of this movement we have ventured to consider is of a cause growing, pushing, and developing in all the nations upon the face of the earth, representing new experiences and untrammeled hopes. It is everywhere surprisingly spontaneous and universal. It not only appears simultaneously in various nations in both hemispheres, but manifests itself in widely separated groups within the same nation, embracing the smart set and the hard driven working woman; sometimes the movement is sectarian and dogmatic, at others philosophic and grandiloquent; it may be amorphous and sporadic, or carefully organized and consciously directed; but it is always vital and is constantly becoming more widespread.

14. "My Experiences as a Progressive Delegate"

1912

In 1912 Jane Addams took part in the creation of Theodore Roosevelt's Progressive Party and campaigned for Roosevelt against Wilson and Taft. To do so, she had to overcome her objections to Roosevelt's militarism, as she conceived it, and to the party's lily-white policy in the South. Some of her friends thought she went too far on the path of compromise, particularly on the latter point. When she failed to demand from the platform committee a declaration of racial equality as the price of her support, her friends "stood outside her door at the Congress Hotel and wept in the night hours." "It seemed as though she could not do anything," said Sophonisba Breckinridge, a former Hull-House resident, "that was in the nature of an exercise of compulsion or control."[1]

During the convention of the Progressive party in Chicago, one constantly encountered members of the American Economic Association, the National Conference of Charities and Corrections, the Civil Service Reform League, and similar bodies, until one feared that a few students of social conditions were endeavoring, through the new party, to secure measures which, although worthy, have after all recommended themselves to only a very small group out of all the nation. To an

---

From Jane Addams, "My Experiences as a Progressive Delegate," *McClure's*, XL (November 1912), 12–14.

[1] *Unity*, CXV (July 15, 1935), 191.

incorrigible democrat this was, naturally, very alarming. I was first reassured when I met a friend, whom I had last seen at the earlier Chicago convention before the Resolutions Committee, where he was presenting a plank which later left a slight residuum in the compressed labor paragraph adopted by the Republican party, and where I was presenting an equal suffrage plank which left no residuum at all. I remarked, in passing, that we were both getting a better hearing than we did in June, and he replied that we were not in the usual position of bringing men around to a new way of thinking, but that we were being met more than half way by men definitely committed to progress along all lines.

I gradually discovered that the situation was, in reality, the very reverse of what I had feared. The dean of a university law school acted as chairman of the Committee on Resolutions, and men conversant with the later developments in social legislation supplied information concerning similar legislation abroad; but these men with the so-called practical members of the committee, were not representing the opinion of any individual, nor the philosophy of any group. They were trying, as conscientious American citizens, to meet that fundamental obligation of adapting the legal order to the changed conditions of national life—in the words of a Kansas member, "to formulate our own intrinsic, self-vindicating laws." The members of the committee had all experienced the frustration and disappointment of detached and partial effort. They had come to this first national convention of the Progressive party, not only to urge the remedial legislation which seemed to them so essential to the nation's welfare, but to test its validity and vitality by the "inner consent" of their fellow citizens, to throw their measures into the life of the nation itself for corroboration.

The program of social legislation placed before the country by the Progressive party is of great significance to the average voter, irrespective of the party which may finally claim his allegiance. Aristotle is reported to have said that politics is a school wherein questions are studied, not for the sake of knowledge, but for the sake of action. He might have added that politics are most valuable as a school because the average man has an inveterate tendency not to study at all unless he sees the prospect of action ahead of him. During the present campaign, measures of social amelioration will be discussed up and down the land, as only party politics are discussed, in the remotest farm-house to which the rural free delivery brings the weekly newspaper; certain economic principles will become current, and new phrases will enter permanently into popular speech.

The discussion of the Progressive party platform will further surprise many a voter into the consciousness that the industrial situation in America has developed by leaps and bounds, without any of the restraining legislation which has been carefully placed about in Europe. He will be told, for instance, that although twenty-nine European countries prohibit all night work for women, only three of our States have taken such action. He will learn of the long hours and overstrain to which the working-women of America may be subjected. If he is convinced that a girl who pushes down a lever with her right foot eight or nine thousand times a day is making so poor a preparation for motherhood that her work reacts in an "impaired second generation," he will be quick to see that it is the business of government to protect her, certainly in a republic whose very continuance depends upon the intelligence and vigor of its future citizens.

Such matters, doubtless, have a technical aspect, but they are in essence human, and intimately allied to the experiences of the average voter. But it is only when such needs are discussed in politics that he sees "where he comes in" and begins to be "worried."

The members of the Resolutions Committee were possessed of knowledge which it is, after all, a great responsibility not to submit to the nation. If a man knows, for instance, that fifteen thousand of his fellow citizens are killed in industry every year,—as if every adult male in a city of seventy-five thousand were put to death,—and that half a million of men are crippled,—as if every adult male in a State the size of Minnesota were annually maimed,—it is not sufficient for his peace of mind to know that a small group of public-spirited citizens are constantly agitating in various State legislatures for a system of industrial insurance, and that a yet smaller group of manufacturers successfully oppose such effort because their interests are threatened. The members of the committee knew that such problems belong to the nation as well as to the State, and that only by federal control, through the Inter-State Commerce Regulations, can great corporations be made to assume the injury of workmen as one of the risks of industry; only when human waste shall automatically involve a reduction in profits will a comprehensive system of safeguards be developed, as Germany has clearly demonstrated. Such facts should be made public to the entire country, for it is no abstract theory which would lead one State after another to act upon this knowledge; it is self-preservation. Legislation forced by actual conditions is like the statutory laws, which in the first instance were reactions to felt needs.

It did not seem strange that women were delegates to this first convention of the Progressive party, and it would have been much more unnatural if they had not been there, when such matters of social welfare were being considered.

When a great political party asks women to participate in its first convention, and when a number of women deliberately accept the responsibility, it may indicate that public-spirited women are ready to give up the short modern rôle of being good to people and to go back to the long historic rôle of ministration to big human needs. After all, our philanthropies have cared for the orphans whose fathers have been needlessly injured in industry; have supported the families of the convict whose labor is adding to the profits of a prison contractor; have solaced men and women prematurely aged because they could find no work to do; have rescued girls driven to desperation through overwork and overstrain. Remedial legislation for all these human situations is part of the Progressive party platform; and as the old-line politician will be surprised to find during this campaign that politics have to do with such things, so philanthropic women, on their side, will be surprised to find that their long concern for the human wreckage of industry has come to be considered politics. When we develop the courage to commit our principles to reality, we will not only enlarge our concept of truth, but we will give it a chance to become humanized and vital. It is as if we thrust a dry stick of a principle into moist, fruitful earth, and as if it returned to our hands so fresh and blooming that we no longer have an impulse to use it as a chastening rod upon the evildoer, but, wondering, hold it as a new-born pledge of the irresistible power of life to quicken and to heal.

In spite of many reassuring experiences on the part of the women who identified themselves with the Progressive party, during the three days of the convention there were inevitable moments of heart-searching and compunction. But, because one felt curiously at home, there was the utmost freedom of speech and a quick understanding of hidden scruples which one was mysteriously impelled to express.

We were, first and foremost, faced with the necessity of selecting from our many righteous principles those that might be advocated at the moment, and of forcing others to wait for a more propitious season. To illustrate from my own experience: For many years I have advocated international peace; to that end, I have been a member, sometimes an official, of various international, national, and local peace societies, and have zealously written and spoken upon the stirring theme of international arbitration. But, when I sat as a delegate in the convention of the Progressive party, I voted to adopt a plat-

form, "as a whole," which advocated the building of two battleships a year, pending an international agreement for the limitation of naval forces.

I confess that I found it very difficult to swallow those two
battleships. I know only too well the outrageous cost of building and maintaining them—that fatal seventy cents out of
every dollar of federal taxes which is spent indirectly for war;
and I would fain that the Progressive party had added no
more to this preposterous and unnecessary burden, that it had
been ready to commit the future to arbitration.

It was a serious matter even to appear to desert the cause
and the comrades with which I had been for so many years
identified. Believing, however, as I do, that we prepare ourselves for sudden deeds by an infinite series of minor decisions
we have previously made, and that our convictions are, after
all, determined by our sincerest experiences, I read over the
documents of my long advocacy of peace, to find that I had
consistently pursued one line of appeal. I contended that peace
is no longer an abstract dogma, but that marked manifestations of "a newer dynamic peace" are found in that new internationalism promoted by the men of all nations who are determined upon the abolition of degrading poverty, disease, and
intellectual weakness, with their resulting inefficiency and
tragedy.

It is therefore not surprising that I should have been attracted to a party which pledged itself to work unceasingly
for "effective labor legislation looking to the prevention of
industrial accidents, occupational diseases, overwork, involun-
tary unemployment, and other injurious effects incident to
modern industry." The men in every-day contact with the
economic conditions of our industrial cities have estimated that
the total number of casualties suffered by our industrial army
is sufficient to carry on perpetually two such wars, at the same
time, as our Civil War and the Russo-Japanese War; that the
casualties in the structural iron trade, in the erection of bridges

and high buildings, bear the same percentage to the number of men engaged as did the wounded to the total number of troops in the battle of Bull Run. After all, when a choice was presented to me between protesting against the human waste in industry or against the havoc in warfare, the former made the more intimate appeal, and I identified myself with the political party which not only protests against such waste, but advances well considered legislation to prevent it.

Industrial Insurance Acts to protect the thousands of young immigrants who each year take the return journey across the Atlantic, maimed and crippled because the republic to which they have given their young strength failed to protect them as they would have been safeguarded at home, may but precede the successful conclusion of arbitration treaties.

Perhaps that ancient kindliness which "sat beside the cradle of the race" can not assert itself, in our generation, against warfare, so long as we stultify ourselves by our disregard of the shocking destruction in industry. The federal government through its own recent experience is leaning to the new humanitarianism. The wonderful sanitary system and daily regimen which preserved the life and health of the workers who dug the Panama Canal ought to make it very difficult for the same government to build upon the same spot huge fortifications whose very existence threatens with destruction that same human stuff which it has so painstakingly kept alive.

During the three days of the Progressive convention, one felt not only the breakdown of the old issues which had furnished both parties with their election cries for half a century, but the inevitable emergence of a new position.

A new code of political action has been formulated by men who are striving to express a sense of justice, socialized by long effort to secure fair play between contending classes; men who have learned that it can not be done by *a priori* reasoning, but must be established upon carefully ascertained facts.

Through the action of the Progressive party, remedial legislation is destined to be introduced into Congress and into every State legislature, by men whose party is committed to the redress of social wrongs and who have promised their constituents specific measures adapted to the changing and varied conditions of our industrial life.

15. "The Progressive Party and the Negro"

1912

In the following article, Miss Addams confronted the most delicate question raised by her support of the Progressive Party. Once again she argued along pragmatic lines. The Republicans, she contended, paid lip service to the idea of equality, and the Progressives could have followed their example; but the practical result of the Republican policy had been simply to strengthen the one-party system in the South. The Republicans, indeed, had no intention either of forcing the issue of Negro suffrage or of creating a real Republican Party in the South, when the present arrangement gave them a solid bloc of votes in national conventions that could be manipulated as the party managers saw fit. The silence of the Progressives seemed to Jane Addams preferable to the empty rhetoric of the Republicans. The Progressives, moreover, aimed at becoming a national party; the Republicans were content to remain sectional. But nothing was clearer than that the race problem was national, not sectional, in scope. By avoiding a direct challenge to white supremacy in the South, the Progressives might eventually establish themselves in that section, thereby undermining the monopoly of the Democrats. Only then, she reasoned, would it be possible to overthrow the whole system of paternalism, of which white supremacy was a part.

These arguments assumed that the Progressive Party would be

a permanent feature of the political landscape. In fact, it proved to be no more than a vehicle for the personal ambitions of Theodore Roosevelt. When Roosevelt led his followers back into the Republican fold in 1916, the party collapsed, and with it, the dream of a two-party South.

At the Progressive convention held in Chicago last August disquieting rumors arose concerning the Negro delegates. It was stated that although two groups from Florida, one of colored men and one of white men, had been excluded because of a doubt as to which had been authorized to elect delegates, that the colored men only from Mississippi had been excluded; and that this was done in spite of the fact that the word "white" had been inserted in the call for the State convention which elected the accredited delegates. It did not seem sufficient to many of us that the credentials committee in seating the Mississippi delegation had merely protested against the use of the word "white," and some of us at once took alarm on behalf of the colored men.

With several others, who were also members of the National Association for the Advancement of Colored People, I appeared before the resolutions committee to point out the inconsistency of pledging relief to the overburdened workingman while leaving the colored man to struggle unaided with his difficult situation, if, indeed, the action of the credentials committee had not given him a setback.

In reply we were told that colored men were sitting as delegates in the convention, not only from such Northern States as Rhode Island, but that the Progressives of West Virginia, Maryland, Tennessee and Kentucky had also elected colored delegates, setting a standard which it was hoped the States south of them would attain when the matter was left to those men of the South who are impatient in the thraldom of war issues

---

From Jane Addams, "The Progressive Party and the Negro," *Crisis*, V (November 1912), 30–31.

and old party alignments. It was pointed out that such are the limitations of local self-government that free political expression can only be secured to the colored man through the co-operative action of the patriotic and far-seeing citizens of the States in which he lives; that only when white men and colored men together engage upon common political problems will the colored man cease to be regarded as himself a problem. We were reminded that under so-called Republican protection the colored man has practically lost his vote in certain States, not only through the grandfather clause,[1] but through sheer intimidation in those counties where the line of party cleavage follows the line of race antagonism, all the whites being Democrats who vote, all the blacks Republicans who do not. We were further told that if there was any disposition to continue old shams, that it would be a very simple matter to insert in the Progressive platform the glittering phrases which had done valiant service for so long a time, not only to blind the colored man himself, but to enable the manager of a Republican convention to determine the result through the colored vote. By the simple device of appointing to federal offices colored men in the sections where there is no Republican party, these men elect themselves delegates to the national conventions and naturally repay their party by voting as their office-holding interests require. Certainly self-government is not being promoted by such political recognition on the part of the Republicans of the North any more than it is by the disenfranchising action on the part of the Democrats of the South. The Progressive convention took neither point of view and

---

[1] The strategy of Negro disfranchisement in the South was to lay down strict qualifications for voting in the form of literacy tests and other devices and then to invent loopholes that would exempt whites but not Negroes from these requirements. One of the loopholes was the grandfather clause, whereby all males who, according to the Louisiana statute, had been able to vote in 1867—a time when Negroes had been unable to vote—could vote now, and so could their sons and grandsons [Ed.].

challenged one and at the same time the traditional shibbo-
leths of both parties.

When I asked myself most searchingly whether my Aboli-
tionist father would have remained in any political convention
in which colored men had been treated slightingly, I recalled
an incident of my girlhood which was illuminating and somewhat comforting. I had given my father an explanation of a
stupid decision whereby I had succeeded in bungling the plans
of a large family party, and I ended my apology with the honest statement that I had tried to act upon what I thought his
judgment would have been. His expression of amused bewilderment changed to one of understanding as he replied: "That
probably accounts for your confusion of mind. You fell into
the easy mistake of substituting loyalty and dependence upon
another's judgment for the very best use of your own faculties.
I should be sorry to think that you were always going to com-
plicate moral situations, already sufficiently difficult, by trying
to work out another's point of view. You will do much better
if you look the situation fairly in the face with the best light
you have."

Certainly the Abolitionists followed the best light they had,
although it differed from that possessed by the framers of the
Constitution, whose light had also come from the eighteenth
century doctrines of natural rights and of abstract principles,
when ideas were pressed up to their remotest logical issues,
without much reference to the conditions to which they were
applied. Shall we be less fearless than they to follow our own
moral ideals formed under the influence of new knowledge,
even, although the notion of evolution has entered into social
history and politics, and although "abstract" in the tongue of
William James, has come to imply the factitious, the academic,
and even the futile?

We all believe that a wide extension of political power is
the only sound basis of self-government and that no man is
good enough to vote for another, but we surely do not become

mere opportunists when we try to know something of the process by which the opinion of the voter has been influenced and his vote secured. If it is done through bribery, we easily admit that the whole system of representative government has broken down, and we are not accounted to have lost our patriotism when we estimate how much of a given vote is due to the liquor interests or to manufactured opinion; only on the political status of the colored man is it still considered unpatriotic to judge, save as one who long ago made up his mind.

Even in that remarkable convention where, for the moment, individual isolation was dissolved into a larger consciousness and where we caught a hint of the action of "the collective mind," so often spoken of and so seldom apprehended, I was assailed by the old familiar discomfort concerning the status of the colored man. Had I felt any better about it, I speculated, when I had tried in vain for three consecutive years to have the question discussed by a great national association[2] to whose purposes such a discussion was certainly germain? Was I more dissatisfied with this action than I had often been with no action at all? I was forced to acknowledge to myself that certainly war on behalf of the political status of the colored man was clearly impossible, but that there might emerge from such federal action as the interference with peonage, perhaps, a system of federal arbitration in interracial difficulties, somewhat analagous to the function of the Hague tribunal in international affairs. In fact, it has already been discovered at the Hague that many difficulties formerly called international were in reality interracial. Through such federal arbitration it may in time be demonstrated that to secure fair play between races living in the same nation is as legitimate as it is when irrational race hatred breaks out on those fringes of empire which the Hague calls "spheres of influence." The action of the Progressive party had at least taken the color question away from

---

[2] The Progressive Party [Ed.].

sectionalism and put it in a national setting which might clear the way for a larger perspective. Possibly this is all we can do at the present moment.

Viewing the third-party movement as a consistent, practical effort toward the "barn raising of a new party in the nation," which in its organization and program should not be along the old Civil War cleavages, we can predict but one outcome. The issues were those of political democracy and industrial justice—a merging of the political insurgency in the West and country districts with the social insurgency of the cities. Imbedded in this new movement is a strong ethical motive, and once the movement is crystallized, once as a body of people it gets a national foothold, once as a propaganda the rank and file are transfused with the full scope and meaning of social justice, it is bound to lift this question of the races, as all other questions, out of the grip of the past and into a new era of solution.

PART IV

DEMOCRACY AND EDUCATION

---

16. "A Toast to John Dewey"

1929

The concept of education had a very broad meaning for Jane Addams, as many of the preceding selections have shown. Education extended far beyond the realm of formal classroom instruction; for it was Jane Addams' contention, as it was the contention of other progressive educators, that learning was a continuous process —a process, moreover, that was implicit in any situation that brought a person into contact with the unexpected and the unfamiliar. Education was as broad as experience itself; education *was* experience. And it was the failure of professional educators to come to grips with this fact, in Jane Addams' opinion, that accounted for the sterility of much of American education. Education, at some point in its recent history, had divorced itself from "life." The task of educators was to reestablish the connection.

Jane Addams' early life once again provides a clue to the development of her ideas. She experienced her college training as "the snare of preparation"—an endless process of cultivation that had merely postponed her entrance into the real world. During her long years of waiting—the years between Rockford Seminary and Hull-House—she had plenty of time to brood upon the consequences of too much culture, the habit of seeing everything at second hand. Hull-House only confirmed her misgivings about the

American school and the American university in particular. She saw learned men come to lecture the immigrants in the language of the classroom—a language totally removed from their experience—and she sensed that academic instruction had as little relation to the needs of the poor as it had to the needs of the young women like herself. The schools, she concluded, had identified education with a self-perpetuating scholarship, with the accumulation of knowledge for its own sake; whereas, the real question for educators was how knowledge was to be used to improve the quality of life.

Finally, there was her own immediate experience as a settlement worker—the shock of plunging unprepared into another culture. Other charity workers had assumed that it was their duty to instruct and uplift the poor. Jane Addams, because she did not think of Hull-House as a charity in the first place, found that the process worked the other way around: she herself was the pupil; her neighbors, the teachers. From this experience she generalized that education ought to be conceived as a mutual relation. Not the transmission of knowledge, intact and untested by exposure to experience, but the interaction between teacher and pupil, under the conditions of life itself—this, for Jane Addams, became the essence of education.

These ideas paralleled and supported the educational theories of John Dewey. It is difficult to say whether Dewey influenced Jane Addams or Jane Addams influenced Dewey. They influenced each other and generously acknowledged their mutual obligations. Hull-House and Dewey's experimental school at the University of Chicago constantly exchanged ideas and personnel. One of the teachers in Dewey's school was a Hull-House resident. Dewey himself delivered a series of lectures at Hull-House on social psychology. Like William James, he admired Jane Addams' uncanny instinct for social observation. When she showed him the manuscript of "A Modern Lear," he exclaimed, "It is one of the greatest things I ever read both as to its form and its ethical philosophy."[1]

She reciprocated with many acknowledgments of Dewey's influence on her own thought. The following essay clearly states the

---

[1] John Dewey to Jane Addams, January 19, 1896; Jane Addams MSS (Swarthmore College Peace Collection, Swarthmore, Pennsylvania).

connection between Dewey's work and hers. As usual, however, Jane Addams was too modest about her own accomplishments. She credits Dewey's book, *School and Society*, with having had a deep effect on the relations not only between teacher and child, but between the social worker and his client; but she herself, in "The Subjective Necessity for Social Settlements," had already argued that the social worker had as much to learn from his clients as he had to teach them. And "A Function of the Social Settlement," published simultaneously with *School and Society* in 1899, contained a full statement of the educational implications of the settlement movement. Her obligation to Dewey was not, perhaps, as sweeping as she wished people to believe.

John Dewey was a member of the first board of Hull-House trustees. It consisted of two or three business men, two or three philanthropic women, and the philosopher, to keep us from becoming either hard-boiled or sentimental in this new undertaking, which the English somewhat heavily called "residential study of the problems of poverty." Unlike many trustees, he actually worked on the job: he took Julia Lathrop's[2] Plato Club for a series of Sunday afternoons one mid-winter, some days so stormy that only the "cranks" came.

The Plato Club was an epitome of all discussions held on social questions in the nineties. You propounded your theory and stuck to it through thick and thin, and no compromise was permitted! You either believed in heredity or you believed in environment, and the very highschools debated the question with the same fervor brought to bear upon the problem of the priority of the chick or the egg. It was therefore most signifi-

---

From Jane Addams, "A Toast to John Dewey," *Survey*, LXIII (November 15, 1929), 203–204.

[2] Julia Clifford Lathrop (1858–1932) lived at Hull-House in the 1890's. She established the Juvenile Court of Cook County, one of the first of its kind. Later (1912–1921) she became the first chief of the Children's Bureau in the Department of Labor. Jane Addams' last book, *My Friend Julia Lathrop* (New York: The Macmillan Company, 1935), was a memorial to Miss Lathrop [Ed.].

cant when John Dewey, who came to the new University of Chicago in 1894, announced the theory, or rather when the theory slowly leaked out, of an ever changing society in constant need of exploration and rediscovery; but stranger still was his ultimate test of the utility of any social scheme. Even Mr. Dooley said to Mr. Hennessy in the Chicago Tribune itself, "The question is, Hennessy, does it work? The jawing isn't worth a tinker's dam."

It was still more useful then, when John Dewey began a little practice school which he established near the University of Chicago, and demonstrated among other things the interaction between the individual and his environment. He studied the response of each child, not to a static environment but to various surroundings largely produced by the child himself. An historic period having made itself at home in the child's imagination, he energetically dug, built, wove and cooked according to his needs in a primitive hut or a moated castle.

John Dewey's little yellow-covered book, School and Society, made so clear the necessity for individualizing each child that it is quite fair, I think, to say that his insistence upon an atmosphere of freedom and confidence between the teacher and pupil, of a common interest in the life they led together, profoundly affected all similar relationships, certainly those between the social worker and his client. We were used to saying that the welfare of the community is a mutual responsibility, but John Dewey told us that the general intelligence is dormant, with its communications broken and faint, until it possesses the public as its medium.

He, who had so highly individualized the children in his school as to drive their parents into alarmed protest, warned us not to make exceptions of ourselves in regard to the experiences of life. But as he had socialized the children by giving them an almost empirical consciousness of the race life, so he individualized us by the corollary that the dear public itself—for which we were so much concerned—comes into existence through the extension of the acts of individuals beyond those personally involved.

Perhaps the entire psychological approach to the problems of social welfare was implicit in the situation when that group of brilliant men formed the Department of Philosophy at the new University of Chicago. Most of them had been attached in some way to the University of Michigan. There were James Tufts, John Dewey, George Mead and James Angell, if I may be permitted to use Quaker nomenclature. This philosophic department was one of those which incorporated pedagogy within itself. Many educators had been philosophers and a few philosophers had been educators, but this department broke down those invisible walls which so stubbornly separate one academic department from another. There is nothing in all creation like it, excepting the unbreakable division walls between the different departments of the United States government.

Perhaps we may trace back to this group of men the movement now culminating in the brand new psychiatric social worker and in the institutes of juvenile research. It began, in Chicago at least, when a student of John Dewey's was put in charge of the Child Study Department in the public schools. It was largely the prestige of Dr. Dewey himself which enabled the department to come into existence and perhaps it is not a mere coincidence that it was Chicago that founded the first psychopathic clinic attached to its Juvenile Court which in its turn had been the pioneer ten years earlier, because children were entitled to a court adapted to their own needs. We are impatient for the time when such a treatment may be extended to the adult criminal. At the moment the data supplied by the psychologists is often left on the hands of the embarrassed judge as extra-legal material; he cannot permit it to affect the judicial decision, although it may be convincing enough to weigh heavily upon his conscience.

Whatever may be the outcome of these newer experiments, many of John Dewey's contemporaries are certain of one thing: that the problems of social welfare in our own time have never been so squarely faced as by the philosopher who deliberately made the study of men and their intelligences a foundation for the study of the problems with which men have to deal. In those years when we were told by the scientists, or at least by the so-called scientists, that the world was in the grasp of sub-human forces against which it was absurd to oppose the human will, John Dewey calmly stated that the proper home of intelligence was the world itself and that the true function of intelligence was to act as critic and regulator of the forces which move the world.

Perhaps the greatest tribute to this worldly wisdom of his— the most impressive acknowledgement of his contribution to social welfare—has been the confidence with which one distracted nation after another has called him into their councils. We were in China only a few months after the Deweys had been there. The Philosophy Club at Peking was voluble with admiration, insisting that the philosophy of Dewey and his concepts of conduct could be compared to no one but to Confucius himself. It may have been this pious juxtaposition which moved one of these nascent philosophers gravely to remark, that it was a pity that when America needed a new religion the citizens had not called upon John Dewey to found it instead of Mrs. Eddy. Following the Dewey technique, Alice Dewey had inaugurated the office of Dean of Women at the National University at Nanking, to make clear that co-education was feasible in China as elsewhere. I shall always remember the tribute of affectionate appreciation given by her Chinese successor.

I do not know much personally of Dr. Dewey's journey to Turkey, although I have no doubt it was as successful as his others were, but I do wish that I might reproduce to you the enthusiasm on the part of the young Mexicans; of Saenz, the present minister of education; of Vasconsalez, who previously held that office; of the school of gifted artists who, as they decorate the vast walls of the educational buildings with scenes from the history of the Aztecs and other Indians, always bear in mind the educational theory as they conceive John Dewey propounded it to Mexico. They showed us a wall in a boys' school upon which the paintings had been deliberately defaced because they violated the canons of the new education and had imitated the frivolities of a dead art.

It is hard to exaggerate the gratitude of the young Russian intelligentsia in this country for the report that Dr. Dewey gave of the contemporary Russian experiment not only in education but in rebuilding the social structure itself. The representatives of a misunderstood and unpopular cause are devoted above all others to the recognized authority who becomes the champion of their cause through a clear and objective statement of the facts. He has done this many times. Years ago, before trade unions had proved their social utility and when it was scarcely respectable to be identified with them, John Dewey made it clear for them and for all their Chicago friends. Later he entered into a contest with the unions themselves that they might not curtail freedom in their educational enterprises.

That John Dewey should take an active part in the successful movement for the outlawry of war, is perhaps a corollary of his wide acquaintance with this world of ours and his desire for a stable foundation for those superstructures of social welfare of which we venture to dream.

Only once in a public crisis did I find my road taking a sharp right angle to the one he recommended. That fact in and of itself gave me pause to think, and almost threatened my confidence in the inevitability of that road. Our rough journeyings thereon often confirmed John Dewey's contention that unless truth indicates itself in practice it easily slips into futile dogma.

Advocates of peace in time of war, we were perforce thrust into the position of the doctrinaire, although the Dewey teaching saved us from resorting to the ineffable solace vouchsafed to the self-righteous, and as we struggled in one country after another for a foothold in reality and actually found it, we were grateful to him for having taught us a method.

Of course, even in those days when I first knew John Dewey, he bore certain earmarks of the traditional absent-minded philosopher. I vividly remember when he lost a newly acquired doctor's hood at the fifty years' celebration of the founding of the University of Wisconsin. At the moment I was walking with the venerated president of the University of Michigan, down that path which seems to connect the somber dome of the university with the gilded dome of the State House. Angell and Addams had "swapped" stories of foreign visitors whom we had entertained and we had almost reached a decision to collaborate on a book entitled, Famous People whose Boots We have Blacked, for at that time distinguished foreigners— innocent of the domestic system prevailing on the broad and democratic prairies—confidingly flung their boots outside their bedroom doors, little suspecting that only their hosts would deign to pick them up. President Angell, whose diplomatic services had taken him well over the world, whose tolerant and kindly spirit had appraised many men of many lands, listened delightedly when asked if he had lost a hood, and replied, "Of course, it is Dewey's. The occasion wouldn't be complete unless he *had* lost it!" Turning to me he remarked, "Dewey, of all men on this campus today, will probably make the greatest contribution, in spite of the fact that they have combed the universities from Oxford down for this occasion."

Although Dr. Dewey is not easy to read, nor in the Chautauqua sense, a popular lecturer, through the conscious use of his luminous mind he has almost made over the connotations on the very word philosopher for thousands of people. May we quote his own words which one of his students[3] has placed on the title page of his last book: "Better it is for philosophy to err in active participation in the living struggles and issues of its own age and times, than to maintain an immune monastic impeccability. To try to escape from the snares and pitfalls of time by recourse to traditional problems and interests—rather than that, let the dead bury their own dead." It is such winged words as these which have endeared John Dewey to those who live in settlements or undertake other lines of social welfare.

I remember during certain strenuous days in Chicago when we were under cross-fire in a bewildering situation of a strike turned into a lockout, that I thought with primitive green envy of university professors on the other side of town secure from the bludgeonings of both trade unionists and capitalists. But at least one of these professors promptly entered the industrial arena. It was part of his life-long effort to embody truth in conduct. He has qualified for a preeminent position among all those committed to the long struggle for social betterment.

It is a toast rather than a topic—John Dewey and Social Welfare!

17. "A Function of the Social Settlement"

1899

This essay, later reprinted in slightly altered form as the chapter "Socialized Education" in *Twenty Years at Hull-House,* is the most

---

[3] Joseph Ratner, who edited a number of Dewey's works [Ed.].

comprehensive statement of Jane Addams' educational theories. It explicitly compares the settlement to the university, and the comparison serves to point up Jane Addams' chief criticism of the latter—its failure to apply knowledge to life. Note especially the reference (page 193, n) to "the always getting ready for life which seems to dog the school," and which a settlement must seek at all costs to avoid.

At the same time she makes it clear that she does not conceive of applied knowledge in any narrowly utilitarian sense. What she has in mind is the use of knowledge to enrich the lives of people to whom the traditional advantages have been denied; and, conversely, the use of the human environment as a test of knowledge itself. Following William James and John Dewey, Jane Addams believed that the validity of an idea could not be divorced from its consequences. Thus the validity of the theory of democracy—to give an example that was always in the forefront of her consciousness—could be ascertained only by observing how the theory worked out in practice, at the neighborhood level. It is this proposition that Miss Addams sought to capture in the somewhat mystifying definition of the settlement as an attempt "to express the meaning of life in terms of life itself" (see p. 187).

The word "settlement," which we have borrowed from London, is apt to grate a little upon American ears. It is not, after all, so long ago that Americans who settled were those who had adventured into a new country, where they were pioneers in the midst of difficult surroundings. The word still implies migrating from one condition of life to another totally unlike it, and against this implication the resident of an American settlement takes alarm.

We do not like to acknowledge that Americans are divided into "two nations," as her prime minister once admitted of England. We are not willing, openly and professedly, to assume

---

From Jane Addams, "A Function of the Social Settlement," *Annals of the American Academy of Political and Social Science*, XIII (May 1899), 323–355.

that American citizens are broken up into classes, even if we make that assumption the preface to a plea that the superior class has duties to the inferior. Our democracy is still our most precious possession, and we do well to resent any inroads upon it, even although they may be made in the name of philanthropy.

And yet because of this very democracy, superior privileges carry with them a certain sense of embarrassment, founded on the suspicion that intellectual and moral superiority too often rest upon economic props which are, after all, matters of accident, and that for an increasing number of young people the only possible way to be comfortable in the possession of those privileges, which result from educational advantages, is in an effort to make common that which was special and aristocratic. Added to this altruistic compunction one may easily discover a selfish suspicion that advantages thus held apart slowly crumble in their napkins, and are not worth having.

The American settlement, perhaps, has represented not so much a sense of duty of the privileged toward the unprivileged, of the "haves" to the "have nots," to borrow Canon Barnett's phrase, as a desire to equalize through social effort those results which superior opportunity may have given the possessor.

The settlement, however, certainly represents more than compunctions. Otherwise it would be but "the monastery of the nineteenth century," as it is indeed sometimes called, substituting the anodyne of work for that of contemplation, but still the old attempt to seek individual escape from the common misery through the solace of healing.

If this were the basis of the settlement, there would no longer be need of it when society had become reconstructed to the point of affording equal opportunity for all, and it would still be at the bottom a philanthropy, although expressed in social and democratic terms. There is, however, a sterner and more enduring aspect of the settlement which this paper would attempt to present.

It is frequently stated that the most pressing problem of modern life is that of a reconstruction and a reorganization of the knowledge which we possess; that we are at last struggling to realize in terms of life all that has been discovered and absorbed, to make it over into healthy and direct expressions of free living. Dr. John Dewey, of the University of Chicago, has written: "Knowledge is no longer its own justification, the interest in it has at last transferred itself from accumulation and verification to its application to life." And he adds: "When a theory of knowledge forgets that its value rests in solving the problem out of which it has arisen, that of securing a method of action, knowledge begins to cumber the ground. It is a luxury, and becomes a social nuisance and disturber."

We may quote further from Professor [William] James, of Harvard University, who recently said in an address before the Philosophical Union of the University of California: "Beliefs, in short, are really rules of action, and the whole function of thinking is but one step in the production of habits of action," or "the ultimate test for us of what a truth means is indeed the conduct it dictates or inspires."

Having thus the support of two philosophers, let us assume that the dominating interest in knowledge has become its use, the conditions under which, and ways in which it may be most effectively employed in human conduct; and that at last certain people have consciously formed themselves into groups for the express purpose of effective application. These groups which are called settlements have naturally sought the spots where the dearth of this applied knowledge was most obvious, the depressed quarters of great cities. They gravitate to these spots, not with the object of finding clinical material, not to found "sociological laboratories," not, indeed, with the analytical motive at all, but rather in a reaction from that motive, with a desire to use synthetically and directly whatever knowledge they, as a group, may possess, to test its validity and to discover the conditions under which this knowledge may be employed.

That, just as groups of men, for hundreds of years, have organized themselves into colleges, for the purpose of handing on and disseminating knowledge already accumulated, and as other groups have been organized into seminars and universities, for the purpose of research and the extension of the bounds of knowledge, so at last groups have been consciously formed for the purpose of the application of knowledge to life. This third attempt also would claim for itself the enthusiasm and advantage of collective living. It has become to be a group of people who share their methods, and who mean to make experience continuous beyond the individual. It may be urged that this function of application has always been undertaken by individuals and unconscious groups. This is doubtless true, just as much classic learning has always been disseminated outside the colleges, and just as some of the most notable discoveries of pure science have been made outside of the universities. Still both these institutions do in the main accomplish the bulk of the disseminating, and the discovering; and it is upon the same basis that the third group may establish its value.

The ideal and developed settlement would attempt to test the value of human knowledge by action, and realization, quite as the complete and ideal university would concern itself with the discovery of knowledge in all branches. The settlement stands for application as opposed to research; for emotion as opposed to abstraction, for universal interest as opposed to specialization. This certainly claims too much, absurdly too much, for a settlement, in the light of its achievements, but perhaps not in the light of its possibilities.

This, then, will be my definition of the settlement: that it is an attempt to express the meaning of life in terms of life itself, in forms of activity. There is no doubt that the deed often reveals when the idea does not, just as art makes us understand

and feel what might be incomprehensible and inexpressible in the form of an argument. And as the artist tests the success of his art when the recipient feels that he knew the thing before, but had not been able to express it, so the settlement, when it attempts to reveal and apply knowledge, deems its results practicable, when it has made knowledge available which before was abstract, when through use, it has made common that knowledge which was partial before, because it could only be apprehended by the intellect.

The chief characteristic of art lies in freeing the individual from a sense of separation and isolation in his emotional experience, and has usually been accomplished through painting, writing and singing; but this does not make it in the least impossible that it is now being tried, self-consciously and most bunglingly we will all admit, in terms of life itself.

A settlement brings to its aid all possible methods to reveal and make common its conception of life. All those arts and devices which express kindly relation from man to man, from charitable effort to the most specialized social intercourse, are constantly tried. There is the historic statement, the literary presentation, the fellowship which comes when great questions are studied with the hope of modifying actual conditions, the putting forward of the essential that the trivial may appear unimportant, as it is, the attempt to select the more typical and enduring forms of social life, and to eliminate, as far as possible, the irrelevant things which crowd into actual living. There are so-called art exhibits, concerts, dramatic representations, every possible device to make operative on the life around it, the conception of life which the settlement group holds. The demonstration is made not by reason, but by life itself. There must, of course, be a certain talent for conduct and unremitting care lest there grow to be a divergence between theory and living, for however embarrassing this divergence may prove in other situations, in a settlement the artist throws away his tools as soon as this thing happens. He is constantly transmitting by means of his human activity, his notion of life to others. He hopes to produce a sense of infection which may ultimately result in identity of interest. . . .

. . . The phrase "applied knowledge" or science has so long been used in connection with polytechnic schools that it may be well to explain that I am using it in a broader sense. These schools have applied science primarily for professional ends. They are not so commercial, but they may easily become quite as specialized in their departments as the chemical laboratories attached to certain large manufacturing concerns. In the early days of Johns Hopkins University, one of the men in the biological department invented a contrivance which produced a very great improvement in the oyster raft at that time in use in the Chesapeake Bay. For months afterward, in all the commencement orations and other occasions when "prominent citizens" were invited to speak, this oyster raft was held up as the great contribution of the University to the commercial interest of the city, and as a justification of the University's existence, much to the mortification of the poor inventor. This . . . is an excellent example of what I do not mean.

The application which I have in mind is one which cannot be measured by its money-making value. I have in mind an application to a given neighborhood of the solace of literature, of the uplift of the imagination, and of the historic consciousness which gives its possessor a sense of connection with the men of the past who have thought and acted, an application of the stern mandates of science, not only to the conditions of sewers and the care of alleys, but to the methods of life and thought; the application of the metaphysic not only to the speculations of the philosopher, but to the events of the passing moment; the application of the moral code to the material life, the transforming of the economic relation into an ethical relation until the sense that religion itself embraces all relations, including the ungodly industrial relation, has become common property.

An ideal settlement would have no more regard for the "commercial" than would the most scientific of German seminars. The word application must be taken quite aside from its commercial or professional sense.

In this business of application, however, a settlement finds itself tending not only to make common those good things which before were partial and remote, but it finds itself challenging and testing by standards of moral democracy those things which it before regarded as good, if they could but be universal, and it sometimes finds that the so-called good things will not endure this test of being universalized. This may be illustrated by various good things. We may take first the so-called fine arts.

Let us consider the experience of a resident of a settlement who cares a great deal for that aspect and history of life, which has been portrayed in the fine arts. For years she has had classes studying through photographs and lectures the marbles of Greece, the paintings, the renaissance of Italy and the Gothic architecture of mediaeval Europe. She has brought into the lives of scores of people a quality of enjoyment, a revelation of experience which they never knew before. Some of them buy photographs to hang in their own houses, a public school art society is started, schoolroom walls are tinted and hung with copies of the best masters; so that in the end hundreds of people have grown familiar with the names of artists, and with conceptions of life which were hidden from them before. Some of these young women were they students of a freshwater college could successfully pass an examination in the "History of Art." The studio of Hull House is well filled with young men and women who successfully copy casts and paint accurately what they see around them, and several of them have been admitted to the Chicago Art Institute upon competitive scholarships. Now, the first of these achievements would certainly satisfy the average college teacher whose business it is faithfully to transmit the accumulations of knowledge upon a given subject, and, of course, if possible, to add to the sum total of that knowledge in the matter of arrangement or discovery. The second achievement would certainly satisfy the ordinary philanthropic intent, which is to give to others the good which it possesses. But a settlement would have little vitality if it were satisfied with either of these achievements, and would at once limit its scope to that of the school on the one hand, or that of philanthropy on the other. And a settlement is neither a school nor a philanthropy, nor yet a philanthropic school or a scholarly philanthropy.

A settlement looks about among its neighbors and finds a complete absence of art. It sees people working laboriously without that natural solace of labor which art gives; they have no opportunity of expressing their own thoughts to their fellows by means of that labor. It finds the ambitious members of the neighborhood over-anxious and hurried. Wrapping up bars of soap in pieces of paper might at least give the pleasure of accuracy and repetition if it could be done at leisure but, when paid for by the piece, speed is the sole requirement, and the last suggestion of human interest has been taken away. The settlement soon discovers how impossible it is to put a fringe of art on the end of a day thus spent. It is not only bad pedagogics, but is an impossible undertaking, to appeal to a sense of beauty and order which has been crushed by years of ugly and disorderly work. May I relate an experience of a friend of Hull House, who took a party of visitors to the Art Institute of Chicago? In a prominent place upon that excellent building there have been carved in good stone, and with some degree of skill, several fine, large skulls of oxen. The bulk of the settlement party had no armor of erudition with which to protect themselves against such hideousness, and the leader of the party carefully explained that in Greece, after a sacrifice was made, skulls of the animals were hung upon the temples. But when he came to tell why they were upon the Art Institute of Chicago, he found his discourse going lame. That they were once religious symbols charged with meaning, was hardly a sufficient defence. They struck no response, certainly gave no delight nor sense of infection to the bewildered group who stood in front of them. It may be well to say in passing that this group were too unsophisticated to take great pride in the mere fact that they knew what this meant, as a club in search of culture would certainly have done. In his chagrin the Hull House friend found himself reflecting that the sacrifices, after all, did represent brotherhood and he made an attempt to compare them with the present symbols of brotherhood which are found upon the engraved charters hanging upon those walls which shelter the meetings of labor organizations. These charters make a sincere attempt to express the conviction of brotherhood, yet they have but the crudest symbolic representation, two hands clasping each other. It is not only that the print is cheap, but the hands are badly drawn and badly modeled; they express no tenderness nor firmness, and are done without any interpretive skill. The hands upon the old-fashioned tombstones which indicated a ghostly farewell might be interchanged with this pair of hands which indicate vital standing together, and no one would detect the difference. It occurred to this Hull House friend, with a sense of shame and chagrin, that the artists of Chicago had been recreant to their trust, that they had been so caught by a spirit of imitation that they slavishly represented the symbols of animal sacrifice which no longer existed, and kept away from a great human movement, which in America at least, has not yet found artistic expression. If the skulls had been merely an obsolete symbol of the brotherhood which had survived and developed its own artistic symbols, they might easily have been made intelligible and full of meaning. The experience of the resident who teaches the history of art, of the good friend who is ashamed of the lack of democracy and interpretive power among modern artists, added to many other bits of experience and emotion has resulted in the establishment of a Chicago Arts and Crafts

Society, which was founded at Hull House more than a year ago. This society has developed an amazing vitality of its own. And perhaps a quotation from its constitution will show its trend:

"To consider the present state of the factories and the workmen therein, and to devise lines of development which shall retain the machine in so far as it relieves the workmen from drudgery, and tends to perfect his product but which shall insist that the machine be no longer allowed to dominate the workman and reduce his production into a mechanical distortion."

The Chicago Arts and Crafts Society has challenged the present condition and motive of art. Its protest is certainly feeble and may be ineffective, but it is at least genuine and vital. Under the direction of several of its enthusiastic members a shop has been opened at Hull House where articles are designed and made. It is not merely a school where people are taught and then sent forth to use their teaching in art according to their individual initiative and opportunity, but where those who have been carefully trained and taught may remain, to express the best they may in wood or metal. A settlement would avoid the always getting ready for life which seems to dog the school, and would begin with however small a group to really accomplish and to live.[1]

This may indeed bring us quite naturally to the attitude of the settlement toward the organized education with which it is brought in contact, the two forms of organization being naturally the public school and university extension lectures.

---

[1] All of us who have been through the old-fashioned school and college can remember the tedium and confusion of always getting ready for something, of preparing for the life which was to follow school. We may remember how it affected our moral natures as well. We were in a hurry now, but we would be more leisurely and kindly when we finished school. We came to have a firm belief that a new and strong moral nature would be given to us at the time we received our diplomas; and this attitude of preparation is easily carried over into life beyond the school.

The resident finds the use of the public school constantly limited because it occupies such an isolated place in the community. The school board and the teachers have insensibly assumed that they have to do exclusively with children, or a few adult evening classes, only in certain settled directions. The newly arrived South Italian peasants who come to the night schools are thoroughly ill-adjusted to all their surroundings. To change suddenly from picking olives to sewer extension is certainly a bewildering experience. They have not yet obtained control of their powers for the performance of even the humblest social service, and have no chance to realize within themselves the social relation of that service which they are performing. Feeling this vaguely perhaps, but very strongly as only a dull peasant mind can feel, they go to the night schools in search of education. They are taught to read and write concerning small natural objects, on the assumption that the undeveloped intellect works best with insects and tiny animals, and they patiently accept this uninteresting information because they expect "education" to be dull and hard. Never for an instant are their own problems of living in the midst of unfamiliar surroundings even touched upon. There seems to be a belief among educators that it is not possible for the mass of mankind to have experiences which are of themselves worth anything, and that accordingly, if a neighborhood is to receive valuable ideas at all, they must be brought in from the outside, and almost exclusively in the form of books. Such scepticism regarding the possibilities of human nature as has often been pointed out results in equipping even the youngest children with the tools of reading and writing, but gives them no real participation in the industrial and social life with which they come in contact.

The residents in a settlement know that for most of their small neighbors life will be spent in handling material things either in manufacturing or commercial processes, and yet little is done to unfold the fascinating history of industrial evolution or to illuminate for them the materials among which they will live. The settlement sees boys constantly leave school to enter the factory at fourteen or fifteen without either of the requirements involved in a social life, on the one hand "without a sense of the resources already accumulated," and on the other "without the individual ability to respond to those resources."

If it is one function of a settlement to hold a clue as to what to select and what to eliminate in the business of living, it would bring the same charge of overwrought detail against the university extension lectures. A course of lectures in astronomy, illustrated by "stereopticon slides," will attract a large audience the first week who hope to hear of the wonders of the heavens, and the relation of our earth thereto, but instead of that they are treated to spectrum analyses of star dust, or the latest theories concerning the milky way. The habit of research and the desire to say the latest word upon any subject overcoming any sympathetic understanding of his audience which the lecturer might otherwise develop.

The teachers in the night schools near Hull House struggle with Greeks and Armenians, with Bohemians and Italians, and many another nationality. I once suggested to a professor of anthropology in a neighboring university that he deliver a lecture to these bewildered teachers upon simple race characteristics and, if possible, give them some interest in their pupils, and some other attitude than that all persons who do not speak English are ignorant. The professor kindly consented to do this, but when the time came frankly acknowledged that he could not do it—that he had no information available for such a talk. I was disappointed, of course, and a little chagrined when, during the winter, three of his pupils came to me at different times, anxiously inquiring if I could not put them on the track of people who had six toes, or whose relatives had been possessed of six toes. It was inevitable that the old charge should occur to me, that the best trained scientists are inclined to give themselves over to an idle thirst for knowledge which lacks any relation to human life, and leave to the charlatans the task of teaching those things which deeply concern the welfare of mankind.

Tolstoy points out that the mass of men get their intellectual food from the abortive outcasts of science, who provide millions of books, pictures and shows, not to instruct and guide, but for the sake of their own profit and gain, while the real student too often stays in a laboratory, occupied in a mysterious activity called science. He does not even know what is required by the workingmen. He has quite forgotten their mode of life, their views of things and their language. Tolstoy claims that the student has lost sight of the fact that it is his duty, not to study and depict, but to serve. This is asking a great deal from one man, or even from one institution. It may be necessary that the university be supplemented by the settlement, or something answering thereto; but let the settlement people recognize the value of their own calling, and see to it that the university does not swallow the settlement, and turn it into one more laboratory: another place in which to analyze and depict, to observe and record. A settlement which performs but this function is merely an imitative and unendowed university, as a settlement which gives all its energies to classes and lectures and athletics is merely an imitative college. We ourselves may have given over attending classes and may be bored by lectures, but to still insist that working people shall have them is to take the priggish attitude we sometimes allow ourselves toward children, when we hold up rigid moral standards to them, although permitting ourselves a greater latitude. If without really testing the value of mental pabulum, we may assume it is nutritious and good for working people, because some one once assumed that it was good for us, we throw away the prerogative of a settlement, and fall into the rigidity of the conventional teacher.

The most popular lectures we ever had at Hull House were a series of twelve upon organic evolution, but we caught the man when he was but a university instructor, and his mind was still eager over the marvel of it all. Encouraged by this success we followed the course with other lectures in science, only to find our audience annihilated by men who spoke with dryness of manner and with the same terminology which they used in the class room.

A settlement might bring the same charge against university extension as against the public schools, that it is bookish and remote. Simple people want the large and vital—they are still in the tribal stage of knowledge, so to speak. It is not that simple people like to hear about little things; they want to hear about great things, simply told. We remember that the early nomads did not study the blades of grass at their feet, but the stars above their heads—although commercially considered, the study of grass would have been much more profitable.

These experiences would seem to testify that there is too much analysis in our thought, as there is too much anarchy in our action. Perhaps no one is following up this clue so energetically as Professor Patrick Geddes in Edinburgh, who is attempting, not only to graphically visualize a synthesis, an encyclopedia of orderly knowledge, but in his own words—is endeavoring "to outline a correspondingly detailed synergy of orderly actions." The "regional survey" of knowledge which he takes from his outlook tower would thus pass into "regional activity."

So far as my experience goes a settlement finds itself curiously more companionable with the state and national bureaus in their efforts in collecting information and analyzing the situation, than it does with university efforts. This may possibly be traced to the fact that the data is accumulated by the bureaus on the assumption that it will finally become the basis for legislation, and is thus in the line of applicability. The settlements from the first have done more or less work under the direction of the bureaus. The head of a federal department quite recently begged a settlement to transform into readable matter a certain mass of material which had been carefully collected into tables and statistics. He hoped to make a connection between the information concerning diet and sanitary conditions, and the tenement house people who sadly needed this information. The head of the bureau said quite simply that he hoped that the settlements could accomplish this, not realizing that to put information into readable form is not nearly enough. It is to confuse a simple statement of knowledge with its application.

Permit me to illustrate from a group of Italian women who bring their underdeveloped children several times a week to Hull House for sanitary treatment, under the direction of a physician. It has been possible to teach some of these women to feed their children oatmeal instead of tea-soaked bread, but it has been done, not by statement at all but by a series of gay little Sunday morning breakfasts given to a group of them in the Hull House nursery. A nutritious diet was thus substituted for an inferior one by a social method. At the same time it was found that certain of the women hung bags of salt about their children's necks, to keep off the evil eye, which was supposed to give the children crooked legs at first, and in the end to cause them to waste away. The salt bags gradually disappeared under the influence of baths and cod liver oil. In short, rachitis was skillfully arrested, and without mention that disease was caused not by evil eye but by lack of cleanliness and nutrition, and without passing through the intermediate belief that disease was sent by Providence, the women form a little centre for the intelligent care of children, which is making itself felt in the Italian colony. Knowledge was applied in both cases, but scarcely as the statistician would have applied it.

We recall that the first colleges of the Anglo-Saxon race were established to educate religious teachers. For a long time it was considered the mission of the educated to prepare the mass of the people for the life beyond the grave. Knowledge dealt largely in theology, but it was ultimately to be applied, and the test of the successful graduate, after all, was not his learning, but his power to save souls. As the college changed from teaching theology to teaching secular knowledge the test of its success should have shifted from the power to save men's souls to the power to adjust them in healthful relations to nature and their fellow men. But the college failed to do this, and made the test of its success the mere collecting and disseminating of knowledge, elevating the means into an end and falling in love with its own achievement. The application of secular knowledge need be no more commercial and so-called practical than was the minister's when he applied his theology to the delicate problems of the human soul. This attempt at application on the part of the settlements may be, in fact, an apprehension of the situation.

It would be a curious result if this word "applied science," which the scholar has always been afraid of, lest it lead him into commercial influences, should have in it the salt of saving power, to rescue scholarship from the function of accumulating and transmitting to the higher and freer one of directing human life.

Recognizing the full risk of making an absurd, and as yet totally unsubstantiated claim, I would still express the belief that the settlement has made a genuine contribution in this direction by its effort to apply knowledge to life, to express life itself in terms of life. . . .

18. *The Second Twenty Years at Hull-House*

1930

The Second Twenty Years at Hull-House, from which the following chapter is taken, is rambling and diffuse in style and generally inferior to Jane Addams' earlier works. The chapter on education contains little in the way of theory that Jane Addams had not said better in "A Function of the Social Settlement," but it does contain a good deal of illustrative material that helps to clarify the theory. It also makes clear, as even the preceding essay does not, the breadth of Jane Addams' concept of education. Education, here, is any experience that tends to unite people instead of dividing them. Education is shared experience. Current events are educative because people experience them directly, but also because they experience them collectively; and such experience beomes a demonstration, a reminder, of their common humanity.

The point might be restated more concretely. Only when a social problem becomes national in scope, only when it impresses itself on the public consciousness as a whole, is it susceptible of solution. Only then do the slogans of democracy encounter the practical test of common experience. Thus the Negro problem, as long as it remained purely a Southern problem, presented itself to the rest of the nation as an abstraction, a question of rights. Only when Negroes began to move to the cities of the North, after the First World War, could people begin to understand the cultural consequences of racial segregation. Only then could they see, for instance, the degree to which the Negroes, in comparison with other minorities, had been culturally impoverished by the loss of their own traditions, on the one hand, and their isolation from American society, on the other. Only then, in short, could the abstract issue of injustice take on tangible meaning.

But as Miss Addams herself admits, "mere information is not enough." It needs to be "constantly supplemented"—by what, she does not say. It is the area beyond which information is not enough that remains obscure, in her analysis of the Negro problem and in her analysis of education in general. Jane Addams believed—in common with many progressives—that the substitution of educative controls for outright coercion was precisely the mark of progressive societies, and she did not linger very long over the possibility that such issues as the Negro question might in the long run have to be settled by a resort to some kind of force. History—a superficial reading of history—seemed to bear out the view that social progress tended to eliminate the need for force. Dueling had given way to courts of law; the gallows were no longer a public amusement. What had really happened, however, was not that coercion had been eliminated but that crude methods of social control had given way to more subtle ones. Education itself was a case in point. The birch rod had disappeared from the common schools, but that was in part because progressive educators had taken control of the schools. In American society as a whole, they enjoyed no such power. Even in the school system, the progressives would soon be replaced by educational bureaucrats who used progressive methods for conservative ends—to induce conformity to the "American way of life." And in society at large, the progressives were opposed from the start by powerful interests that could not simply be educated into a more altruistic point of view. The leap from the school and the settlement to the reform of the social structure as a whole was a much greater leap than the progressives imagined. The techniques that worked so well in a controllable environment, when projected into an environment that could not so easily be controlled —if it could be controlled at all—proved quite inadequate to the emergencies that so shortly overwhelmed not only the United States but the entire Western world.

The settlements early founded their educational theories upon a conviction that in every social grade and class in the whole circle of genuine occupations there are mature men and women of moral purpose and specialized knowledge, who because they have become efficient unto life, may contribute an enrichment to the pattern of human culture. We knew that much of this possible enrichment was lost because he who would incorporate these experiences into the common heritage must constantly depend upon fresh knowledge and must further be equipped with a wide and familiar acquaintance with the human spirit and its productions. The difficulties in-

Reprinted with the permission of The Macmillan Co. from *The Second Twenty Years at Hull-House* by Jane Addams, pp. 380–386, 396–413. Copyright 1930 by The Macmillan Co., renewed 1940 by John A. Britain.

volved would be almost insurmountable but that life has a curious trick of suddenly regarding as a living moral issue, vital and unappeasable, some old outworn theme which has been kicked about for years as mere controversial material. The newly moralized issue, almost as if by accident, suddenly takes fire and sets whole communities in a blaze, lighting up human relationships and public duty with new meaning. The event suddenly transforms abstract social idealism into violent political demands, entangling itself with the widest human aspiration.

When that blaze actually starts, when the theme is heated, molten as it were with human passion and desire, the settlement can best use it in its unending effort to make culture and the issue of things go together. From time to time during the last twenty years, when such a blaze did start it seemed for the moment that the peculiar aspect of the world which marks each age for what it is—the summary of its experiences, knowledge and affections, in which are found the very roots of its social existence was fused into a glowing whole. At such a moment, it seemed possible to educate the entire community by a wonderful unification of effort and if the community had been able to command open discussion and a full expression of honest opinion the educational opportunity would have been incomparable.

As an example of sudden interest, resulting in widespread education upon a given theme, the trial at Dayton, Tennessee, upon the general subject of the theory of evolution, forms a striking example.[1]

---

[1] In 1925 the state of Tennessee passed a law forbidding any teacher "to teach . . . that man has descended from a lower order of animals." With the backing of the American Civil Liberties Union, John T. Scopes, a biology teacher in Dayton, defied the law, and the resulting trial provided a forum for the opponents of the legislation. Clarence Darrow defended Scopes; William Jennings Bryan, the people of Tennessee. Scopes was found guilty and fined $100. The state supreme court later rescinded the fine on a legal technicality [Ed.].

I had been in England the summer of the trial and had been so often challenged as to our situation in contrast to theirs, because Huxley and Dean Wace presided over by Bishop Wilberforce had publicly discussed the so-called conflict between science and religion in an atmosphere of scholarly tolerance. I had tried to point out that the United States could doubtless at any moment stage a debate between a polished churchman and a kindly scientist, but that such a debate would leave the situation very much where it was before; that what made the Tennessee incident so significant was the fact that legislative action had been taken against the teaching of the theory of evolution in tax-supported schools, by people who had a chance to express their actual desires through their government representatives. I was quite sure that Englishmen could be found in remote quarters of the British Isles who believed exactly what these Tennessee mountaineers believed in regard to the acts of creation; thousands of them had received their education, as had these Americans, through those who had expounded the "Book" as a sole and abiding authority. Such men in England were as totally untouched by scholarly debates as were the Tennessee mountaineers; there was this difference, however, that the latter found self-expression through the processes of local government and eagerly determined what their children should be taught upon the subject that they regarded as the most important in the world.

During the trial the situation was so sharply defined that it brought before the entire country a public discussion of fundamentalism versus evolution. That such a situation arose was in one sense a demonstration of our democratic purpose, which is, after all, an attempt at self-expression for each man. Democracy believes that the man at the bottom may realize his aim only through an unfolding of his own being, and that he must have an efficacious share in the regulation of his own life. While there was no doubt that the overwhelming public opinion concerning the Tennessee trial was on the side of liberality both in politics and religion, the group of so-called narrow-minded men had made their own contribution to our national education. In the first place, they had asserted the actuality of religion. It is always difficult to convince youth that reality reaches upward as well as outward, and that the higher planes of life contain anything but chilly sentiments. The educator dealing with religious topics often finds that young people receive his statements with polite attention, but when it comes to action, they who are fretting with impatience to throw themselves into the stream of life and to become a part of its fast-flowing current, carefully imitate the really desirable world inhabited by successful men of affairs. But suddenly there came from a group of remote mountaineers a demonstration of a vivid and sustained interest in matters of religion, resulting in a sharp clash of doctrine between themselves and thousands of our fellow citizens, who all hung upon the issues of the trial with avid interest.

It was at times almost comic to hear the "hard-boiled" city youth in his bewilderment talk about the situation. In the first place, modern economics had taught him—or he thought that it had—that a man was abjectly dependent upon the material world about him and must succumb to the iron clamp which industry imposes upon life; moreover, the youth himself gravely asserted that man's very freedom, morality and progress is determined by the material conditions which surround him and he had bodily taken over this theory into ethics and philosophy. He quoted those students of the social order who in what they considered the scientific spirit had collected and arranged data, to demonstrate the sole reaction of economic forces upon human life. These young people had for the most part lightly disregarded all teleological considerations, as they had long before renounced the theological explanations of a final cause. And yet many of them were secretly glad of this opportunity for discussion with old Jewish fathers who had never ceased to attest to the life of the spirit and who on their side caught their first glimpse in those sons hotly defending the theory of evolution, of the same zeal which they and their fathers had expended upon religion. These same young men so devoted to economic determinism as a theory of life had been already somewhat disconcerted by a recent movement in psychiatry with the emphasis upon the emotional and subconscious life versus the exclusive response to environmental stimuli. But if they were startled they were also much interested in this ardent inner life which was apparently to be found among so many different types of people who were everywhere responding to the blaze of interest started in Tennessee.

The repercussions of the trial were the more interesting because the incident brought into the circle of their discussion a large number of people who had hitherto been quite outside their zone of interest. These remote farmers were isolated, save on the occasional Sundays when a circuit rider came to preach, by their discouraging occupation of extracting a living from a rock-bound soil. Nothing could have been further from the experiences and mental processes of the intelligentsia of a cosmopolitan city than these mountaineers, nothing more diverse than the two methods of approach to the time-old question of the origin of man. Only a molten current event could have accomplished a simultaneous discussion upon the same theme by these two bodies of people.

Although these young Chicago intelligentsia I have been describing lived among colonies of immigrants, each one with its own history and conscious religious background, and had moreover naturally been interested in the normative sciences, they had known little about such descendants of early Americans so Anglo-Saxon and "Nordic" in background that they still had remnants of Elizabethan English in their daily speech. It was interesting to hear these young men talk of the effects of isolation whether the group were encompassed by mountains or by the invisible boundaries of a ghetto. . . .

Another instance of education through the discussion of current social developments, took place in regard to the problem of race relations when the industrial needs of war-time and the immigration restriction following the war, resulted in a great increase of Negroes in the urban populations throughout the country. This was brought to a head in Chicago as in many other places by the question of housing, when real estate values became confused as always with the subject of segregation. Whatever may be the practical solution it is still true that a complete segregation of the Negro in definite parts of the city, tends in itself to put him outside the immediate action of that imperceptible but powerful social control which influences the rest of the population. Those inherited resources of civilization which are embodied in custom and kindly intercourse, make more for social restraint than does legal enactment itself.

One could easily illustrate this lack of inherited control by comparing the experience of a group of colored girls with those of a group representing the daughters of Italian immigrants or of any other South European peoples. The Italian girls very much enjoy the novelty of factory work, the opportunity to earn money and to dress as Americans do, but only very gradually do they obtain freedom in the direction of their own social affairs. Italian fathers consider it a point of honor that their daughters shall not be alone upon the street after dark, and only slowly modify their social traditions. The fathers of colored girls, on the other hand, are quite without those traditions, and fail to give their daughters the resulting protection. If colored girls yield more easily to the temptations of a city than the Italian girls do, who shall say how far the lack of social restraint is responsible for it? The Italian parents represent the social traditions which have been worked out during centuries and although such customs often become a deterrent to progress through the very bigotry of their adherents, nevertheless it is largely through a modification of these customs and manners that alien groups are assimilated into American life. The civilizations in Africa are even older than those in

Italy and naturally tribal life everywhere has its own traditions and taboos which control the relations between the sexes and between parents and children. But of course these were broken up during the period of chattel slavery for very seldom were family ties permitted to stand in the way of profitable slave sales. It was inevitable that the traditions were lost and that customs had to be built up anew. It gives an American community less justification for withholding from a colony of colored people those restraints and customs which can only be communicated through social understanding. Another result of race antagonism is the readiness to irritation which inevitably results when one race is forced to demand as a right from the other those things which should be accorded as a courtesy. Every chance meeting between representatives of the two races is easily characterized either by insolence or arrogance. To the friction of city life and the complications of modern intercourse is added this primitive race animosity.

Happily in the midst of this current event discussion, there came to Chicago a distinguished Negro singer, various plays concerning colored people which portrayed something of that inner life upon which the kinship of races is founded and the Race Relations Committee of the Chicago Woman's Club arranged for a week of exhibits at the Art Institute and for recitals and lectures by well-known artists, poets and scholars. We have no exact knowledge of what has been and is being lost by the denial of free expression on the part of the Negro, it is difficult even to estimate it. One can easily suggest the sense of humor, unique and spontaneous, so different from the wit of the Yankee or the inimitable story telling prized in the South; the natural use of rhythm and onomatopoeia which is now so often travestied in the grotesqueness of long words: the use of varied colors which makes it natural perhaps that the only scientific study made in America of the use of common clay as coloring material in the building of simple houses should have been done by a Negro so that we may hope some day to rival the pinks, yellows and blues of those European houses which afford the traveler such perpetual joy.

There is one exception to this lack of recognition, in the admiration of those melodies which we have learned to call the only American folk-songs and which have become the basis of the Negroes' contribution to American music. Perhaps because an oppressed people have always been sustained by their dreams the spirituals became the support of their failing spirits. It may be that the wish-fulfillment was too slowly transferred to actual life but certainly an ever-increasing respect is coming from the Negroes' own achievements in the arts. Through their plays they have found the stimulus for conduct in the very field where it was possible to make the initial step toward social efficiency. It may be significant that the curtain falls on an advanced play like "Porgy" while the Negroes of Catfish Row are singing, "I'm on my way."

But even though fine demonstrations have been made by smaller groups of cultivated Negroes, we cannot truthfully say, however much we should like to do so, that recognition lies with the colored man himself and that the worthy will be worthily received. To make even the existing degree of recognition more general requires first of all a modicum of leisure and freedom from grinding poverty. An investigation made in 1929 by the Woman's Bureau of the Department of Labor gives an analysis of *Colored Women in Industry* from studies made in fifteen states. Their earnings were found to be far below the earnings of most white women, although they too must somehow meet the expenses of food, shelter and clothing. A great American industrialist had said, almost at the moment of the publication of the report, "American industry must for the future be based not on a living wage alone, nor on a saving wage, but on a cultural wage." No one needs the benefit of this dictum more than the ambitious Negro.

Because we are no longer stirred as the Abolitionists were, to remove fetters, to prevent cruelty, to lead the humblest to the banquet of civilization, we have allowed ourselves to become indifferent to the gravest situation in our American life. The abolitionists grappled with an evil intrenched since the beginning of recorded history and it seems at moments that we are not even preserving what was so hardly won. To continually suspect, suppress or fear any large group in a community must finally result in a loss of enthusiasm for that type of government which gives free play to the self-development of a majority of its citizens. It means an enormous loss of capacity to the nation when great ranges of human life are hedged about with antagonism. We forget that whatever is spontaneous in a people, in an individual, a class or a nation, is always a source of life.

In the world-wide effort to relieve the colored races from the odium and discrimination which white races have placed upon them, no man living on the planet today has done more than has Mahatma Gandhi, first in South Africa in the struggle for civil rights against the Transvaal Government, which absorbed his energy for almost twenty years, and later in the undertaking, the most difficult of all, directed against customs intrenched in the religious traditions of India, to free the fifty million untouchables or pariahs, who are subject to many harsh rules of segregation. While the differences of race between the Brahmans and Pariahs is not the sole basis of the insupportable division between them, the situation is essentially the same as that which faces any effort to break down barriers of race or caste. Gandhi's most striking success in his protest against untouchability was the opening of the roads, which because they passed near the temples were forbidden to the Pariahs. His followers faced a cordon of police for twelve hours every day during a year and four months before the orthodox Brahmans yielded. Such devotion opened to the untouchables not only that one forbidden road but all the roads that had been forbidden to them in southern India and gave the doctrine of untouchability its severest blow. Such a long and courageous effort may indicate that only sustained moral energy will be able to break through long-established restrictions. Perhaps it is only protests such as these which could offset those protests made in Paris restaurants and elsewhere by Americans whose influence it is said is gradually breaking down the traditional Latin attitude toward race equality. It looks at moments as if we should be late in the movement to abolish race discrimination as we were very late in the abolition of slavery. We were more than thirty years behind England who abolished her colonial slavery in 1832.

We were all very grateful when the Inquiry undertook the study of race relations not by employing a group of experts but by helping people to study effectively their own experiences and desires, although all they may have known about their desire for study was an uneasy feeling on their part that friction was gradually developing between white and colored sections of the community and that something ought to be done about it. The cause of the reported friction may be primarily due to industrial competition or to a housing shortage, or again to the machinations of a small minority of troublemakers. In any case, what is needed is a technique for helping people to find the sore spot and to secure a quick and effective diagnosis.

The Inquiry through its commission on Race Relations has endeavored to find the causes of inter-racial friction in economic competition by interesting groups in different centers to bring to light those factors that make for racial antagonism— whether these are found in the policies of the industries themselves, in the attitudes of their workers or in the traditional racial experiences of the whole community. The committee has discovered that problems of race relations may arise in situations where a group of people regard themselves, or are regarded by others, as racially homogeneous, even where such an assumption does not correspond to scientific reality. Merely to inform people that such and such a group conflict is based upon an ethnological misunderstanding, will not do away either with the conflict or its emotional associations in the minds of those implicated. The entire race situation demonstrates once more that mere information is not enough and that the various research bodies need to be constantly supplemented.

This was something we learned in the early days of Hull-House. We used to say that the settlement had a distinct place in the educational field and we were even bold enough to compare ourselves with universities and colleges. It was the business of the universities, we said, to carry on research, they were committed to an unwearying effort to reduce the black region of ignorance by bringing to light that which would increase the sum total of human knowledge. It was the business of the colleges, broadly speaking, to hand down the knowledge that had thus been accumulated and if they kindled an ardor for truth, each succeeding generation would add to the building of civilization. It was the business of the settlements to do something unlike either of these things. It was the function of the settlements to bring into the circle of knowledge and fuller life, men and women who might otherwise be left outside. Some of these men and women were outside simply because of their ignorance, some of them because they led lives of hard work that narrowed their interests, and others because they were unaware of the possibilities of life and needed a friendly touch to awaken them. The colleges and universities had made a little inner circle of illuminated space beyond which there stretched a region of darkness, and it was the duty of the settlements to draw into the light those who were out of it. It seemed to us that our mission was just as important as that of either the university or the college.

It is easy for young settlements, as it is for all youth, to be boastful. It is easy to say what you are going to do before you have had a chance to try. Our achievement was halting but I still think there was something fine in that youthful statement, and that our contention was well-founded that the man who breaks new soil and makes it ready for the seed, may be quite as useful as the sower himself or even the triumphant harvester. We came rather slowly to the conviction that this could best be done through the use of the current event.

During its first two decades, Hull-House with other American settlements, issued various studies and fact-finding analyses of the city areas with which they were most familiar. The settlements had antedated by three years the first sociological departments in the universities and by ten years the establishment of the first Foundations so that in a sense we were the actual pioneers in field research. We based the value of our efforts not upon any special training, but upon the old belief that he who lives near the life of the poor, he who knows the devastating effects of disease and vice, has at least an unrivaled opportunity to make a genuine contribution to their understanding.

We used to say that it would be easy to throw away that opportunity, either because we shirked intellectual effort, because we lacked courage or because we failed to see our obligations.

These early efforts of the settlements in research, gradually made for a cordial coöperation between the social workers and the university men. The School of Civics and Philanthropy founded by Graham Taylor of the Chicago Commons, with which Julia Lathrop of Hull-House was early associated, after a useful career of twenty years, was taken over by the University of Chicago, and has developed into a graduate school of "Social Service Administration," of which the dean, Edith Abbott, and Sophonisba Breckinridge, long-time residents of Hull-House, are the executives; two other former residents of Hull-House are identified with the studies in social and family welfare carried on at the Northwestern University where Professor Arthur Todd is head of the department in which William B. Bryon is also teaching.

The early companionship between the settlements and the

universities has been described by Charles Beard "as exerting beyond all question a direct and immediate influence on American thinking about industrial questions, and on the course of social practice." It was partly due to the custom of the early setttlements—in Chicago at least this was true of the Chicago Commons and Hull-House—of giving the radicals in the city an opportunity to debate upon a free floor, believing that no one can be really useful in the long and delicate task of social amelioration unless he knows the changes being urged by various bodies of people for a world which they honestly believe to be upon the brink of destruction. The newspapers tended to judge these men as disturbers of the peace and for a long time they unintelligently insisted that because the settlements promoted free discussion, they therefore endorsed what everybody said. They little realized that had we endorsed all these conflicting beliefs we should have been burst asunder as was the chameleon placed upon a piece of plaid.

In one sense it was easier to be patient with the radicals during the first two decades than to prove the thesis which emerged in the third decade of our existence as a sort of settlement creed that the processes of social amelioration are of necessity the results of gradual modification. We learned to act upon a belief that the hoary abominations of society can only be done away with through the "steady effort to accumulate facts and exalt the human will." But because such an undertaking requires the coöperation of many people and because with the best will in the world it is impossible to get the interest of the entire community centered upon any given theme, we gradually discovered that the use of the current event is valuable beyond all other methods of education. In time we came to define a settlement as an institution attempting to learn from life itself in which undertaking we did not hesitate to admit that we encountered many difficulties and failures. But this effort to interpret the contemporaneous situation and to make it usable demanded an ever-widening public who should have a sympathetic understanding of those social problems which are of such moment to all of us. To allow a large number of persons to remain outside the circle of those interests because they have not been given a sense of participation would at last not only cripple our national life but limit our human possibilities.

We had discovered the use of a genuine interest in life itself by accident, in the early days of Hull-House, in such a simple matter as teaching English to our foreign-born neighbors. We were surrounded by a great many Italians in those days when unified Italy was still comparatively new and many of our neighbors had taken part in that great movement for nationalism. In our first Hull-House reading club for foreign-born students we tried to read an English translation of Mazzini's on *The Duties of Man*. It was very good reading but not always easy reading, although a shared interest that is genuine is the best possible basis for a class. When we had finished reading *On The Duties of Man*, the class with much bilingual oratory presented to Hull-House a bust of Mazzini—perhaps in gratitude that the course was over! Hull-House was opened three years before a great massacre occurred at Kishinev, Russia. A large number of Russians of Jewish origin came to this country, and hundreds of them settled in our neighborhood. Partly because of our personal contacts with some of their relatives and partly because of our knowledge of the ability of those who had been persecuted and driven away from their own country, we felt an enormous interest in the whole situation. We were also concerned with the effect upon our national existence of the sudden coming of a large number of persons who might easily be filled with hatred and a spirit of revenge. I read with a group of those Russians a book of Tolstoy's in English translation in which he works out cogently his theory of non-resistance. When I think of that group I have an impression of something very vivid. They had an intense desire to master the English language because they had something very vital to say, and could not say it unless they could find the English words. It is surprising what a stimulus such a situation provides!

I think that our attitude toward the foreign-born was permanently modified by such experiences. We may make foreign birth a handicap to them and to us, or we may make it a very interesting and stimulating factor in their development and ours. There is a theory of culture which contends that when people journeyed on foot or on camels or by other means into a strange part of the world, their contact with the established civilization there produced a curious excitement that often resulted in the creation of a new culture that never had existed before. I believe that we may get, and should get, something of that revivifying and upspringing of culture from our contact with the groups who come to us from foreign countries, and that we can get it in no other way. It implies of course a mutual interest in the life which is being lived in various parts of the globe. The settlement makes a constant effort through books, through the drama and through exhibits, to connect passing experiences with those expressions of permanent values which lie at the basis of world culture. If this is well done, it should heighten the sense of companionship in the neighborhood itself. The Italians have a saying that probably originated with St. Francis that the poor little brethren gathered with us under the Madonna's cloak, keep us warm quite as much as the great blue mantle itself.

Settlements are trying through all these years, to build up a technique, although with only a few scientific generalizations to go upon in order to use the group itself for educational ends. Perhaps the best efforts in this direction have been carried out through the National Federation of Settlements. A national association is driven to find a new technique if its annual meetings are to be in any real sense a conference. Certain enthusiasts for creative discussion, such as the national Y.W.C.A., in their widespread organization of committees, boards, and clubs, have accepted the growing change of basis in modern life from individual to organized activities, and seek ways by which people in group relations shall find the mutual stimulus and enhancement of shared purposes and pooled resources. In such undertakings the settlements inevitably encounter more difficulties than the more homogeneous organizations do, for from the nature of the case settlement activities must respond to the diversity of their clientele.

The settlements have often been accused of scattering their forces; as institutions they are both philanthropic and educational; in their approach to social problems they call now upon the sociologist, now upon the psychiatrist; they seek the services of artists, economists, gymnasts, case-workers, dramatists, trained nurses; one day they beg the anthropologist for a clue to a new immigration, and the next they boast that one of their pupils is playing in the symphony orchestra. In response to the irrefutable charge of weakness in multiform activity, we are accustomed to reply that even so we are not as varied and complex as life itself. I recall my sense of relief the first time I heard a sociologist use the phrase, "vortex causation"; the universities were at last defining the situation and it was possible that they would later enter this inter-related field of personal difficulties, bewildering legal requirements, ill health and conflicting cultures which the settlements find so baffling.

The very recent attempts of several graduate schools to find a methodology applicable to more than one field of science promises to throw light on those problems of frustrated human beings with which a settlement becomes so painfully familiar. In spite of the fact that a large proportion of the children of immigrants avail themselves of the educational opportunities which America offers—in a Hull-House club of twenty-four Russian Jewish boys, all of whose parents were immigrants, eleven have graduated from universities or from professional schools—nevertheless, a neighborhood such as ours contains many men and women who have been left behind. The social relationships in a modern city are hastily made and often superficial. Common sense, the household tradition, the inherited custom, the desultory reading by which so much of life is directed, the stream of advice constantly poured over the radio, break down the restraints long sustained in smaller communities by public opinion, and in the end certain areas of city life seem to be in a state of dire confusion.

I do not believe that throughout America there are any groups more grateful than ours for the Social Science Research Council and its investigations of the scientific aspect of human migrations, broadening into general population studies and for the notable series of reports on international and domestic topics, produced by the Institute of Economics in Washington. All these demonstrate that education should be continued throughout life and should play a leading rôle in the interpretation of contemporaneous developments. Possibly education in a democracy must in the end depend upon action, for raw theory cannot immediately be applied to life without grave results. In addition to the League of Nations Commission upon Intellectual Coöperation with its headquarters in Washington where one of the former Hull-House residents is acting as secretary, all these national research bodies are inevitably carried into the international aspects of their subjects. They demonstrate that each current event in this interrelated world may be the result of a repercussion from any part of the globe, or due to the same impulse manifesting itself in widely separated areas.

Dr. Dewey has told us that the general intelligence is dormant with its communications broken and faint until it possesses the public as its medium. It seems at moments as if we were about to extend indefinitely what we call our public, and that unless it were stretched to world dimensions, the most significant messages of our times might easily escape us.

PART V
PEACE

---

19. *Newer Ideals of Peace*

1907

It is generally agreed that apart from her work in the field of social settlements Jane Addams made her greatest contribution to the cause of peace. Yet the nature of that contribution is easily misunderstood. Jane Addams was not a sentimental pacifist. Nor did she oppose war on religious grounds. She was not a Quaker—and even her Quaker father was not a pacifist. Officially she was a Presbyterian, but in fact her formal affiliations were extremely vague; her closest acquaintances were not even sure whether she believed in a life after death.

She opposed war on the pragmatic grounds that it was a wasteful and ineffective method of solving social problems; that, indeed, it created more problems than it solved. In her first book on the subject, *Newer Ideals of Peace*—the introduction to which is given below—she tried hard to distinguish the modern peace-movement from "the older dovelike ideal," and her services to the peace movement must be judged by the degree to which she succeeded in putting the case for peace on a solid foundation of political and economic theory.

The weakness of the following argument, if anything, is that it is *too* theoretical. It owes too much to an extension of the Darwinian theory of evolution into the social sphere; to the view, reinforced by the writings of men like Jeremy Bentham, that "the

218

subsidence of war was inevitable as society progressed." Jane Addams' pacifism was of a piece with her theory of education. Both rested on the assumption that physical force had ceased to be functional and would therefore disappear. Even so, her pacifism was far more robust than that of most of her contemporaries. The measure of the difference between them was that hers survived the test of war, whereas theirs crumbled at the first hint of crisis.

The following pages present the claims of the newer, more aggressive ideals of peace, as over against the older dovelike ideal. These newer ideals are active and dynamic, and it is believed that if their forces were made really operative upon society, they would, in the end, quite as a natural process, do away with war. The older ideals have required fostering and recruiting, and have been held and promulgated on the basis of a creed. Their propaganda has been carried forward during the last century in nearly all civilized countries by a small body of men who have never ceased to cry out against war and its iniquities and who have preached the doctrines of peace along two great lines. The first has been the appeal to the higher imaginative pity, as it is found in the modern, moralized man. This line has been most effectively followed by two Russians, Count Tolstoy in his earlier writings and Verestchagin[1] in his paintings. With his relentless power of reducing all life to personal experience Count Tolstoy drags us through the campaign of the common soldier in its sordidness and meanness and constant sense of perplexity. We see nothing of the glories we have associated with warfare, but learn of it as it appears to the untutored peasant who goes forth at the mandate of his

---

From Jane Addams, *Newer Ideals of Peace* (New York: The Macmillan Company, 1907), pages 3–5, 7–19, 23–27.

[1] Vasili Vasilievich Verestchagin (1842–1904) was a Russian artist known for his paintings of war, which were frankly designed to arouse opposition to war. He did a series on the Napoleonic campaign in Russia in 1812—the subject also of one of his books. These paintings (1893) are said to have inspired Tolstoy's *War and Peace* [Ed.].

superior to suffer hunger, cold, and death for issues which he does not understand, which, indeed, can have no moral significance to him. Verestchagin covers his canvas with thousands of wretched wounded and neglected dead, with the waste, cruelty, and squalor of war, until he forces us to question whether a moral issue can ever be subserved by such brutal methods.

High and searching as is the preaching of these two great Russians who hold their art of no account save as it serves moral ends, it is still the appeal of dogma, and may be reduced to a command to cease from evil. And when this same line of appeal is presented by less gifted men, it often results in mere sentimentality, totally unenforced by a call to righteousness.

The second line followed by the advocates of peace in all countries has been the appeal to the sense of prudence, and this again has found its ablest exponent in a Russian subject, the economist and banker, Jean de Bloch.[2] He sets forth the cost of warfare with pitiless accuracy, and demonstrates that even the present armed peace is so costly that the burdens of it threaten social revolution in almost every country in Europe. Long before the reader comes to the end of de Bloch's elaborate computation he is ready to cry out on the inanity of the proposition that the only way to secure eternal peace is to waste so much valuable energy and treasure in preparing for war that war becomes impossible. Certainly no theory could be devised which is more cumbersome, more roundabout, more extravagant, than the *reductio ad absurdum* of the peace-secured-by-the-preparation-for-war theory. This appeal to prudence was constantly emphasized at the first Hague Conference and was shortly afterward demonstrated by Great Britain when she went to war in South Africa, where she was fined one

---

[2] Jean de Bloch (Ivan Stanislavovitch Bloch, 1836–1902), Polish financier and pacifist, made a fortune in lumber and railroads and then devoted his life to the cause of peace. His major work, *The Future of War*, was published in 1898 in seven volumes [Ed.].

hundred million pounds and lost ten thousand lives. The fact that Russia also, and the very Czar who invited the Conference, disregarded the conclusions of the Hague Tribunal makes this line of appeal at least for the moment seem impotent to influence empires which command enormous resources and which lodge the power of expenditure in officials who have nothing to do with accumulating the treasure they vote to expend. . . .

. . . It is difficult to formulate the newer dynamic peace, embodying the later humanism, as over against the old dogmatic peace. The word "non-resistance" is misleading, because it is much too feeble and inadequate. It suggests passivity, the goody-goody attitude of ineffectiveness. The words "overcoming," "substituting," "re-creating," "readjusting moral values," "forming new centres of spiritual energy" carry much more of the meaning implied. For it is not merely the desire for a conscience at rest, for a sense of justice no longer outraged, that would pull us into new paths where there would be no more war nor preparations for war. There are still more strenuous forces at work reaching down to impulses and experiences as primitive and profound as are those of struggle itself. That "ancient kindliness which sat beside the cradle of the race," and which is ever ready to assert itself against ambition and greed and the desire for achievement, is manifesting itself now with unusual force, and for the first time presents international aspects.

Moralists agree that it is not so much by the teaching of moral theorems that virtue is to be promoted as by the direct expression of social sentiments and by the cultivation of practical habits; that in the progress of society sentiments and opinions have come first, then habits of action and lastly moral codes and institutions. Little is gained by creating the latter prematurely, but much may be accomplished to the utilization of human interests and affections. The Advocates of Peace would find the appeal both to Pity and Prudence totally unnecessary, could they utilize the cosmopolitan interest in human affairs with the resultant social sympathy that at the present moment is developing among all the nations of the earth.

By way of illustration, I may be permitted to cite the London showman who used to exhibit two skulls of Shakespeare—one when he was a youth and went poaching, another when he was a man and wrote plays. There was such a striking difference between the roystering boy indulging in illicit sport and the mature man who peopled the London stage with all the world, that the showman grew confused and considered two separate acts of creation less improbable than that such an amazing change should have taken place. We can easily imagine the gifted youth in the little group of rustics at Stratford-on-Avon finding no adequate outlet for his powers save in a series of break-neck adventures. His only alternative was to sit by the fire with the village cronies, drinking ale so long as his shillings held out. But if we follow him up to London, through all the charm and wonder of the stage which represented his unfolding mind, if we can imagine his delight as he gradually gained the freedom, not only of that big town, but of the human city as well, we can easily see that illicit sport could no longer attract him. To have told the great dramatist the night Hamlet first stepped upon the boards that it was a wicked thing to poach, to have cautioned him that he must consider the cost of preserving the forest and of raising the deer, or to have made an appeal to his pity on behalf of the wounded creatures, would have been the height of folly, because totally unnecessary. All desire, almost all memory of those days, had dropped from him, through his absorption in the great and exciting drama of life. His effort to understand it, to portray it, had utilized and drained his every power. It is equally true of our contemporaries, as it was of the great playwright, that the attainment of this all-absorbing passion for multiform life, with the desire to understand its mysteries and to free its capacities, is gradually displacing the juvenile propensities to warfare.

From this standpoint the advocates of the newer Ideals of Peace would have little to do but to insist that the social point of view be kept paramount, realizing at the same time that the social sentiments are as blind as the egoistic sentiments and must be enlightened, disciplined and directed by the fullest knowledge. The modern students of human morality have told us that primitive man, by the very necessities of his hard struggle for life, came at last to identify his own existence with that of his tribe. Tribal life then made room within itself for the development of that compassion which is the first step towards sensibility and higher moral sentiment. If we accept this statement then we must assume that the new social morality, which we so sadly need, will of necessity have its origin in the social affections—we must search in the dim borderland between compassion and morality for the beginnings of that cosmopolitan affection, as it is prematurely called.

The life of the tribal man inevitably divided into two sets of actions, which appeared under two different ethical aspects: the relation within the tribe and the relation with outsiders, the double conception of morality maintaining itself until now. But the tribal law differed no more widely from inter-tribal law than our common law does from our international law. Until society manages to combine the two we shall make no headway toward the Newer Ideals of Peace.

If we would institute an intelligent search for the social conditions which make possible this combination we should naturally seek for them in the poorer quarters of a cosmopolitan city where we have, as nowhere else, the conditions for breaking into this double development; for making a fresh start, as it were, toward a synthesis upon a higher moral line which shall include both. There is every opportunity and necessity for compassion and kindliness such as the tribe itself afforded, and there is in addition, because of the many nationalties which are gathered there from all parts of the world, the opportunity and necessity for breaking through the tribal bond. Early associations and affections were not based so much on ties of blood as upon that necessity for defense against the hostile world outside which made the life of every man in a tribe valuable to every other man. The fact of blood was, so to speak, an accident. The moral code grew out of solidarity of emotion and action essential to the life of all.

In the midst of the modern city which, at moments, seems to stand only for the triumph of the strongest, the successful exploitation of the weak, the ruthlessness and hidden crime which follow in the wake of the struggle for existence on its lowest terms, there come daily—at least to American cities— accretions of simple people, who carry in their hearts a desire for mere goodness. They regularly deplete their scanty livelihood in response to a primitive pity, and, independent of the religions they have professed, of the wrongs they have suffered, and of the fixed morality they have been taught, have an unquenchable desire that charity and simple justice shall regulate men's relations. It seems sometimes, to one who knows them, as if they continually sought for an outlet for more kindliness, and that they are not only willing and eager to do a favor for a friend, but that their kindheartedness lies in ambush, as it were, for a chance to incorporate itself in our larger relations, that they persistently expect that it shall be given some form of governmental expression. This is doubtless due partly to the fact that emotional pity and kindness are always found in greatest degree among the unsuccessful. We are told that unsuccessful struggle breeds emotion, not strength; that the hard-pressed races are the emotional races; and that wherever struggle has long prevailed emotion becomes the dominant force in fixing social relations. Is it surprising, therefore, that among this huge mass of the unsuccessful, to be found in certain quarters of the modern city, we should have the "medium," in which the first growth of the new compassion is taking place?

In addition to this compassion always found among the unsuccessful, emotional sentiment runs high among the newly arrived immigrants as a result of the emotional experiences of parting from home and kindred, to which he [*sic*] has been so recently subjected. An unusual mental alertness and power of perception also results from the upheaval. The multitudes of immigrants flooding the ˌAmerican cities have many times sundered social habits cherished through a hundred generations, and have renounced customs that may be traced to the habits of primitive man. These old habits and customs have a much more powerful hold than have mere racial or national ties. In seeking companionship in the new world, all the immigrants are reduced to the fundamental equalities and universal necessities of human life itself, and they inevitably develop the power of association which comes from daily contact with those who are unlike each other in all save the universal characteristics of man.

When looked at too closely, this nascent morality disappears, and one can count over only a thousand kindly acts and neighborly offices. But when meditated upon in the whole, there at once emerge again those vast and dominant suggestions of a new peace and holiness. It would seem as if our final help and healing were about to issue forth from broken human nature itself, out of the pathetic striving of ordinary men, who make up the common substance of life: from those who have been driven by economic pressure or governmental oppression out of a score of nations.

These various peoples who are gathered together in the immigrant quarters of a cosmopolitan city worship goodness for its own value, and do not associate it with success any more than they associate success with themselves; they literally "serve God for nought." If we would adduce evidence that we are emerging from a period of industrialism into a period of humanitarianism, it is to such quarters that we must betake ourselves. These are the places in which it is easiest to study the newer manifestations of government, in which personal welfare is considered a legitimate object; for a new history of government begins with an attempt to make life possible and human in large cities, in those crowded quarters which exhibit such an undoubted tendency to barbarism and degeneracy when the better human qualities are not nourished. Public baths and gymnasiums, parks and libraries, are provided first for those who are without the security for bare subsistence, and it does not seem strange to them that it should be so. Such a community is made up of men who will continue to dream of Utopian Governments until the democratic government about them expresses kindliness with protection. Such men will continue to rely upon neighborly friendliness until organized charity is able to identify impulsive pity with well-considered relief. They will naïvely long for an education for their children that will fit them to earn money until public education shall come to consider industrial efficiency. As their hopes and dreams are a prophecy of the future development in city government, in charity, in education, so their daily lives are a forecast of coming international relations. Our attention has lately been drawn to the fact that it is logical that the most vigorous efforts in governmental reform, as well as the most generous experiments in ministering to social needs, have come from the larger cities and that it is inevitable that they should be to-day "the centers of radicalism," as they have been traditionally the "cradles of liberty."[3]

If we once admit the human dynamic character of progress, then it is easy to understand why the crowded city quarters become focal points of that progress.

---

[3] *The Growth of Cities in the Nineteenth Century.* A. T. Weber, p. 432.

A deeper and more thorough-going unity is required in a community made up of highly differentiated peoples than in a more settled and stratified one, and it may be logical that we should find in this commingling of many peoples a certain balance and concord of opposing and contending forces; a gravitation toward the universal. Because of their difference in all external matters, in all of the non-essentials of life, the people in a cosmopolitan city are forced to found their community of interests upon the basic and essential likenesses of their common human nature; for, after all, the things that make men alike are stronger and more primitive than the things that separate them. It is natural that this synthesis of the varying nations should be made first at the points of the greatest congestion, quite as we find that selfishness is first curbed and social feeling created at the points where the conflict of individual interests is sharpest. One dares not grow too certain as to the wells of moral healing which lie under the surface of the sullen work-driven life which the industrial quarters of the modern city present. They fascinate us by their mere size and diversity, as does the city itself; but certain it is, that these quarters continually confound us by their manifestations of altruism. It may be that we are surprised simply because we fail to comprehend that the individual, under such pressure, must shape his life with some reference to the demands of social justice, not only to avoid crushing the little folk about him, but in order to save himself from death by crushing. It is an instance of the irresistible coalescing of the altruistic and egoistic impulse which is the strength of social morality. We are often told that men under this pressure of life become calloused and cynical, whereas anyone who lives with them knows that they are sentimental and compassionate.

It is possible that we shall be saved from warfare by the "fighting rabble" itself, by the "quarrelsome mob" turned into kindly citizens of the world through the pressure of a cosmopolitan neighborhood. It is not that they are shouting for peace

—on the contrary, if they shout at all, they will continue to shout for war—but that they are really attaining cosmopolitan relations through daily experience. They will probably believe for a long time that war is noble and necessary both to engender and cherish patriotism; and yet all of the time, below their shouting, they are living in the kingdom of human kindness. They are laying the simple and inevitable foundations for an international order as the foundations of tribal and national morality have already been laid. They are developing the only sort of patriotism consistent with the intermingling of the nations; for the citizens of a cosmopolitan quarter find an insuperable difficulty when they attempt to hem in their conception of patriotism either to the "old country" or to their adopted one. There arises the hope that when this newer patriotism becomes large enough, it will overcome arbitrary boundaries and soak up the notion of nationalism. We may then give up war, because we shall find it as difficult to make war upon a nation at the other side of the globe as upon our next-door neighbor. . . .

. . . Speculative writers, such as Kant, Bentham, and Buckle, long ago pointed out that the subsidence of war was inevitable as society progressed. They contended that every stage of human progress is marked by a further curtailment of brute force, a limitation of the area in which it is permitted. At the bottom is the small savage community in a perpetual state of warfare; at the top an orderly society stimulated and controlled by recognized ideals of social justice. In proportion as the savage society comes under the dominion of a common moral consciousness, it moves up, and in proportion as the civilized society reverts to the use of brute force, it goes down. Reversion to that brute struggle may at any moment cost the destruction of the painfully acquired bonds of equity, the ties of mutual principle, which are wrought with such effort and loosed with such ease. But these earlier philosophers could not possibly have foreseen the tremendous growth of industry

and commerce with their inevitable cosmopolitanism which
has so recently taken place, nor without knowledge of this
could they possibly have prognosticated the leap forward and
the aggressive character which the concern for human welfare
has latterly evinced. The speculative writers among our contemporaries are naturally the only ones who formulate this
new development, or rather bid us heed its presence among
us. An American philosopher[4] has lately reminded us of the
need to "discover in the social realm the moral equivalent for
war—something heroic that will speak to men as universally
as war has done, and yet will be as compatible with their
spiritual natures as war has proved itself to be incompatible."
It may be true that we are even now discovering these moral
substitutes, although we find it so difficult to formulate them.
Perhaps our very hope that these substitutes may be discovered has become the custodian of a secret change that is
going on all about us. We care less each day for the heroism
connected with warfare and destruction, and constantly admire
more that which pertains to labor and the nourishing of human
life. The new heroism manifests itself at the present moment
in a universal determination to abolish poverty and disease, a
manifestation so widespread that it may justly be called
international.

In illustration of this new determination one immediately
thinks of the international effort to rid the face of the earth of
tuberculosis, in which Germany, Italy, France, England and
America are engaged with such enthusiasm. This movement
has its international congresses, its discoverers and veterans,
also its decorations and rewards for bravery. Its discipline is
severe; it requires self-control, endurance, self-sacrifice and
constant watchfulness. Its leaders devote hours to careful
teaching and demonstration, they reclaim acres of bad houses,
and make over the food supply of huge cities. One could

---

[4] William James, Professor of Philosophy at Harvard University.

instance the determination to do away with neglected old age, which finds expression in the Old Age Pension Acts of Germany and Australia, in the State Savings Banks of Belgium and France, in the enormous number of Mutual Benefit Societies in England and America. In such undertakings as these, with their spontaneous and universal manifestations, are we beginning to see the first timid forward reach of one of those instinctive movements which carry onward the progressive goodness of the race.

It is possible that this substitution of nurture for warfare is analogous to that world-wide effort to put a limit to revenge which one nation after another essayed as each reached a certain stage of development. To compel the avenger to accept blood-money in lieu of the blood of his enemy may have been but a short step in morals, but at least it destroyed the stimulus to further shedding of blood which each avenged death had afforded, and it laid the foundations for court adjudications. The newer humanitarianism is more aggressive and substitutes emotional stimuli as well as codes of conduct. We may predict that each notion quite as a natural process will reach the moment when virile good-will will be substituted for the spirit of warfare. The process of extinguishing war, however, compared to the limiting of revenge, will be amazingly accelerated. Owing to the modern conditions of intercourse, each nation will respond, not to an isolated impulse, but will be caught in the current of a world-wide process.

We are much too timid and apologetic in regard to this newer humanitarianism, and do not yet realize what it may do for us in the way of courage and endurance. We continue to defend war on the ground that it stirs the nobler blood and the higher imagination of the nation, and thus frees it from moral stagnation and the bonds of commercialism. We do not see that this is to borrow our virtues from a former age and to fail to utilize our own. We find ourselves in this plight because our modern morality has lacked fibre, because our humanitarianism has been much too soft and literary, and has given itself over to unreal and high-sounding phrases. It appears that our only hope for a genuine adjustment of our morality and courage to our present social and industrial developments, lies in a patient effort to work it out by daily experience. We must be willing to surrender ourselves to those ideals of the humble, which all religious teachers unite in declaring to be the foundations of a sincere moral life. . . .

20. *Peace and Bread in Time of War*

1 9 2 2

According to the theories advanced in *Newer Ideals of Peace*, the First World War should never have happened. When it did happen, most of the prewar pacifists managed nevertheless to convince themselves that it would never happen again. The war, they argued, was a war to end war. Jane Addams, in her gentle way, dismissed such arguments as the intellectual rubbish they were and faced up to the fact that the war was a disaster, unmitigated except for the possibility that even war might teach a few lessons in international cooperation. What followed—the disintegration of the peace movement, the isolation of those who stood against the war, their mounting sense that the nation had become deaf to all rational appeals, and above all the double danger of self-pity and self-righteousness which was the lot of those who found themselves almost single-handedly opposing the rest of their countrymen—these things are the subject of the "Personal Reactions" below.

After the war, Jane Addams went to Europe for the second conference of the Women's International League for Peace and Freedom, of which she was one of the founders. This experience forced her to the painful conclusion, set forth in the second of the following excerpts (part of Chapter 8 of *Peace and Bread*), that nationalism had become a destructive force in the world, rather than the liberalizing influence that social reformers had expected. The courage with which Jane Addams faced this possibility distinguished her once again from other progressives, who were seeking comfort in the thought that nationalism had become as outmoded as war itself. Jane Addams was willing to reckon with the possibility that the war had, if anything, strengthened the force of nationalism at the same time that it had brought to the surface all its uglier emotions.

PERSONAL REACTIONS DURING WAR

After the United States had entered the war there began to appear great divergence among the many types of pacifists, from the extreme left, composed of non-resistants, through the middle-of-the-road groups, to the extreme right, who could barely be distinguished from mild militarists. There were those people, also, who although they felt keenly both the horror and the futility of war, yet hoped for certain beneficent results from the opportunities afforded by the administration of war; they were much pleased when the government took over the management of the railroads, insisting that governmental ownership had thus been pushed forward by decades; they were also sure that the War Labor Policies Board, the Coal Commission and similar war institutions would make an enormous difference in the development of the country, in short, that militarism might be used as an instrument for advanced social ends. Such justifications had their lure and one found old pacifist friends on all the war boards and even in the war department itself. Certainly we were all eager to accept whatever progressive social changes came from the quick reorganization demanded by war, and doubtless prohibition was one

---

From Jane Addams, *Peace and Bread in Time of War* (New York: The Macmillan Company, 1922), pp. 132–151, 173–177.

of these, as the granting of woman suffrage in the majority of the belligerent nations, was another. But some of us had suspected that social advance depends as much upon the process through which it is secured as upon the result itself; if railroads are nationalized solely in order to secure rapid transit of ammunition and men to points of departure for Europe, when that governmental need no longer exists what more natural than that the railroads should no longer be managed by the government?

My temperament and habit had always kept me rather in the middle of the road; in politics as well as in social reform I had been for "the best possible." But now I was pushed far toward the left on the subject of the war and I became gradually convinced that in order to make the position of the pacifist clear it was perhaps necessary that at least a small number of us should be forced into an unequivocal position. If I sometimes regretted having gone to the Woman's Congress at The Hague in 1915, or having written a book on Newer Ideals of Peace in 1911 which had made my position so conspicuously clear, certainly far oftener I was devoutly grateful that I had used such unmistakable means of expression before the time came when any spoken or written word in the interests of Peace was forbidden.

It was on my return from The Hague Congress in July, 1915, that I had my first experience of the determination on the part of the press to make pacifist activity or propaganda so absurd that it would be absolutely without influence and its authors so discredited that nothing they might say or do would be regarded as worthy of attention. I had been accustomed to newspaper men for many years and had come to regard them as a good natured fraternity, sometimes ignorant of the subject on which they asked an interview, but usually quite ready to report faithfully albeit somewhat sensationally. Hull-House had several times been the subject of sustained and inspired newspaper attacks, one, the indirect result of an exposure of the inefficient sanitary service in the Chicago Health Department had lasted for many months; I had of course known what it was to serve unpopular causes and throughout a period of campaigning for the Progressive Party I had naturally encountered the "opposition press" in various parts of the country, but this concerted and deliberate attempt at misrepresentation on the part of newspapers of all shades of opinion was quite new in my experience. After the United States entered the war, the press throughout the country systematically undertook to misrepresent and malign pacifists as a recognized part of propaganda and as a patriotic duty. We came to regard this misrepresentation as part of the war technique and in fact an inevitable consequence of war itself, but we were slow in the very beginning to recognize the situation, and I found my first experience which came long before the United States entered the war rather overwhelming.

Upon our return from the Woman's International Congress at The Hague in 1915, our local organization in New York City with others, notably a group of enthusiastic college men, had arranged a large public meeting in Carnegie Hall. Dr. Anna Howard Shaw[1] presided and the United States delegates made a public report of our impressions in "war stricken Europe" and of the moral resources in the various countries we visited that might possibly be brought to bear against a continuation of the war. We had been much impressed with the fact that it was an old man's war, that the various forms of doubt and opposition to war had no method of public expression and that many of the soldiers themselves were far from enthusiastic in regard to actual fighting as a method of settling international difficulties. War was to many of them much more anachronistic than to the elderly statesmen who

---

[1] Anna Howard Shaw (1847–1919) was a Boston feminist and president of the National American Woman Suffrage Association (1904–1915). Not a pacifist, she nevertheless supported a league of nations and died after overexerting herself speaking on its behalf [Ed.].

were primarily responsible for the soldiers' presence in the trenches.

It was the latter statement which was my undoing, for in illustration of it I said that in practically every country we had visited, we had heard a certain type of young soldier say that it had been difficult for him to make the bayonet charge (enter into actual hand to hand fighting) unless he had been stimulated; that the English soldiers had been given rum before such a charge, the Germans ether and that the French were said to use absinthe. To those who heard the address it was quite clear that it was not because the young men flinched at the risk of death but because they had to be inflamed to do the brutal work of the bayonet, such as disembowelling, and were obliged to overcome all the inhibitions of civilization.

Dr. Hamilton[2] and I had notes for each of these statements with the dates and names of the men who had made them, and it did not occur to me that the information was new or startling. I was, however, reported to have said that no soldier could go into a bayonet charge until he was made half drunk, and this in turn was immediately commented upon, notably in a scathing letter written to the New York Times by Richard Harding Davis, as a most choice specimen of a woman's sentimental nonsense. Mr. Davis himself had recently returned from Europe and at once became the defender of the heroic soldiers who were being traduced and belittled. He lent the weight of his name and his very able pen to the cause, but it really needed neither, for the misstatement was repeated, usually with scathing comment, from one end of the country to the other.

I was conscious, of course, that the story had struck athwart the popular and long-cherished conception of the nobility and

---

[2] Alice Hamilton (1869–   ), a physician and professor of medicine, was chiefly noted for her studies of industrial diseases and for her autobiography, *Exploring the Dangerous Trades* (1943) [Ed.].

heroism of the soldier as such, and it seemed to me at the time that there was no possibility of making any explanation, at least until the sensation should have somewhat subsided. I might have repeated my more sober statements with the explanation that whomsoever the pacifist held responsible for war, it was certainly not the young soldiers themselves who were, in a sense, its most touching victims, "the heroic youth of the world whom a common ideal tragically pitted against each other." Youth's response to the appeal made to their self-sacrifice, to their patriotism, to their sense of duty, to their high-hearted hopes for the future, could only stir one's admiration, and we should have been dull indeed had we failed to be moved by this most moving spectacle in the world. That they had so responded to the higher appeals only confirms Ruskin's statement that "we admire the soldier not because he goes forth to slay but to be slain." The fact that many of them were obliged to make a great effort to bear themselves gallantly in the final tests of "war's brutalities" had nothing whatever to do with their courage and sense of devotion. All this, of course, we had realized during our months in Europe.

After the meeting in Carnegie Hall and after an interview with President Wilson in Washington, I returned to Chicago to a public meeting arranged in the Auditorium; I was met at the train by a committee of aldermen appointed as a result of a resolution in the City Council. There was an indefinite feeling that the meeting at The Hague might turn out to be of significance, and that in such an event its chairman should have been honored by her fellow citizens. But the bayonet story had preceded me and every one was filled with great uneasiness. To be sure, a few war correspondents had come to my rescue—writing of the overpowering smell of ether preceding certain German attacks; the fact that English soldiers knew when a bayonet charge was about to be ordered because rations of rum were distributed along the trenches. Some people began to suspect that the story, exaggerated and grotesque as it had become, indicated not cowardice but merely an added sensitiveness which the modern soldier was obliged to overcome. Among the many letters on the subject which filled my mail for weeks, the bitter and abusive were from civilians or from the old men to whom war experiences had become a reminiscence, the larger number and the most understanding ones came from soldiers in active service.

Only once did I try a public explanation. After an address in Chautauqua, New York, in which I had not mentioned bayonets, I tried to remake my original statement to a young man of the associated press only to find it once more so garbled that I gave up in despair, quite unmoved by the young man's letter of apology which followed hard upon the published report of his interview.

I will confess that the mass psychology of the situation interested me even then and continued to do so until I fell ill with a serious attack of pleuro-pneumonia, which was the beginning of three years of semi-invalidism. During weeks of feverish discomfort I experienced a bald sense of social opprobrium and wide-spread misunderstanding which brought me very near to self pity, perhaps the lowest pit into which human nature can sink. Indeed the pacifist in war time, with his precious cause in the keeping of those who control the sources of publicity and consider it a patriotic duty to make all types of peace propaganda obnoxious, constantly faces two dangers. Strangely enough he finds it possible to travel from the mire of self pity straight to the barren hills of self-righteousness and to hate himself equally in both places.

From the very beginning of the great war, as the members of our group gradually became defined from the rest of the community, each one felt increasingly the sense of isolation which rapidly developed after the United States entered the war into that destroying effect of "aloneness," if I may so describe the opposite of mass consciousness. We never ceased to miss the unquestioning comradeship experienced by our fellow citizens during the war, nor to feel curiously outside the enchantment given to any human emotion when it is shared by millions of others. The force of the majority was so overwhelming that it seemed not only impossible to hold one's own against it, but at moments absolutely unnatural, and one secretly yearned to participate in "the folly of all mankind." Our modern democratic teaching has brought us to regard popular impulses as possessing in their general tendency a valuable capacity for evolutionary development. In the hours of doubt and self-distrust the question again and again arises, has the individual or a very small group, the right to stand out against millions of his fellow countrymen? Is there not a great value in mass judgment and in instinctive mass enthusiasm, and even if one were right a thousand times over in conviction, was he not absolutely wrong in abstaining from this communion with his fellows? The misunderstanding on the part of old friends and associates and the charge of lack of patriotism was far easier to bear than those dark periods of faint-heartedness. We gradually ceased to state our position as we became convinced that it served no practical purpose and, worse than that, often found that the immediate result was provocative.

We could not, however, lose the conviction that as all other forms of growth begin with a variation from the mass, so the moral changes in human affairs may also begin with a differing group or individual, sometimes with the one who at best is designated as a crank and a freak and in sterner moments is imprisoned as an atheist or a traitor. Just when the differing individual becomes the centro-egotist, the insane man, who must be thrown out by society for its own protection, it is impossible to state. The pacifist was constantly brought sharply up against a genuine human trait with its biological basis, a trait founded upon the instinct to dislike, to distrust and finally to destroy the individual who differs from the mass in time of danger. Regarding this trait as the basis of self-preservation it becomes perfectly natural for the mass to call such an individual a traitor and to insist that if he is not for the nation he is against it. To this an estimated nine million people can bear witness who have been burned as witches and heretics, not by mobs, for of the people who have been "lynched" no record has been kept, but by order of ecclesiastical and civil courts.

There were moments when the pacifist yielded to the suggestion that keeping himself out of war, refusing to take part in its enthusiasms, was but pure quietism, an acute failure to adjust himself to the moral world. Certainly nothing was clearer than that the individual will was helpless and irrelevant. We were constantly told by our friends that to stand aside from the war mood of the country was to surrender all possibility of future influence, that we were committing intellectual suicide, and would never again be trusted as responsible people or judicious advisers. Who were we to differ with able statesmen, with men of sensitive conscience who also absolutely abhorred war, but were convinced that this war for the preservation of democracy would make all future wars impossible, that the priceless values of civilization which were at stake could at this moment be saved only by war? But these very dogmatic statements spurred one to alarm. Was not war in the interest of democracy for the salvation of civilization a contradiction of terms, whoever said it or however often it was repeated?

Then, too, we were always afraid of fanaticism, of preferring a consistency of theory to the conscientious recognition of the social situation, of a failure to meet life in the temper of a practical person. Every student of our time had become more or less a disciple of pragmatism and its great teachers in the United States had come out for the war and defended their positions with skill and philosophic acumen. There were moments when one longed desperately for reconciliation with one's friends and fellow citizens; in the words of Amiel,[3] "Not to remain at variance with existence but to reach that understanding of life which enables us at least to obtain forgiveness." Solitude has always had its demons, harder to withstand than the snares of the world, and the unnatural desert into which the pacifist was summarily cast out seemed to be peopled with them. We sorely missed the contagion of mental activity, for we are all much more dependent upon our social environment and daily newspaper than perhaps any of us realize. We also doubtless encountered, although subconsciously, the temptations described by John Stuart Mill: "In respect to the persons and affairs of their own day, men insensibly adopt the modes of feeling and judgment in which they can hope for sympathy from the company they keep."

The consciousness of spiritual alienation was lost only in moments of comradeship with the like minded, which may explain the tendency of the pacifist in war time to seek his intellectual kin, his spiritual friends, wherever they might be found in his own country or abroad.

It was inevitable that in many respects the peace cause should suffer in public opinion from the efforts of groups of people who, early in the war, were convinced that the country as a whole was for peace and who tried again and again to discover a method for arousing and formulating the sentiment against war. I was ill and out of Chicago when the People's Council held a national convention there, which was protected by the city police but threatened with dispersion by the state troops, who, however, arrived from the capital several hours after the meeting had adjourned. The incident was most sensational and no one was more surprised than many of the

---

[3] Henri Frédéric Amiel (1821–1881), French essayist, wrote, among other things, a well-known private journal [Ed.].

members of the People's Council who thus early in the war had supposed that they were conducting a perfectly legitimate convention. The incident gave tremendous "copy" in a city needing rationalizing rather than sensationalizing at that moment. There is no doubt that the shock and terror of the "anarchist riots" occurring in Chicago years ago have left their traces upon the nervous system of the city somewhat as a nervous shock experienced in youth will long afterwards determine the action of a mature man under widely different circumstances.

On the whole, the New York groups were much more active and throughout the war were allowed much more freedom both of assembly and press, although later a severe reaction followed expressed through the Lusk Committee and other agencies. Certainly neither city approximated the freedom of London and nothing surprised me more in 1915 and again in 1919 than the freedom of speech permitted there.

We also read with a curious eagerness the steadily increasing number of books published from time to time during the war, which brought a renewal of one's faith or at least a touch of comfort. These books broke through that twisting and suppressing of awkward truths, which was encouraged and at times even ordered by the censorship. Such manipulation of news and motives was doubtless necessary in the interest of war propaganda if the people were to be kept in a fighting mood. Perhaps the most vivid books came from France, early from Romain Rolland, later from Barbusse, although it was interesting to see how many people took the latter's burning indictment of war merely as a further incitement against the enemy. On the scientific side were the frequent writings of David Starr Jordan and the remarkable book of Nicolai[4] on

---

[4] Georg Friedrich Nicolai (1874–   ), German writer and critic, wrote *The Biology of War* (1918) [Ed.].

"The Biology of War." The latter enabled one, at least in one's own mind, to refute the pseudo-scientific statement that war was valuable in securing the survival of the fittest. Nicolai insisted that primitive man must necessarily have been a peaceful and social animal and that he developed his intelligence through the use of the tool, not through the use of the weapon; it was the primeval community which made the evolution of man possible, and coöperation among men is older and more primitive than mass combat which is an outgrowth of the much later property instinct. No other species save ants, who also possess property, fights in masses against other masses of its own kind. War is in fact not a natural process and not a struggle for existence in the evolutionary sense. He illustrated the evolutionary survival of the fittest by two tigers inhabiting the same jungle or feeding ground, the one who has the greater skill and strength as a hunter survives and the other starves, but the strong one does not go out to kill the weak one, as the war propagandist implied; or by two varieties of mice living in the same field or barn; in the biological struggle, the variety which grows a thicker coat survives the winter while the other variety freezes to extinction, but if one variety of mice should go forth to kill the other, it would be absolutely abnormal and quite outside the evolutionary survival which is based on the adjustment of the organism to its environment. George Nasmyth's[5] book on Darwinism and the Social Order was another clear statement of the mental confusion responsible for the insistence that even a biological progress is secured through war. Mr. Brailsford[6] wrote constantly on the economic results of the war and we got much

---

[5] George William Nasmyth (1882–1918), English diplomat, wrote *Nationalism and War in the Near East* (1915) [Ed.].

[6] Henry Noel Brailsford (1873–1958) was an English journalist and Fabian socialist. His book *The War of Steel and Gold* (1915) gave an economic interpretation of the origins of World War I [Ed.].

comfort from John Hobson's[7] "Toward International Government," which gave an authoritative account of the enormous amount of human activity actually carried on through international organizations of all sorts, many of them under governmental control. Lowes Dickinson's[8] books, especially the spirited challenge in "The Choice Before Us," left his readers with the distinct impression that "war is not inevitable but proceeds from definite and removable causes." From every such book the pacifist was forced to the conclusion that none save those interested in the realization of an idea are in a position to bring it about and that if one found himself the unhappy possessor of an unpopular conviction, there was nothing for it but to think as clearly as he was able and be in a position to serve his country as soon as it was possible for him to do so.

But with or without the help of good books a hideous sensitiveness remained, for the pacifist, like the rest of the world, has developed a high degree of suggestibility, sharing that consciousness of the feelings, the opinions and the customs of his own social group which is said to be an inheritance from an almost pre-human past. An instinct which once enabled the man-pack to survive when it was a question of keeping together or of perishing off the face of the earth, is perhaps not underdeveloped in any of us. There is a distinct physical as well as moral strain when this instinct is steadily suppressed or at least ignored.

The large number of deaths among the older pacifists in all the warring nations can probably be traced in some measure

---

[7] John A. Hobson (1864–1940) was an English economist and pacifist. His works include *The Evolution of Modern Capitalism* (1894) and *Imperialism, A Study* (1902) [Ed.].

[8] G. Lowes Dickinson (1862–1932), English author and pacifist, wrote several books against war, including *The War and the Way Out* (1914) [Ed.].

to the peculiar strain which such maladjustment implies. More than the normal amount of nervous energy must be consumed in holding one's own in a hostile world. These older men, Kier Hardie[9] and Lord Courtney in England, Jenkin Lloyd Jones,[10] Rauchenbusch,[11] Washington Gladden[12] in the United States, Lammasch and Fried in Austria, had been honored by their fellow citizens because of marked ability to interpret and understand them. Suddenly to find every public utterance wilfully miscontrued, every attempt at normal relationship repudiated, must react in a baffled suppression which is health-destroying even if we do not accept the mechanistic explanation of the human system. Certainly by the end of the war we were able to understand, although our group certainly did not endorse the statement of Cobden, one of the most convinced of all internationalists: "I made up my mind during the Crimean War that if ever I lived in the time of another great war of a similar kind between England and another power, I would not as a public man open my mouth on the subject, so convinced am I that appeals to reason, conscience or interest have no force whatever on parties engaged in war, and that exhaustion on one or both sides can alone bring a contest of physical force to an end."

On the other hand there were many times when we stubbornly asked ourselves, what after all, has maintained the

---

[9] Keir Hardie (1856–1915), English socialist, was one of the founders of the British Labour Party and an opponent of World War I [Ed.].

[10] Jenkin Lloyd Jones (1843–1918), English diplomat, wrote *Nationalism and War in the Near East* (1915) [Ed.].

[11] Walter Rauchenbusch (1861–1918), Baptist clergyman, was one of the proponents of the "social gospel" in the United States. He wrote, among other things, *Christianity and the Social Crisis* (1907) and *Dare We Be Christians?* (1914), the latter an indictment of World War I [Ed.].

[12] Washington Gladden (1836–1918), Congregational clergyman, was another preacher of the "social gospel." He wrote many books, including *Social Salvation* (1902) and *The Church and Modern Life* (1908) [Ed.].

human race on this old globe despite all the calamities of nature and all the tragic failings of mankind, if not faith in new
possibilities, and courage to advocate them. Doubtless many
times these new possibilities were declared by a man who,
quite unconscious of courage, bore the "sense of being an exile,
a condemned criminal, a fugitive from mankind." Did every
one so feel who, in order to travel on his own proper path had
been obliged to leave the traditional highway? The pacifist,
during the period of the war could answer none of these questions but he was sick at heart from causes which to him were
hidden and impossible to analyze. He was at times devoured
by a veritable dissatisfaction with life. Was he thus bearing
his share of blood-guiltiness, the morbid sense of contradiction
and inexplicable suicide which modern war implies? We certainly had none of the internal contentment of the doctrinnaire,
the ineffable solace of the self-righteous which was imputed to
us. No one knew better than we how feeble and futile we were
against the impregnable weight of public opinion, the appalling
imperviousness, the coagulation of motives, the universal confusion of a world at war. There was scant solace to be found
in this type of statement: "The worth of every conviction consists precisely in the steadfastness with which it is held," perhaps because we suffered from the fact that we were no longer
living in a period of dogma and were therefore in no position
to announce our sense of security! We were well aware that
the modern liberal having come to conceive truth of a kind
which must vindicate itself in practice, finds it hard to hold
even a sincere and mature opinion which from the very nature
of things can have no justification in works. The pacifist in war
time is literally starved of any gratification of that natural
desire to have his own decisions justified by his fellows.

That, perhaps, was the crux of the situation. We slowly
became aware that our affirmation was regarded as pure
dogma. We were thrust into the position of the doctrinnaire,
and although, had we been permitted, we might have cited

both historic and scientific tests of our so-called doctrine of Peace, for the moment any sanction even by way of illustration was impossible.

It therefore came about that ability to hold out against mass suggestion, to honestly differ from the convictions and enthusiasms of one's best friends did in moments of crisis come to depend upon the categorical belief that a man's primary allegiance is to his vision of the truth and that he is under obligation to affirm it.

IN EUROPE DURING THE ARMISTICE

My experience in Europe in 1919 was in marked contrast to my impressions received thirty-four years earlier, in 1885. Nationalism was also the great word then, but with quite another content. At that moment in all political matters the great popular word had been Unity; a coming together into new national systems of little states which had long been separated. The words of Mazzini, who had died scarcely a decade before, were constantly on the lips of ardent young orators, the desire to unite, to overcome differences, to accentuate likenesses, was everywhere a ruling influence in political affairs. Italy had become united under Victor Emanuel; the first Kaiser and Bismarck ruled over a German Empire made of many minor states. It rather smacked of learning, in those days, to use the words Slavophile and Panslavic, but we knew that the movement stood for unity in the remoter parts of Europe where Bohemia was the most vocal, although she talked less of a republic of her own than of her desire to unite with her fellow Slavs. The most striking characteristic of all these nationalistic movements had been their burning humanitarianism, a sense that the new groupings were but a preparation for a wider synthesis, that a federation of at least the European states was a possibility in the near future.

In 1885 I had seen nationalistic fervor pulling scattered people together, but in 1919 it seemed equally effective in pushing those apart who had once been combined—a whole ring of states was pulling out of Mother Russia, Bavaria was threatening to leave Germany, and Italy, in the name of nationalism was separating a line of coast with its hinterland of Slavs, from their newly found brethren. Whereas nationalism thirty years earlier had seemed generous and inclusive, stressing likenesses, it now appeared dogmatic and ruthless, insisting upon historic prerogatives quite independent of the popular will. Had the nationalistic fervor become overgrown and over-reached itself, or was it merely for the moment so self-assertive that the creative impulse was submerged into the possessive instinct? Had nationalism become dogmatic and hardened in thirty-five years? It was as if I had left a group of early Christians and come back into a flourishing mediaeval church holding great possessions and equipped with well tried methods of propaganda. The early spontaneity had changed into an authoritative imposition of power. One received the impression everywhere in that moment when nationalism was so tremendously stressed, that the nation was demanding worship and devotion for its own sake similar to that of the mediaeval church, as if it existed for its own ends of growth and power irrespective of the tests of reality. It demanded unqualified obedience, denounced as heretics all who differed, insisted that it alone had the truth, and exhibited all the well known signs of dogmatism, including a habit of considering ordinary standards inapplicable to a certain line of conduct if it were inspired by motives beyond reproach.

We saw arriving in Rotterdam, from the German colonies in Africa and the Pacific, hundreds of German families who had been driven from their pioneer homes and their colonial business undertakings, primarily because they belonged to the outlaw nation; in many of the railroad stations in Germany there were posted directions for the fugitives coming from Posen, from Alsace, from the new Czecho-Slovakia and from the Danzig corridor. As we had opportunity to learn of their experiences, they told of prohibition of language, of the forced sale of real estate, of the confiscation of business, of the expulsion from university faculties and the alienation of old friends. There was something about it all that was curiously anachronistic like the expulsion of the Jews from Spain, or Cromwell's drive through Ireland when the Catholics took refuge in the barren west country, or of the action by which France had made herself poorer for generations when she banished her Huguenots. It is as if nationalism, through the terms of the Peace Conference itself, had fallen back into an earlier psychology, exhibiting a blind intolerance which does not properly belong to these later centuries.

After all, the new Nationalism—even counting its rise as beginning three hundred years ago—is still in its early history. It might be possible for its representatives to meet in frank and fearless discussion of its creeds as the early church in its first centuries called its Ecumenical Councils.

These creeds would easily divide into types: the hypernationalism, if one may call it such, of the suppressed nations, as Ireland, Poland or Bohemia; the imperialistic nationalism of empires like Great Britain in which colonial expansion had become the normal expression and is no longer challenged as a policy; the revolutionary type, such as Russia attempting an economic state. Every nation would show traces of all types of nationalism, and it would be found that all types have displayed the highest devotion to their ideals.

It is possible that such a hypothetical Council would discover that as the greatest religious war came at the very moment when men were deciding that they no longer cared intensely for the theological creeds for which they had long been fighting, so this devastating war may have come at a similar moment in regard to national dogmas. The world, at the very verge of the creation of the League of Nations may be entering an era when the differing types will no longer suppress each other but live together in a fuller and richer comity than has ever before been possible. But the League of Nations must find a universal motive which shall master the overstimulated nationalism so characteristic of Europe after the war.

We came home late in August, inevitably disappointed in the newly formed League, but eager to see what would happen when "the United States came in!"

21. Later Reflections on Peace

1 9 3 2

This final selection is the text of a radio interview between Jane Addams and William Hard, a prowar liberal who in the postwar period had become more pacifistic. His questions are given here somewhat abridged; Miss Addams' answers are printed in full. They illustrate what might be called the soft side of Jane Addams' pacifism, as distinguished from the more searching analysis revealed in the preceding excerpts from *Peace and Bread*. The best arguments against war were those which analyzed its effect on American society and, beyond that, which insisted upon the sheer destructiveness of modern warfare. The worst were surely those which argued from the premise that the "gradual moralization of our international relations" was the necessary precondition of world peace. If that were the case, the world might as well resign itself to war.

Question: Miss Addams, you have recently appeared before the Resolutions Committee of the Republican National Convention and also before the informal Resolutions Committee of the approaching Democratic National Convention as an

---

From Jane Addams, "How to Build a Peace Program," *Survey,* LXVIII (November 1, 1932), 550–553.

advocate of "increased participation in the work of the League of Nations." Now it is well known that the Covenant, or Constitution, of the League of Nations embraces a possible resort to force for the preservation of peace. It is equally well known that you are far from being an advocate of force.

Will you illustrate to us what you mean when you speak of a closer American cooperation with the League.

Answer: The League of Nations was established so soon after the war, Mr. Hard, that certain participants, like the sorely tried French, were still suffering from shellshock. It was quite natural at such a moment that the League should provide military sanctions to be invoked to bring a recalcitrant nation into line. In the entire history of the League of Nations, however, such military sanctions, so provided for, have never been used although the League has been faced by a number of severe crises.

As time goes on, it is less and less probable that military sanctions will be used. You yourself said the other day, Mr. Hard, in your address before the Foreign Policy Association that the French, when faced by the recent situation in the East, found themselves as unwilling to send their sons to Manchuria as the Americans would be to send their boys to settle a difficulty in Jugoslavia.

To many of us the notion of military power connected with the League of Nations has been an anachronism from the first. The very existence of the League is a departure from such methods, as the early establishment of the Supreme Court of the United States was a declaration of a new type of relation between the thirteen colonies. Of course you will recall that each colony gradually dropped its own army, slowly at first— it took New York two and a half years—because each became convinced that in case of any difficulty it could appeal to the Supreme Court, and the United States Constitution itself finally forbade the states to maintain armies and navies.

At different times three former residents of Hull-House have been identified with the League of Nations: Julia Lathrop as an assessor of the Child Welfare division, followed later by another of our residents, Grace Abbott, the present chief of the Children's Bureau, and Dr. Alice Hamilton, now a professor in the Harvard Medical School, who served on a health commission. It was quite as natural for these three women, appointed by the United States government in the fashion appointments were then made, to go to Geneva in their effort to forward the welfare of children, as they had already gone from Chicago to Washington. In fact, the American participation in the League has come about naturally. Whenever there is a genuine situation which can be furthered by participation in the League, I hope America will continue to cooperate. It would seem to me simpler that she should become a member of the League, pay her share of the expenses, and be entitled to a vote with the rest, but the essential thing is that she should cooperate with the other nations.

To say that the League is remote from our daily experiences is absurd. I recall one of the early meetings in Geneva on migratory labor, called by the Labor Office of the League of Nations. A number of Italian workmen came in to see me about it—very much excited because such care was to be taken on behalf of their friends. At that time the Italians had a habit of going to South America in the early winter, which was of course the time the crops south of the Equator were ripening, and they would work their way up through South and Central America and the United States into Manitoba, harvesting all the way. But sometimes they would get into difficulties in remote places where they could find no Italian consul and the whole undertaking was fraught with many difficulties, some of them purely legalistic. It seemed to them the most natural thing in the world that somewhere the nations should meet and discuss this awkward situation which could not be remedied by Italy alone nor even by the powerful United States, but could only be taken care of through international agreement.

The interests of the League touch us intimately in one way or another almost every day of our lives, but those interests lie in the way of protection for the helpless, the welfare of children and a thousand other aspects of life which have nothing to do with the use of force. In fact, the use of military force is possible to the League of Nations only under such very remote and exceptional circumstances that it may never be invoked, as it never has been. The League would have been a thousand times stronger if the possibility were removed, as many of its friends contended from the first. Perhaps the entrance of the United States, which is so enthusiastic at the moment for changing constitutions, would make this possible.

Question: . . . In the peace program which you have suggested to the Republican and Democratic Parties you have included this: that there should be an agreement by the United States government to consult with other governments in case of a violation of the Kellogg-Briand Pact or of other threats to world peace.[1] In the Republican platform a pledge to that effect, to that substantial effect, was included. May I ask you: If and when an international conference meets to consider a possible outbreak of war, what measures do you think it can effectively take in the field of moral as distinguished from physical force? And what confidence do you think we should have in such "moral" measures?

Answer: As a Chicagoan, I am naturally very proud of the fact that the Pact of Paris—the Kellogg Pact as we like to call

---

[1] The Kellogg-Briand Pact, signed by the major world powers at Paris in 1928, outlawed war as an instrument of national policy. The pact came about partly through the efforts of Salmon O. Levinson (1865–1941), a Chicago lawyer who campaigned throughout the 1920's for the outlawry of war, enlisting in his crusade such eminent people as John Dewey and Senator William E. Borah [Ed.].

it—resulted so directly from Mr. Levinson's campaign for the Outlawry of War. Seldom has any campaign moved more quickly to success. It was a great advance toward an organized and peaceful world when the Pact was signed by the leading nations of the world. The very warlike events in Manchuria, because of the Pact, have resulted in one of the most striking pronouncements of modern times, which Secretary Stimson sent in despatches to China and Japan and reaffirmed later in his letter to Senator Borah.[2] He made clear that illegal force shall not result in legal gains; i. e., territorial adjustments reached by methods contrary to the agreement of the Pact of Paris could have no standing with the United States. He made this announcement January 7, 1932, and the Assembly of the League of Nations solemnly adopted it on March 11. This turned out extremely well because the League of Nations in this instance followed the lead of the United States; but perhaps it would have been more reasonable and courteous to have reached this conclusion together, although no doubt it is natural that the United States should consider the Kellogg Pact its own child and be very quick to resent its repudiation.

I think you will agree that Mr. Stimson used moral energy as distinguished from physical force. I firmly believe that nothing else will prevail but this gradual moralization of our international relations. Quite as the truculent citizen no longer settles a quarrel with his neighbor by means of his fists but takes his case into court for legal adjustment, so the nations must learn gradually to substitute law for war. This might be illustrated by the vigilance committees which were inevitably

---

[2] When Japan invaded Manchuria in 1931, Secretary of State Henry L. Stimson announced the "Stimson doctrine." The United States, he said, would simply refuse to recognize the Japanese conquest. Stimson himself would have preferred to go further, not being himself a believer in "moral energy as distinguished from physical force." Indeed, in his open letter to Senator Borah he hinted that Japan's violation of her treaty obligations might release the United States from her promise not to fortify the Philippine islands—an empty threat, given the state of public opinion, but a threat nevertheless [Ed.].

found in California and other new communities of men who had no time to establish civil governments. The vigilance committee hung a horse-thief on the nearest tree, acting as judge, jury and executioner all in one, and the community approved. But gradually, when courts were established and sheriffs elected, to use violence in such a way was itself made illegal.

Nations are rapidly moving in this same direction. That they should move together, understanding each other's motives through conferences and mutual deliberations, seems but the natural outcome of the moral appeal.

Question: . . . In your talks to the Resolutions Committees of the Republican and Democratic Conventions, you spoke of the growing "uselessness" of armaments. May I inquire of you: How far would you have the United States go in that direction? And on what terms? In other words, do you really hope that there might be an international agreement for getting rid of armies and navies altogether?

Answer: Although nations like men are not very logical, as you doubtless know, Mr. Hard, the present situation brought about through the American secretary of state naturally suggests, does it not, that some day a nation will at last ask itself the question: Why do we seek to gain by going to war something which the world refuses to concede? Why impoverish a nation for elaborate defence when the organized opinion of the world stands ready to deny the agressor [*sic*] the fruits of his agression [*sic*]? In short, why prepare for war under these changed circumstances?

In this fast-moving world disarmament, twenty-five years ago, was a wild dream. Until yesterday it was a laborious matter of matching tonnage and war planes. The President of the United States gave it a tremendous impetus by his very recent suggestion of a one third reduction all around. Is it too much to hope that in the future—perhaps the near future—it will become the obvious course to get altogether rid of what is no longer useful! The present armament situation is also harmful:

As the chief obstacle to a resort to arms and to the success of the pacific means of settlement pledged in the Kellogg Pact.

We wish the United States might enunciate another principle of international law, which President Hoover has already enunciated in relation to Haiti, and President Taft and President Coolidge had already intimated in connection with the United States troops in Nicaragua: the protection of nationals and their property in foreign countries, no matter what they do, shall be taken care of through civil processes without the intervention of the Navy and the Marines. We believe that such a doctrine, made universal, would deal a body blow at imperialism all over the world, and imperialism, as you know, is the mother of modern militarism. During 1931 the world spent five billion dollars on useless armaments. In that very year half the governments were bankrupt, millions of men and women were unemployed, with myriads of children undernourished. It will be increasingly difficult to defend such folly, not only to those who are facing starvation but to every one of us.

I would have disarmament come about through international agreement, and would be very proud if the United States—perhaps the most secure and powerful of all the nations—would lead the movement as rapidly as possible. In point of fact, we do not realize that a number of the nations are already proceeding to disarm: Denmark almost completely by votes of successive parliaments; Sweden with a Department of Defense substituted for the Department of War; Germany and the other Central Powers by international agreements; Iceland, an island accessible to all the navies of the world, but with the oldest government in Europe, celebrating its one thousandth anniversary a year ago, without a single warship.

The situation is moving rapidly on the line which the peace people advocated in the years before the World War:

1. The establishment of machinery for the arbitration and adjudication of all differences between nations.

2. A sense of security which would result from the use of this machinery.

3. Disarmament gradually occurring because arms were no longer essential for security—but a deadly menace to it.

Question: . . . I note that in your suggestions for platform planks for the Republican and Democratic Parties, you included "the nationalization of munitions." You wish, I take it, to eliminate the munitions business, the armaments business, as a private business. You wish to confine the producing of armaments and the possessing of armaments and the trading in armaments, to the world's governmental authorities. Will you tell us your reasons for that proposal?

Answer: We have come to regard with horror the results of unrestricted trade in armaments and of the profits derived from their manufacture and sale because we see that private profits accruing from the great armament factories are a powerful hindrance to the abolition of war, and we therefore urge as a first step that governments agree to the nationalization of arms and munitions. It has already been proposed to the Disarmament Conference at present sitting in Geneva, that:

1. No new orders for war material should be permitted for an agreed number of years.

2. During this time the estimated need for every country for small arms (police, frontier guards, sports, etc.) shall be registered at the Secretariat of the League of Nations; new estimates to be presented at fixed intervals.

Such an agreement would sound like the dictates of a supergovernment to the United States of America, but would be a great improvement over what happens now. When Massachusetts some years ago attempted to minimize the sale of firearms, especially to minors, word came to the legislature from the United States War Department that such legislation would be unfortunate because it was desirable to keep up the sales of small-arms factories so that they might be going concerns in case of war and able to manufacture arms for the United States government.

We further believe that the nationalization of munitions would not only eliminate private profits accruing to the great armament factories but would also reduce war scares. That such scares are from time to time deliberately fomented was made quite clear by an American citizen representing munition interests at a recent international conference for the reduction of armaments.

Question: Miss Addams, your discussion of the private trade in munitions takes us over naturally into the field of economics. Your recommendations to the Republicans and to the Democrats had economic as well as what we call political features. You argued for instance, that the world should have lower tariff walls between its several countries. Yet you were not speaking from a solely economic point of view. You seemed to believe that a lowering of tariff walls would conduce to peace. You seemed to believe that altitudinous tariffs are in some degree dangerous to peace. Will you tell our auditors, in a little more detail, your reasons for that view?

Answer: We believe first, Mr. Hard, that unrestricted intercourse between nations must in the long run make for better understanding and good-will. A protective tariff is in and of itself a purely nationalistic measure although it becomes more and more evident that the mobility of goods and the freedom of trade intercourse is essential even to national prosperity. We cannot expect to sell our wheat to nations to whom we make it impossible that they should sell us manufactured goods. We believe that a revival of world trade depends among other things upon a drastic reduction in tariffs. I was in Austria in 1921 when tariffs throughout southeastern Europe were being used as an instrument in a sort of static warfare, which indeed they may easily become. In Vienna that summer it was cheaper to buy wheat from the Argentine, although Austria had no seaport of its own, than it was to buy it from the Great Basin of the Danube—at the moment under the control of the

Hungarians—although the Viennese had fed from that Basin for a thousand years.

The lowering of an excessive nationalistic tariff will probably take place first, for reasons which you yourself so cogently explained last Friday, through some sort of a customs union in Europe, beginning possibly in the Southeast where the tariffs have been so unfair. It is perhaps one of the finest indications we have of the return of good-will between recent enemies that the Balkan States may be willing to live and let live, in their trade relations.

Question: Miss Addams, one further question in the field of economics. You have advocated here in Chicago, to the delegates of our national conventions, the cancellation of reparations from the vanquished in the late Great War to the victors and also the cancellation of the debts from the European victors to the government of the United States. Do you think that the good feeling produced by these cancellations would outweigh the injustice which it is claimed they would impose upon American taxpayers? Or do you think that they imply no such injustice?

Answer: You know, Mr. Hard, I did not advocate, to put it mildly, the entrance of the United States into the World War; but our government having become an associated power with the Allies, it seems to me that it undertook financial obligations as well as the military ones for which money was spent so freely.

An analysis of the debts would show that much of the indebtedness is for material and munitions bought in this country at excessive war prices, and which was used, as the Europeans believe, in a common cause. If it had been taken for granted from the beginning that the United States sent supplies in the same spirit that it sent its soldiers, the public would not have gotten into this attitude of a righteous creditor claiming his own, irrespective of the debtor's ability to pay or the consequences to the creditor himself in case he did pay.

This attitude would not be of great consequence if it were not clear that the adjustment of the whole question of war-debts and reparations is essential to world prosperity. While we realize that the United States is receiving no reparations, nevertheless the two things are so closely allied that it is impossible to separate them actually, although it may be done by the use of pure logic. Let us in any event have a national commission—and when possible an international conference linked up with disarmament—to go into the whole question and at least disentangle the validity of the various demands. The inherent difficulty in repayment arises from the fact that the materials the United States shipped to Europe designed for munitions as well as the manufactured munitions sent over from here, were all blown up and left nothing behind in the way of property, not even for collateral; and that the food was fed to men who were engaged in destroying property; so that on the whole it became impossible to make a payment for "value received," all values having been destroyed.

A leading economist very soon after the war made a statement which then appeared to be very foolish but which now begins to sound like economic wisdom. He said that the only way Europe could repay the war debts to the United States without dislocating trade and upsetting the whole structure of exchange, was to continue to make munitions to which they were accustomed and which would keep them at work for governmental wages, buying material from the United States of America when necessary, and then shipping enough munitions to our shores to pay the debts in full. The United States, however, must agree to select some safe spot on the Atlantic coast and, as one shipload after another arrived, must promptly set off these European munitions in huge bonfires. That would keep our trade balance secure and not upset matters, as would surely ensue if Europe tried to pay in useful manufactured goods for material which had been wantonly and systematically destroyed. I am not enough of an economist to know if he was right or wrong, but I suspect that there may be something in this reasoning. It seems only fair, in any event, that the war-debts part of the war situation should reflect something of the glamor of those sterling war virtues of loyalty and generous treatment of companions in arms. Instead of this, however, the war debts are being treated in the coldest possible spirit of commercialism.

Perhaps what the world needs more than anything else at this moment is an outbreak of good-will and human understanding, so genuine, so powerful, that it may overwhelm the suspicion and distrust which has paralyzed trade and has poisoned every relationship. Nothing could achieve this so quickly and so powerfully as a statement by the United States that the war debts were being considered generously and impartially. I do not believe that it would work an injustice upon the taxpayer on any other basis than that war debts are always an unfair burden upon him. On the contrary, the action of such a war debt commission might go far towards dispelling that sense of depression with which most of the world is surrounded. We are told that the great achievements of the human race are those which have brought deliverance from some form of terror or of depression. They have been the gains for some new sort of freedom. What an opportunity the world at present presents to the nation which is ready to take it! The good-will the United States attained from China by the renunciation of the Boxer indemnity would be as nothing to what it might have now. ⬤

Question: . . . Your final recommendation to the Republicans was "participation by our government in international conferences on economic problems of vital importance to world recovery, such as the problems of currencies and credits." So may I ask you: What scope would you give to international conferences, what scope would you give to internationalism, in the finding of the answers to the economic evils which produce so much of the human suffering now existent throughout the world?

Answer: There is little doubt that the more often representatives of various nations meet in conference the more they discover that many problems are world-wide in their implications and can only be solved if the nations come together to consider them. They also learn a technique of conferring together, and it is a matter of real regret to many of us that since the war the United States has failed so often to avail itself of the education and adaptation which other nations are developing through annual conferences. And yet, more and more the United States is being drawn into these conferences and is developing "observers" who are fast becoming valuable representatives. You told us on Friday that the United States constantly maintained six consuls at Geneva who act as observers. Perhaps nothing is more needed in the present state of the world than a spot devoted to international conference in which representatives may repair to take counsel together.

The United States has a fine record in regard to international conferences. This history extends from the Arbitral Tribunals established by John Jay in 1794 to the recent establishment of the International Bank at Basle. For more than a hundred years the United States of America rendered its good offices in mediation, international commissions of inquiry, commissions of conciliation—all of which have been universally successful when resorted to. We are now called upon to establish justice and cooperation through this new technique of world conference, and it is hard to understand why we hesitate.

INDEX